OCEANS BRIGHT
WITH STARS

The Journey Mama Writings: Book 2

RACHEL DEVENISH FORD

Other Books By Rachel Devenish Ford:

The Eve Tree: A Novel

Trees Tall as Mountains: The Journey Mama Writings- Book One

First published in 2013
Copyright © 2013 Rachel Devenish Ford

Cover art by Chinua Ford
ISBN-13: 978-0-9895961-1-4

Small Seed Press LLC
PO Box 7775 #48384
San Francisco, CA 94120-7775
racheldevenishford.com

This one is for Solomon, my king of the monsoon.

OCEANS BRIGHT
WITH STARS

INTRODUCTION

In May of 2008 I boarded an airplane with my family to travel overseas all together for the first time. My husband, Chinua, and I had been living in a Christian community in Northern California and had plans to open a meditation center in Goa, South India—we hadn't ever visited Goa, but it would be our new home.

One month later, I wrote, "Sometimes I feel like a salamander that has been whipped around by its tail a few times over some cowboy's head, and then dropped in a puddle." That pretty much sums up what moving overseas did to me. Although I was looking forward to it, although I longed to get back to Asia, nothing prepared me for what moving to India with three kids and a baby on the way would be like. At nineteen and twenty I had been a single backpacker in India. I was used to sleeping in grubby little guesthouses and not caring. But when I got off the plane in Goa with my babies, I could barely push back the panic I felt. My first thoughts were, "What have we done? What have we *done?*"

What we had done was this: We left California, traveled through Turkey and Israel and then into India. In Turkey and Israel, we traveled with good friends. We were surrounded by others who knew us and loved our children. But when we arrived in India, without even a guidebook in hand, Chinua and I were alone with our three kids: Kai, age 5, Kenya, age 4, and Leafy, age 2.

The kids took to traveling like ducks to water, immediately assuming that travel was part of life, and that seeing other countries was a common thing for kids to do. They swam in the Mediterranean and the Sea of Galilee and then in the Arabian Sea. They adjusted to a tropical climate and more bugs and bug bites.

I, however, struggled. A friend had suggested that this would be the way, when I asked her what relocating to a foreign country with a family was like.

She thought for a minute.

"It's easy for the kids," she said. "But it's hard on the mother."

We had been building up to this for so long that I thought I knew what to expect. What I failed to take into account was not only what it meant to adjust to being a mother in a place so foreign to me, but also all the processing I still had to do from the trauma of having two friends and my grandmother pass away in the months before we moved.

And then there was the fact that it was *India*. That's all, that's enough—India would rock anyone's world. I prayed, "Help me not hate it here," every day. I posted on my blog as I learned to live in a new place, writing as often as I could, to open my heart and see things around me. And slowly, slowly, my prayers were answered and my heart opened up enough to take in a new home and a wild new way of living.

These are the best posts from our first two years of living in India, collected and edited. Most of these posts are from Journey Mama, but I have included a few that were written for Fly Fishes Fly, a site Chinua and I began to record our experiences traveling with our family.

I pray that as you read them you will settle more fully into your own home, that you will be able to reach inside yourself and find all the strength you need to inhabit the place where you are.

ON THE WAY

After the craziness of packing and moving across the world, traveling through Turkey and Israel, on our way to India, was strangely blissful. Our travels weren't without incident, but how could they be, with preschoolers and toddlers along? (And would we want them to be? Incidents can be fun.) Chinua and I were impressed and heartened by our first experience of traveling with children. I'm so glad we had Turkish delight, baklava, and memories of the Mediterranean Sea to lead us into the next few years of frequent traveling with many young children and far too many bags.

We took in a rainbow gathering in Turkey— a very rustic and basic communal camping experience. It was short-lived for me, as I found it too hard with the kids. But the welcome of people from around the world, if only for a couple days, was just what we needed to feel received into our new global existence. The kids and I waited out the rainbow gathering in a nearby seaside town, using the time to explore the ice cream and playgrounds of a different country.

I was so unsure of what to expect of our new way of life, as well as tired from my pregnancy, and hopeful about the future. These first weeks of travel were in a way like pregnancy themselves, that precious time during the waiting, before you know all that will become, all that will emerge.

may

May 8, 2008

I am sitting in the traveler section of Istanbul- Sultanahmet- drinking a tiny cup of Turkish tea and trying to put sticky fingers on my feelings about being here. My wonderful and considerate husband suggested that I go out and spend a little time alone.

The plane ride was hectic and long, as anticipated, but the kids were wonderful. They are not angelic or without their kinks, but they are little troopers. We didn't sleep much during the hours that we should have been sleeping, and I was surprised and amazed by how they kept on playing, walking through airports, and standing in line, with a minimum of meltdowns. I was also blown away by just how bone-weary that journey made me. WOW. Being pregnant really adds whole new dimensions to your jet-lag, with tracers.

We are a bit of a spectacle, wherever we go. Chinua already draws a lot of attention, with echoes of "Bob Marley, Bob Marley," following us as we walk down the street. But with the three kids and my round belly, we get even more attention. It's *good* attention;

people everywhere call out, "Very Good!" in Turkish, which is cool, getting points just for dragging our kids around. They probably don't see a lot of tourists with a young entourage like ours.

And the cheek pinching that has been going on! Turkish people are cheek pinchers, let me tell you, and once again, the kids have been responding really well- laughing and ducking their heads. Leafy has been giving people fives when they hold out their hands for handshakes, which just makes him look really enthusiastic, and Kenya has had her hair touched a lot. Will it get old? We'll see. If people keep giving them candy, Turkey may become a favorite place for them.

Yesterday, we were stopped in traffic in the taxi we took from the airport, and a man in the car next to us started smiling and talking to Leafy. Then he picked up a little stuffed frog keychain and gestured for me to take it. I opened my car window and reached across to where he was holding it out. "Thank you! Thank you," we said. It's amazing how people love children here.

We are staying in the crappiest, tiniest little guest house, with artsy iron railings on the stairs and a kitchen that— well, you should just close your eyes before you walk in. The guy working this morning made us a breakfast of bread, jam, cheese, tomatoes and boiled eggs, and later, when Leafy had *finally* woken up (at 10:30 we were starting to wonder if there was something wrong with him, but I think he was just catching up) we found him some food. The manager came in, asking whether the protein was in the yellow or white part of the egg- we fumbled our way through answering him, and he gestured toward Leafy, "I was wanting to make sure he got some protein and I wanted to know what part of the egg to get him."

It's so heartwarming when people look out for your kids' protein intakes and give them toys from the next car, wipe their noses and exclaim over them. It heals that whole children-are-an-embarrassment-in-public vibe that can emerge from American culture at times. And all and all, it seems that we are going to be okay.

Because of course— there I am, wondering whether we'll be okay, picking things to death philosophically, even while we wander the streets of Istanbul and my kids are playing leapfrog over the decorative short poles on the sidewalk, while we eat Turkish Delight (truly delightful) and my kids race each other through the park, while we walk through the Public Bazaar looking at lamps and dishes and rugs, and stand in the shadow of the Hagia Sophia. I am seeing it all, marveling, yawning, shifting from foot to foot, eyes wide and happy, but I am wondering one thing- *Who are we now? Away from where we were? Who will we become?*

And then I remember who we are right now. That we are loved, that we are holding each other's hands tightly. I remember to trust God again, and to live in this day.

And Chinua and I see each other and smile and try to remember not to kiss in public.

May 11, 2008

Today I spent my 28th birthday in Antalya, Turkey. It was... a birthday to beat the band.

I don't know what it is- whether it's spending the time making the kids' birthdays special, or if it's getting older, but I find lately that I just like to do quiet, happy things with my family and friends on my birthday. Which is to say, I've gotten stodgy. No parties for me.

We landed in Antalya, only to go to the guest house that we had picked and find that it was closed. We asked out taxi driver to stop, so we could get out and try to get our bearings, and we happened to be parked right beside a guest house that had two beautiful

7

adjoining rooms for us, run by a Dutch woman who had immense sympathy for me as I waddled in with a sleeping Leafy in my arms.

I felt like maybe Antalya was heaven. The air was balmy, there was a garden for the kids to play in, with real live tortoises for them to feed, and a beautiful room with lots of space! And a shower! We ate a late dinner under the trees (never managing to wake the jet-lagged Leafy Boy up) and met up with a bunch of the friends who we will be camping with, here in Turkey, at the Rainbow Gathering. It was wonderful.

And then, this morning, I woke up to the sun. Oh, well, okay, I actually woke up to the jet-lagged Leafy deciding it was time to play at 5:30, but forget about that~ Chinua got up with the kids at 6:30 and let me sleep longer.

We had Turkish breakfast in the garden: a plate consisting of a boiled egg, some bread, cheese, jam, olives and a couple of fruits and vegetables.

Later we walked around Antalya and picked up some stuffed bread to eat by the water. By the Mediterranean. I think this was the point that I realized how truly amazing it was to be spending my birthday in Antalya.

One of our friends watched the kids while Chinua and I took a little scooter ride around the city, dodging foot traffic and other vehicles. We've driven around on a scooter before, a few times, and it's always so special for us.

And then, the crowning touch. I went to Sefa Hamami, a 600-year-old Turkish Bath, which is a whole story in itself and may have to wait another day. I'll just say that it involved being punched in the backs of the thighs by a strong Turkish woman with oils on her hands, having previously had water thrown on me while I lay on my back in a 600-year-old dome. Also being scrubbed red from top to bottom, and rubbed down with soap like a little baby. Well, that's pretty much the whole story. I guess it didn't have to wait.

May 15, 2008

I wish you could have been here today when we reached a little Kebab restaurant and two Turkish men rushed to pull out a pink satin highchair and then fuss over putting Leafy in it, until he was all strapped in (does anyone even bother with the straps with their third kid?) and had a large chunk of bread in his hand to start stuffing into his mouth. Or when various older men rush out of their shops to give the kids candy, which is so nice of them and also makes this healthy mama cringe a bit, since we're a low candy consumption kind of family.

It just took me an hour to write that paragraph, because I'm using this weird Turkish keyboard and it's really really hard to use.

We have had our moments, for sure. There's Kenya and her various breakdowns over the states of the bathrooms. They're not always in the best condition and she's always had an issue with bathrooms, so every experience is a hurdle for her.

Or there is the way we went out this morning to do some errands and got everything done— shopped at a little market for olives and fresh cheese and Turkish pickles (of course) - got Leafy some pants- and bought some diapers (I think we need to be more settled for potty training to work) and shampoo, only to leave it all on the bus on the way home. And let me just say, in Turkey none of these things are cheap. It was a smooth move, pregnancy brain style. Argh.

And of course, I should be at a Rainbow Gathering right now— it's the reason we came to Turkey. But it was just too hard, there wasn't enough food (a Rainbow Gathering is like a big remote camping experience where everyone throws money together and then a couple of meals a day are cooked over a fire) so Chinua brought Cate, who wasn't feeling so well, and me into a beautiful nearby town. He went back in this morning. We have everything we need, except of course my brain, sufficient patience, and my computer, which is in another town, in storage.

I think I can pray for the first two... I'll just have to wait for the third.

May 16, 2008

In the spirit of throwing money away, today when we were at lunch eating the cheapest food around (pide, which is flat bread with cheese—a pregnant woman's dream) Leafy knocked a bottle of wine onto the concrete floor.

Everyone in the entire restaurant let out a huge collective gasp. Fortunately it wasn't a very expensive bottle of wine, but I felt like a heel as wine trickled all the way down the street in front of the open restaurant. I bought some bread and cheese and olives again, and we have fruit... tomorrow we will probably stay here at the guest house to eat. We seem to be slightly accident prone.

To tell you the truth, my eyes welled up with tears when I felt the eyes of everyone in the restaurant on me. This is not always easy. And I think Leafy is going to give me a heart attack, beautiful harbor or no beautiful harbor. Two-year-olds are not the most relaxing traveling companions, though they sure are cute.

But you should see the beautiful wooden sailboats. Oh my.

May 19, 2008

1. Fethiye seems to be very well known in England. I think that 3 out of 4 tourists here are from the UK. So interesting. I wonder how that happens? Guidebooks?

2. In the interest of adventure and a change of scenery for the

kids, we went on a boat tour yesterday. The boats line the harbor here, all boasting a 12 island tour with lunch included. It was pretty cheap (about $20) and it was free for the kids, so we decided to go for it- hey, lunch is included! We had fun. Or maybe we had funnish. Kenya claims that she didn't have any fun. I had fun trying to keep Leafy from going overboard.

3. The kids did make a friend- a little girl from England named Mia. They squabbled a bit about what things were called: "Do you want any crisps?" "Those are chips." "NO, they're not CHIPS." and so on. We had some good lessons in how words are different in different countries.

4. I absolutely adored swimming in the Mediterranean. I thought this was the Aegean Sea, but I believe we are on the very edge of the Mediterranean. It's fun, pretty cold, but very refreshing. It has a high salt content and buoyancy, so if you let your body relax, with your feet straight down in the water, your head doesn't sink.

5. I am getting so much exercise that I am pretty sure this will be my fittest pregnancy ever, despite a lumpy start. I am not sure how many kilometers we walk each day, but it's a lot, let me tell you. We live up a hill that we climb by a few flights of stairs, too, several times a day.

6. It's a good thing we are walking a lot, because we are also eating a lot of bread and cheese. But we make sure to eat fruit and veggies too. Tomatoes are in season here and we are overdosing on tomatoes.

7. The Turkish breakfast we eat every morning is incredible: a boiled egg, olives, tomatoes and cucumbers, fresh bread, soft cheese, and cherry jam, along with tea or coffee.

8. I got too much sun yesterday during our eight hours on the boat. Whew. Last night the kids rubbed my back with shea butter and made sympathetic noises... "Oh Mama, your poor, poor back."

They were very sweet.

9. I miss my Superstar Husband. He'll be back from the Rainbow Gathering soon, I hope. He tells the best stories, plays the best games, and has the sweetest face.

10. I'm thinking a lot about the beautiful people I met at the Rainbow Gathering. I made friends with people from Iran, from Israel, from Turkey, from Germany, and from Russia. One night around the fire the Israelis sang the Iranians an Iranian folksong that they learned in Farsi. So beautiful. Where does this happen?

May 21, 2008

Last night I put the kids into the double bed in our room and began the nightly routine of breaking up the small fist fights that break out.

Leafy almost always asks to sleep in the double bed with the other two kids, and every night I let him, with the warning that if he starts the pummeling or smacking, he will be moved to the other bed until I can deliver him safely, unconscious and snoring, back to the bed with the brother and sister he abuses so cheerfully.

I sit on the little balcony outside our room, across from the water that is lit by twilight, the lights from the houses and boats starting to shine across it. I read by the light of my small lantern. Last night I started a book that I bought from a book stand. I think I memorized all twenty of the English book titles contained by that little stand and found the book that seemed to be the least smarmy, stupid, violent, or depressing. It was risky, but I can't be without a book to read at night.

Frequently I go back into the room, which smells strongly of citronella and geranium oil from our Burt's Bees bug spray, to tell someone to be quiet, to put Leafy back in his bed, to encourage Kenya to calm down and not be shrieky.

Sometimes I eat an orange. I love oranges.

Last night, as I was getting into my new book, Kai came running out onto the balcony. "Mom, Mom!" he said. "I think I heard Daddy's voice! He was calling- *Rae!*"

"Nooo..." I said. We weren't expecting him until the evening of the next day. But I went out into the hall. He wasn't there. Then I went up the stairs, into the smoky rooftop restaurant and I saw him. The most beautiful face, even dirty and tired. He's back, and we are very, very glad.

May 25, 2008

Do you remember that funny story about how that one time, when I was traveling in Turkey with my husband and kids, a heavy window dropped on my thumb when I was trying to close it before going to sleep? And do you remember the way the sound startled someone outside so that they screamed, and for a split second I thought someone else was hurt, not me, but then I pulled my hand away from the window and my thumb nail was already black, and then I fainted?

And do you remember how I spent the whole night in the tiny bathroom at our guest house, alternatively holding my hand under the cool water and then keeping it out because it hurt too much? It was one of the longest nights of my life, and I tried to sing, and I prayed for all my friends who are sick or in pain, up at night anywhere by themselves trying to breathe deeply, because it's a terrible thing.

And then do you remember how the next morning I went to the Internet room at the guest house to try and see what should be done for nail bed injury, and when I was reading about it with my hand resting on a bag of ice, I fainted again? It was probably the part about putting any severed parts in a plastic bag which got to me.

But the young, long-haired Turkish guy in the Internet room freaked out and ran off to get my husband, yelling, "Your wife! Problem! She is sick! Come now!"

And then there was the bus ride, painful and long, and the hospital visit, surprisingly cheap, where they drilled four holes in my thumb nail and let out big pools of blood and finally... relief!

Yeah, that was a pretty funny story. Oh me.

May 26, 2008

Life is very strange. Here I am, sitting in a café in Jerusalem late at night with a busted thumb, listening to the *Be Good Tanyas* on my headphones, going through hundreds of photos, well aware that I need to keep up with the digitalius. By which I mean the thousands of photos that might disappear into my computer forever if I don't do something with them. And the memories that might float away if I don't pay attention to them.

You'll just have to put up with me. The problem about traveling is that there is so much to write about, and much less time to write about it.

june

June 2, 1008

Tomorrow we step into the next phase of our sojourn. We will walk over the border into Jordan, climb into a taxi destined for the airport, and fly to Doha, in Qatar, where we will wait for our plane headed to India.

But I will never forget Jerusalem.

I won't forget the Western Wall, where I stood on the woman's side, a head or so above every other woman there, laid my hand on the stones, and cried.

Tears for the rolled up pieces of paper with prayers written on them, stuck in the crevices of the stones on stones, tears for the women singing their prayers around me, tears for a city divided into sections with barbed wire between them.

I won't forget the Mount of Olives.

And I won't forget the dear, dear friends here.

It sounds like the border into Jordan will be pretty interesting to cross. Children tend to make things run more smoothly. Hopefully that will be the case tomorrow. Meanwhile, packing again.

GOA

Reaching Goa in the first days of the monsoon, in the wet, dirty, flooded streets, still counts as one of the hardest things that I have ever done, if not the hardest. I immediately panicked, and the panic seemed to come from out of the blue—certainly I wasn't expecting it. I think that after the last stressful months of getting ready to move, I had been waiting for the time to process and relax, waiting for when we would finally reach our new home. When we arrived, however, I found that it was *not* home, it didn't look or feel anything like home, and what was worse, I needed to prepare for the birth of my new baby in just a couple of short months. I still remember fainting in a small market, from stress and fear and panic. I had been picking out some tea bags that were pre-mixed chai. My husband asked me, "Aren't we going to make our own chai?" and that question in that moment was like cold water in my face. It meant we were staying, that this wasn't just a bad dream, that we had to make a home out of this hard, unwelcoming, rainy place.

I wish I could reach back to myself in that moment and whisper, "It's going to be okay. You're going to learn to love it here, more than you've ever loved anywhere before. More than you can imagine."

june

June 5, 2008

Exhausted, but here.

Hot, but here.

A little confused, but here.

Reaching a city in India is like having the layers peeled back that normally protect you from the tragedy and beauty of humanity. The buffer zone is gone, and there it is before you. You've always known, in the back of your mind, that some children play in trash heaps. You've known that there are many different religions in the world. You've known that there are shanty towns, that some people wear bright clothing, like flowers, you've known that in certain places the water is not clean.

In Mumbai, there it was, all of it.

It makes me feel a little like I'm seeing a bit of what God always sees.

Last night we left Mumbai and took a night bus south to Goa. Let's not talk about how badly I needed to pee on that bus.

So, here we are. Intact, loving each other, figuring out the next step.

June 7, 2008

A long time ago, I made the tagline of my blog, "Cultivating Joy," because I believe that joy is something to be cultivated, something that isn't necessarily in the box of crackerjacks when you first open it.

You search with eyes open wide and sometimes full of tears.

I have so many friends who are going through such trials right now, trials that make mine seem small. Especially considering that I walked into mine, almost ran. I am simply homesick. And I don't even know what place I am thinking of when I think of home.

But I am thinking of friends, and family, and a different climate, and a different way of walking down the street. And I am crying in the Internet café. And it is okay to be sad, it is okay to curl into your pillow.

But then comes the time when you need to cultivate joy. My garden is swampy in this monsoon. I need a little shelter for it, something to let it breathe.

I keep thinking of these doves I would see, as I looked out from the balcony of the guesthouse in Turkey. They fluttered and cooed, we heard their cries every morning, we woke up to them. But if you watched at the right moment, you could see one of them halt. It would stop flying, relax like an empty bag, and simply fall.

It would plummet freely toward the ground, and then at some point open its wings and effortlessly return to flight.

I think I am at the descent, the falling point, the part where you relax and allow yourself to drop into what feels like nothing, but is really the very atmosphere that will hold you up when your wings unfurl again. Here we go, falling, looking for joy with eyes wide, sometimes full of tears.

June 9, 2008

Let me just say that kids are the most adjustable creatures in the universe. They are loving life right now, even in our sorta yucky little apartment, even in the rain. They like the rickshaws and the scooter rides and the mangos. They are simply happy.

And I am getting better, little by little. I realize that I had stored up a lot in the last few months of being in America and I am just beginning to process it now. So it could be a while for me. But God sustains.

These are those magical moments, too, when you don't yet know how things will turn out, and later you look back and say, "Do you remember when we first arrived, and we didn't even know this place yet?" and it is incredible to you, that you ever didn't live here.

Sometimes I feel like I hate it here, sometimes I have to breathe deep because I am panicking, and sometimes though, there I am, making oatmeal in the morning and it's okay. It will be.

June 11, 2008

I witnessed something that struck me as such a tender event, as I stood on our balcony hanging clothes on the line yesterday.

We are temporarily in a little flat above a busy chowk (intersection) and yesterday at about 1:30 a whole bunch of kids got out of school. They all wear uniforms: checkered shirts with navy shorts or skirts, and as they flocked out into the chowk, dozens of scooters came by, driven by fathers and mothers picking up their kids. I watched as two or three kids jumped on a scooter with their dads, ready to go home after a day of school. I waved at the girls with long braided hair.

21

In a few minutes most people were gone, and then the rains came, heavy and fast and in sheets.

June 15, 2008

I have more and more normal moments each day; moments where I am just doing what I am doing without that burning feeling in my chest, or the slightly nauseous wrenching that means I am fully aware that I am displaced. I would describe these feelings as a little bit like what a baby goes through when she is playing happily in someone's lap, only to look up and discover, *that's not my mother!*

But they come less and less. More often now I look up and decide that although this lap belongs to a stranger, she seems safe. Maybe even like-able. Maybe even someone who will be my friend.

Loneliness is something that is fairly strange to me. There have been a few times in my life that I have felt lonely; raw, gut-twisting loneliness. The funny thing is that it was usually when I was surrounded by people, but new people. There is a lesson here, I think. There are many lessons.

One time that I can remember is when I was first married. I think I had expectations about finding my other half; about the completion, the wholeness of two people. And then I found myself sitting beside Chinua on our little couch in our little room, realizing *it's still just me in here.* As much as Chinua is my other half more than anyone else in the universe, I stand alone before God. We all do. It was crushing to me at the time, though. I think I had expected more magic and less conversations with the words *"Can you tell me one more time exactly what you mean because I just don't understand?"* in them.

(I've had a series of epiphanies like this; the discovery when I became a mother that I didn't feel any different. I was still just Rae, but 24 hours-on-call Rae who might not possess all of her faculties, and was alternately giddy and weeping. And spouting milk. My grandmother told me once that she used to look in the mirror in her late seventies and feel exactly the same inside as she did at thirty. Her body was like a stranger.)

But mostly, loneliness has not been a big part of life for me. As an introvert who is married with three children and has lived in community for the last ten years, I just don't have time to be lonely. I'm more often looking for solitude. But there are new lessons for all of us, and coming here has been lonely. At least for now. I'm so thankful for my sweet, sweet husband. But we both look at each other at times and wonder where everyone is.

Lessons come for understanding, I think. Right now I want to reach into the solitude of anyone I can and place my hand right between their shoulder blades, and say, in the words of many taxi or rickshaw drivers in India, "I am here." It is good for me to experience the slightest touch of the experience of the lonely traveler. It's from this place that I will invite the traveler into my home, offer him some chai, welcome him to my table.

June 18, 2008

I have these times when I'm lying on my bed in the small flat we're renting, staring at the ceiling fan which is not moving because of a power out, willing it to move, and I'm thinking, *is this really me, eight months pregnant with my fourth child? Because I swear it's someone else.*

We have a game, actually, where we point at the fans and yell, Power ON! and the last person to say it before the power goes back on wins.

Maybe you can tell that this little flat is getting a bit old? Although we thank God every day for a roof over our heads. And the ceiling fans, which usually work. And the food that we make in our little kitchen, even though yesterday I had a bad experience with some peppers that I thought were harmless capsicums—green peppers, you know—but turned out to be of the blow-the-roof-off-of-your-mouth variety. The kids had plain rice for dinner, and I squashed guilty feelings like a bug under my shoe with the thought that even in America kids eat plain rice for dinner sometimes.

India is incense, bathing by candlelight, tooting horns on the street, color everywhere, tropical heat like a sauna.

And here we are, being us, winding up the last of this time in the little flat over the bar on the busy street. Soon we move to our temporary home in a house in the jungle—we'll be living there for about five months, long enough to have the baby and get our feet under us while we look for a more permanent location. The stuff we shipped will arrive soon, and we will no longer have to stick to sudoku (Kenya's getting really good) and origami (Kai is pretty amazing) and the three shows I have downloaded on iTunes. Soon we will have Internet access and phones and homeschool will start up again (we had an early summer break this year) and everything will stabilize a bit.

I look at my kids and my husband and my heart almost breaks with love for them. I feel my baby kicking me and I am so happy to be here, waiting for our sweet little monsoon baby.

June 19, 2008

Since I'm guessing that you don't want to hear about the power outs last night when we were trying to sleep in the crazy humidity, when Chinua and I lay on our backs staring at the ceiling fans, listening to the barking dogs outside—well, you've heard it all before, so maybe I'll tell you about this conversation instead.

The kids come clambering onto our bed, obviously distraught.

Kai- "Mo-om, Kenya's making everything wrecked!'

24

Me- "What's she wrecking, honey?"

Kai- "Well, it's both of our birthdays today, and SHE'S trying to take the first bite out of ALL the cakes, and that's not fair, because I want the first bite.

I stare at him for a minute.

Me- "But don't you think it makes sense for each of you to have your *own* cake, and then each of you can have the first bite of your cake? Since you're both having your birthday?"

Kai- "I want to do that, but every time I try, she just CHOP CHOP CHOPS (quick slashing motion with his hands) it UP, and then she takes the first BITE, of ALL the cakes!"

Me- "Soooo, why don't you make sure that both of you have your own cake, and then Kenya can chop hers up? And both of you can have the first bite?"

Kenya- "I just want a *taste* of his. It's coconut blackberry."

Kai- "NO NO NO, you shouldn't take MINE!"

Kenya- "C'mon, Kai! Let's go get another coconut blackberry one..."

They run off, leaving me shaking my head over the fact that I have perfectly regular conversations sorting out arguments about *invisible cakes made of AIR.*

And then there was the moment, today, when Kenya, touching the back of her knee, said, inexplicably and jubilantly, "Oh! Your *knee pits* help you walk!" like she had solved what had long been a mystery to her.

Oh these kids. Treasure.

The other day my Superstar Husband came home with a garland of jasmine, which smelled like pure heaven, because there is nothing on earth that smells like jasmine other than, well, jasmine. And don't you hate how people never really get it right, when they try to put it into soaps and stuff?

25

Details and cooking adventures (last night I mistakenly tried to make chicken soup from something that turned out to be a lot like chicken spam) and homesickness aside, it's perfect to be able to buy a garland of jasmine wrapped in a banana leaf from a man walking down the street.

June 20, 2008

My smashed thumb has been healing well, which means that the base of the nail is now dying and separating, but has to grow all the way out before it can separate totally.

Nice, huh? In short, it looks disgusting. And the problem is that it's my right thumb. This is a problem because I tend to have a knee jerk reaction of not using this hand to give or receive things to or from people, since I'm very aware of my repulsive thumbnail. And so I use my left hand, which then is culturally offensive.

You see the dilemma that I'm in, don't you?

See, India, and much of the developing world, in fact, use their left hands to perform certain bits of toilet hygiene that render it necessary to politely avoid other uses of this hand. You may not realize, though, that they don't actually USE their hands. Indian people wash their bottoms with water. So do Turkish people, Thai people, West African people. It's really a good idea. So is having a hand that you keep to the less desirable parts of life. It's all about hygiene.

In Turkey, there was a nifty little spigot at the back of the toilet that Kai used during emergency-I-have-no-toilet-paper-in-a-public-place moments. He thought it was awesome. In Thailand, there is usually a spray hose, which many people who are more well off have here. But most often, you'll find a bucket and a little pitcher. Help yourself to some water!

We are using toilet paper, if you're curious. There was a time,

26

when Chinua and I were traveling here with other friends almost seven years ago, that we all stopped using the paper. It was... okay. The only problem I had with it was a little thing that I like to call "wet bum syndrome." What to do? There seemed to be no remedy for it.

So anyway, when I offer my money to the lady, say, at the Internet place, and I forget, and give it to her with my poop hand because I don't want to offend her with my mummy thumbnail, well, it's not good.

Better the mummy thumbnail.

June 24, 2008

We have moved in to our little home in the jungle. I love it. I've started building a little nest, which isn't the easiest because we are housesitting, so there's a whole lot of other people's stuff here. But I think we'll manage fine.

At night sometimes I look up into the dark and see fireflies talking to each other.

Have you ever played War, the card game, with a five-year-old, a four-year-old, and a two-year-old? Where when finally the two-year-old stops crying every time we take his cards away from him to place them on the pile, he ends the game by taking off running through the house with the cards he doesn't want to relinquish in his hands, little bottom in little undies and all?

June 28, 2008

This morning I went to the market to get some food, but the scooter wouldn't start, so I needed to get a taxi. This was alright, because it enabled me to get enough rice to last us several months at a wholesale place. Then after marketing, I wanted to do Internet

27

stuff, so (the scooter was fixed by this time) I drove out to a little beach village, but right when I got started, a planned power outage took away the village's power. So I had to drive to another village. And pay some bills. And now... hmmmm.

Well, lists are fun.

Let's see.

Vegetables and fruits we bought in the market today:
1. Brinzel (eggplant)
2. Tomatoes
3. A dozen mangos
4. Tiny bananas that I adore
5. Lemons (to make lemonade)
6. Chilies
7. Potatoes
8. Ghobi (cauliflower)
9. Palak (spinach)
10. Coriander (cilantro)
11. Onions

Things we bought in the supermarket which is not much like what you would imagine when you think supermarket:
1. Dahl (lentils)
2. Curd (yogurt)
3. Mosquito coils
4. Chini (sugar)
5. Atta (flour)
6. Kismis (raisins)
And much more...

Bodies of Water that Kai has been swimming in in his short lifetime:
1. The Eel River in California
2. The Boiling River in Yellowstone Park

3. The Gulf of Mexico

4. The Pacific Ocean

5. Lake Superior

6. The Mediterranean Sea

7. The Sea of Galilee

8. The Dead Sea

9. The Arabian Sea

10. Cultus Lake, in BC

11. Some little lake in a state park in New Mexico

And I don't know if I'm forgetting any.

Types of vehicles my unborn baby has traveled in:

1. Rickshaw

2. Tractor

3. Scooter

4. Bus

5. Light rail train

6. Taxi

7. Van

8. Car

9. Airplane

10. Boat

Number of bumps we have endured on these vehicles: about eighty million

Number of mayflies that landed on my bed the other morning, causing me to shriek and jump out of bed and not sleep any more: About eighty million

Stinkiest things in India:

1. Trash heaps

2. Dogs

3. The meat side of the market

4. The fish side of the market

5. That bowl of dried shrimp in the sun that a woman tried to sell me today

Number of monkeys the kids have seen in our back yard: 3 or 4

Stoked much? Yes.

Number of birthday parties we have been invited to and attended so far: 1

Number of games of War we have played while waiting for our things to arrive: about eighty million

Estimated number of days until we have Internet: One or two or thirty or never

Estimated number of days until our boxes arrive from the ship: One or two or thirty or never

How much I love my birth center: As much as I love ice cream

Amount of ice cream eaten since arriving in India three and a half weeks ago: one scoop.

july

July 2, 2008

I walk through the market with all its tiny stores lining the street. The vegetable sellers have their stands on either side, with some directly in the middle. Piles of mangos, okra, potatoes, tomatoes... they are everywhere.

I'm looking for something specific, and I'm guessing I'll find it in a shop that sells plastic goods, like buckets and stools and pitchers. I peer into the shops I pass, smiling briefly at people who look concerned when they see me, as if they've never in their life seen something so odd. I know that this is just the famed Indian stare, so it doesn't bother me. Also, Indian women don't go out when they are pregnant, so I *am* rather strange.

I find a little shop and walk inside. It is dark and there are three people sitting in the midst of piles of the things I think will lead me to what I'm looking for. I don't think they'll know the word, so I try using gestures and other words.

"Do you have a small (I gesture the size with my hands) sort of

31

toilet? For a baby?"

They shake their heads. "For a small child? To sit on? To use the bathroom?"

No they don't. They shake their heads again. I gesture again to show the size and shape of what I'm looking for. "For a child? A toilet?" Nope, they sure don't.

"Oh," I say, disappointed. "You don't have a potty."

The one young woman jumps up. "Potty? Yes, we have." And she proceeds to show me the perfect, small, simple potty that I've been hoping for.

Sometimes it works better to just start with the word, rather than becoming some sort of crazed foreign pregnant mime. You know.

July 7, 2008

I've been receiving a lot of *advice* lately. Which is good, because I need it.

This store has great shopping, if you need clean shelves and something that feels sparkly. But normally you should shop at the market in town, because it is way cheaper.

You can get cheap dog food at that shop (leftover pieces of chicken).

This pharmacy has oils and natural products.

Don't swim during monsoon.

Open your windows every day, and keep your fans on 24 hours, to fight the mildew.

Close your windows at dusk, to fight the mosquitoes.

And then, *You'd better get your kids in school, because it's not good to be with them all day.*

I'm not too fond of that last piece of advice, and I feel like I'm opening up a can of worms, but heck. I'm a homeschooler. I love it. LOVE it. It's my favorite part of being a parent. I feel like I see the best sides of my kids when I'm teaching them. The kids love it too.

This little expat community is a lot like a fishing village. You hear so many opinions about what you should or shouldn't do. And it's also an international community, which means that people come from different experiences of a cultural norm. I had a woman say to me, the other day, that she has been bothered here by how little stimulation there is for the kids. And I'm all, hello? Stimulation? In India? There is stimulation galore. It all depends on what you are looking for. And for mine, counting cows as we zoom down the street is awesome. Kenya moos at them. And waves at the dogs.

(On that note, here's a little piece of advice for driving in India: The dogs will observe your horn, but the cows will not. They are entitled to lie in the middle of the road, thanks very much, so you'd better slow the heck down and save your horn, because it will get you nowhere.)

Kenya calls out, "Oh! Pretty!" while we pass a man who is pulling a wagon filled with pots of flowers. There is something to see everywhere you go. My kids have grown up in the *woods*, for goodness' sake.

*

I'm feeling a lot better. Especially as the kids are still waking up laughing, dancing around when it is time for tea, insisting on following the same routine every day, telling me that chapati and mango are their favorite foods, going off to watch a soccer game with Chinua, and visiting a little friend in the next village.

I'm getting a lot of advice about the way things should be done, and it's good, but I'm starting to realize that it's still okay to be me.

When we receive our shipping stuff, and I get my mattress, I think my hips will also be doing a lot better. The mattress I'm sleeping on now feels like a block of cement. I do not kid. Also, there are nothing but straight backed chairs in our house, so I'm going to put a sort of couch together soon. These things will help a fourth time pregnant mama who's feeling a bit tired.

July 10, 2008

The bad news is, they are holding our shipment for a ridiculous amount of ransom money.

The good news is, we now have Internet within our very own home! Luxury.

Last night I thought I would have an absolute Internet glut and read a thousand blogs, but then my mind shut down from all the computer stimulation after about ten minutes and I fell asleep.

This morning the mayflies were back so I jumped out of bed early again. They haven't been back since the first time I wrote about them, and I was kind of missing them. Awww, cute little flying bugs with no mouths who only live for one day and only have reproductive organs. Fodder for fish. So sweet.

July 11, 2008

A conversation:
"Ok, Leafy, what is this letter?"
"A T!"
"That's right! And what's this one?"
"A O!"
"Uh huh! Good, and what's this one?"
"I don't know. It's an umbrella!"
"Well, kind of... It's a U. U is for umbrella."
"Me is for *umbrella*?"
"No, not *you* is for umbrella. The letter U is for umbrella."
"The letter *me* is for umbrella?"
And so on.

As for our shipping: I really think I understand the term *when our ship comes in* now. Our ship contains my entire curriculum, all of our books, all our toys except for the five that are here with us, (that have been with us since Turkey,) our instruments, oh, and the mattress. Sigh. They say two to three weeks for processing through customs. Sigh again. *When our ship comes in.*

July 15, 2008

(I'm including the following post from Chinua because he writes about such a funny and momentous part of our introduction to life in Goa.)

It is another blazing sunny day. In our curious 'non'soon all the torrential rain that we should be swimming in is a planet's width away, throttling retirees in Florida and washing out backyard barbeques by the thousands in the Midwest. I chalk it up to climate change and decide to grab my little crew and head to the beach.

Indian people are natural spectators and a crowd is waiting to precipitate out of thin air at the slightest provocation. If you stand in one place and look at say, a pile of rocks, it's only a matter of time before someone else is wanders over to check out your find. Two people standing somewhere looking at anything is a mighty fine reason to call your buddies and go give them moral support. Two people and a group of buddies looking at something means run on over— could be important. A person running to see something means stampede. Find a pile of rocks in India and try it sometime, I dare you.

Needless to say, a 6'2" African American man with dreadlocks and an assortment of tiny wonder people are naturally a crowd making machine. Kenya's dreadlocks alone could make their own fortune charging for photographs. We make the mistake of stopping to change on the beach. Before I have even put the first kid's shorts

35

on (under a towel of course) a dozen people are standing around us silently waiting for us to entertain them. In the gaps between their bodies, I can see more people throwing caution to the wind and running to meet the freaks for themselves.

To avoid the crowds, we walk far down the beach and change without incident. The water is cool and very refreshing. Kai (who is, in fact, part fish) is soon flopping around without a care. Kenya has invented her own game of run-swim-scream-splash-run with the waves, too interested not to try, but too scared to really get in. I wade in, watching them both carefully, then finally relaxing and having a lot of fun.

Time to toughen Kenya up. I collect her from the line of rolling sea foam and hoist her up to my chest. She holds on tightly at first, then does an experimental kick to the water. *Hey, this could be fun.* A lifeguard waves a flag at us, and I reluctantly come in closer to shore. Kai joins us and we are all together at last, laughing, playing in knee-deep surf, splashing...

...screaming, pulling, thrashing, grabbing each other. It feels like something is branding my legs with white hot wire hangers. I assume that the kids are screaming because I am, I just want to see what is doing this to me, can't they be quiet? Kai happened to be laying in the water when it hit me, and now he is scrabbling at my legs, very upset. Then I see it, nearly invisible elastic strands lashing Kai and I together, even on his face. I grapple with it, wiping everywhere, then throwing a huge impossibly blue blob onto the sand. The kids are screaming so loud. Something is all over us.

Out on the sand, we are all yelling, trying to rub sand on our skin. Kai is actually trying to bury himself in it by writhing like a snake. I am still on super adrenaline, having picked them both up and dashed out of the ocean. I don't know what to do.

Now, if anything is likely to draw a crowd in India, it is several freaks with dreadlocks covered in sand shouting at the tops of their lungs next to a pile of blue goo. You would think someone would offer to help, or tell us why the pain is only getting worse, or even if we were all going to die after foaming at the mouth for a few minutes. But the exact same silent crowd quickly assembled, waiting to see what fun shenanigans we would be up to next.

In extreme pain, I pick up both Kai and Kenya and bolt for the tree line. "Coconut oil!" one beach bar worker shouts. He looks afraid and tells us to go immediately to the hospital. My scooter is far away, we are in no shape to go anywhere. More workers arrive and help us wash off with fresh water. But that is all they can do. The kids are making sounds I have never heard them make.

I decide to run for the bike and ride like the devil for the nearest hospital. On the way, I see the same lifeguard who had waved the flag. Strangely, he is wearing a nonchalant dopey smile. In no great hurry he mentions that this is why he told us to get out of the water. He reaches back and pulls out a plastic bottle with a mini version of the jellyfish that stung us. Was this it? I am flabbergasted at his attitude. My kids are hurt. I am about to take him back to the surf and drape the jellyfish around his dopey head.

But then she appears: the exact person we need at that moment, a grandmother with a huge bosom, wearing a tacky printed dress, knowing exactly what to do. She is like grandmothers everywhere, in command in a way that makes you feel safe, even if she is a bit absurd. I love her right away.

In a flash she swoops in, picks up Kenya first (good choice, Kenya is seconds away from actually snapping a vocal chord) and starts to rub some home brew remedy made with a fleshy red fruit all over her. I did not notice at the time, but Kenya got the worst stings— all of one side of her back, down her backside and on down her little leg.

Grandma has a lot of the red stuff. She sternly tells Kenya to sit, and gives her repeated applications, each dose followed by an entire pot of water being dumped over her screaming head. Kai next, all over his chest and face. The stuff is blood red and looks shocking on their skin.

In bumbles a drunk representative from the cheated crowd. He asks very politely in his drunk guy voice if he could please have a picture. A picture? I am at a loss for words. In Hindi, Grandma tells him exactly where he and his camera can go. She's my hero.

After the kids quiet down from her ministrations, I notice how much I hurt. She does the same for me, coating my legs and dousing me clean. She tells us not to bother with the doctor, just wait a half an hour. I resist the urge to hug her.

We make it to the bike, and Kai is now nerding out on jellyfish facts for the ride home. Did you know that the biggest jellyfish in the world has no tentacles? We got stung by a jellyfish!? A real jellyfish? He asks every five minutes. He's back to normal. Kenya is quiet then asks once if we can please not come to that beach again.

July 17, 2008

Sometimes a husband may need to take a quick trip to Mumbai, a mere 12 hours drive away, for reasons which will no longer be mentioned here, because further mention would be simply draining, but in pig latin would be something like the ipping-shay oblem-pray.

Sometimes a husband and wife may argue over who gets to have the wireless Internet device thingy that usually they share. The discussion may or may not turn to questions of who is more deserving of outside connection and entertainment in the interim that the husband will be in Mumbai. Then the husband and wife will probably think a little about what roaming in Mumbai alone for a few days will be like and the decision to send the Internet device thingy with the husband will be unanimous.

And the wife will be in the house with the children for a couple of days, with no Internet, not knowing that perhaps people are fearing for her safety and the safety of her unborn babe because of giant blue creatures that roam the wide, wide seas, stinging innocent people.

But what concerned people should know is that while innocent people were being stung, this person was safe at home, no doubt eating cookies and re-reading books. Or moaning about the state of her hips. Or fighting with Jaya about who gets to make tea.

And then, when the people, the innocent ones, the stung ones, got home, the un-stung Mama person was able to offer comfort and assistance after all the tears had already been cried, when everyone was tired and talking peacefully about the strange story of the blue sea creature, which, after a little research, turned out to be a blue-bottle, also known as a Portuguese man o' war.

So there are some answers. Here's a question. Should I tell you about the lice? You probably don't really need to know about the dangers of sleeper buses and lice, do you? I'm sure that at some point in your life you've done a little nit-picking yourself. You've gone over things with a fine-tooth comb. Or not, if you're us and a fine-tooth comb wouldn't get through your hair in a million trillion years. You probably don't need to hear about the lice. So I won't tell you.

Don't think it's all strange animals around here, though. Okay, a lot of it is strange animals around here. But there are also the incredible vistas. The green greenness which is astounding. The fruit! The simple pleasure of finding pretty things in the market. Scooter rides every day. Flowers in the night air. Preparing for a new wee one. Making friends. And food! Good food.

July 18, 2008

On the scooter I am not heavy, not trying to lift myself from my
seat on the floor
to chase a naughty toddler.

There is breeze, I am in it, there is release from the humidity
that sometimes threatens to close me in

And there is thunder! Somewhere, in the distance, I hear it
now I notice the sky is darkening, my bags are flapping
full of finds from the market— I'm taking them home to my
family

My time is running out, I'd better get back
The gathering dark keeps me from seeing much beyond the
road, my other senses are heightened
my sense of smell:
There is the night blooming jasmine
There is the dumpster, full and scattered by dogs and cows
There is the smell of the evening dhoop, the heady incense of
the dusk
And dinner is cooking at that house there

Now the night blooming jasmine again and the scent of the
jungle
the greenness of it, the living things

(Sometimes snakes mistakenly crawl out onto the road and live
no more.)

I feel the first drops

That dark green smell means that I am almost home
wind whipping me, honked at and honking
others are making their way hurriedly too
not wanting to be caught in the rush of water that we are all too
thankful for
It has been too dry, this monsoon

But inside I will be even more glad
I am flying, well, at 40 km an hour, I am sort of flying
And the smells are so heady
And they follow me
And I am almost home
And up the red driveway and the rain breaks and chases me
inside
where I collapse, wet and laughing

Full of the night, the smells, the storm that tossed me back into
my family's arms.

July 21, 2008

I bought a crib. Or a cot. A baby bed, depending on where you
live in the world. At first I was debating whether to buy one here,
but I'm not a co-sleeper, I'm just not. Thankfully, for my fourth
baby, with three very well-adjusted and cuddly, loving, and
independent children, I don't have to feel guilty about that. I'm sure
I'll find something else to feel guilty about, but that's beside the
point.

So, something is necessary, and I thought to myself, maybe I'll
just have a little mattress made. Ha ha. And then I came to my
senses and smacked myself a few times as I thought: Rats! Mice!
Cockroaches! Mosquitoes! Ants! Mayflies! All of which have taken

41

up residence in our house and been ousted from our house dead or alive since we've been here.

Crib it is. With a nice, big mosquito net over it.

So I went to this store. It's a very modern store, a place that I don't shop at much, because I find it expensive and I prefer the adventure-like feel of the Municipal Market. But, at this store, I found a crib. I deliberated over whether to buy a wooden one or a pop-up crib with an attachable bassinet, and chose the wooden one because of the mold and fungus that we are constantly fighting in the humidity here.

The pop up crib looked all nice and clean and innocent in the air conditioned store, but I knew, I just knew that as soon as I got it back to our home, spores were going to be all, "WOOOO! FRESH NYLON!" Like that. You should see our backpacks. But that's another story, titled Beating Back the Jungle.

So anyway, I purchased my crib. And that was when the fun began.

There was only one crib and it was the display model. I had hired a little van taxi to do my shopping and bring the crib home, but there was one problem. The store employees really, really didn't want to dismantle the crib.

I can understand. I've watched Chinua dismantle our old one a few times. (So maybe I should say Chinua can understand.) But I needed to get the crib home. What to do?

All the store workers were involved by this point. And then they called my taxi driver in, and everyone discussed it at length. They were speaking Konkani, but I think I can translate.

"Can't you just put it in your taxi?"

"No, there's no way. Can you see how big it is? Why don't you just take it apart?"

"No, this is not possible. We did try to sell her the fold up crib, but she wasn't having it."

"Can't you deliver it?"

"We don't know where she lives."

"She gave you the address, no?"

"Yes but.... Okay, we'll follow you."

"Yes, we'll follow you."

"I'll go!"

"I'll go too!"

"And me!"

They ended up having to take the seats out of their vehicle. How that was easier than taking the crib apart, I'm not sure, but once you're committed, you're committed, I guess. Meanwhile I had stupidly purchased ice cream at the last shop and now it was happily melting in the van. I knew I shouldn't have bought the ice cream. I knew it!

And that is how we ended up leading a jeep full of employees from Poshak (the store) home. There were six, to be exact. Francis, the taxi driver, said succinctly, "They are all coming, like a picnic!"

Chinua wrote a little about the crowds here. There are different kinds. Maybe we can analyze them a little while we are here. There are the observant crowds, like the ones he ran into on the beach. And there are the helpful crowds, like when people stand around and try to help you get your bike out of the mud by yelling instructions. And then there are the "Sounds like fun! Let's join in!" crowds. I can't count the number of times we have stuffed ourselves into a crowded taxi only to find some other guy trying to get in. "Who's that?" we ask.

"Oh, this is my friend. He is coming too."

In India, it is a perfectly sufficient explanation.

July 23, 2008

A Prayer

Dear You,

The Youest of Yous. The dancing One, the Singing in my blood, the One who moves and breathes and loves me always.

So here we are again, we've been here before. I have a theory that You bring me here on purpose. Is it true?

Because this circle comes around again and again, and now I am at the start, where I'm kicking like a baby, resisting change with all of my might.

We box. You block all of my punches and never hit back.

I run to You, then pull away because I am more than a little upset. Why are You always bringing me to my limits? It doesn't feel fair.

Every day lately I wake up with what feels like a fat furry cat sitting on my chest. It's heavy and I can't breathe and there's that stupid cat dander that makes my eyes itch. I struggle to get out of bed because this cat feels like fear. Where is the fear from? Why is it heavy on me? Whose cat is this, anyway?

I remember the pattern from the past. You remind me, most excellent of friends, when I take the time to listen. You say, "We'll get through this." You say, "We'll be a little closer, my love." You say, "You'll drop a few more of those ideas of yours, the ones about your self-sufficiency, your big plans for yourself, your need to be perfect, to keep it all together, to fix everything by your own small self." You say, "Lean into it, don't push away." You say, "There are greener things than you can imagine, sweeter smelling days than you've ever known. Just wait. Just wait."

But I *feel* alone and the fear is ever-present and I'm not sure why I have to do this again. Remind me?

I know there is a changing. There is the kicking and the pushing and then slowly my resistance fades, I go limp, I fall in, and then I learn contentment again. It has been this way so many times before. All the places I have been, the homes I have lived in, all the deserts, all the valleys. Even on the peaks. It is the newness I resist, the loss of what has been. It is the small etchings I have carved into the wood in places all around me, reminding me of who I am, of what my name is. Leaving these things brings a tearing that I don't think I could have imagined.

Now I have only You to remind me. You and the faces of my family. It is enough.

And after the tearing comes a divine healing and Your hands surround me and I have obeyed and You have promised. And there are new things, there are sweet things and the ocean will fold over me and not throw me, it will rock me like a child. It is better than before, it is larger and more spacious than clinging to the old ways. You lead me into ever opening rooms.

It is good that we will have a long time together, my Friend. One day I will look back on all of this and say, "You told me so." So just, please, help me now, when I am still blind and foolish and inwardly about two years old.

All my love. You know You have my heart.

Rae

July 27, 2008

The hand of an acquaintance may tremble and shake, but the grip of a friend is strong.

The eyes of a stranger confuse, but the brow of a dear one is a beacon.

Ten friends may scatter when lice comes into the household, but the eleventh draws near.

(I made those proverbs up, by the way. They're not in the Bible.

45

Just so you know.)

Our friend is here! Renee arrived on Thursday, and we have now had eight cups of chai together, sometimes with digestive biscuits, which are delicious.

Part of the process of deciding to come here was an attempt to relocate a little community to a place where there are many international travelers. We were not trying to give up on community. However, relocation of a community is more difficult than you may imagine, especially if you are leaving the known continent of North America and entering the unknown continent of Monsoon. Or the subcontinent of India. And since we've been here we've realized just how spoiled we've always been, with good friends living close to us and next door and in the house and spilling out of the windows. We long for this enough that we fell on Renee's neck, weeping, when she showed up.

(The monsoon is back. It arrived with Renee and now we are submerged in water. We are very wet. Our sheets are wet, our towels never dry out, our pillowcases are wet, and I am dreaming about having a dryer, since we dry our clothes by hanging them in the kids' room with the fan going at top speed.)

For now, this little community consists of the crazy short ones, Chinua, me, and the brave, formidable, Renee. Soon more friends will join us. Because we all really, really like each other.

And to welcome Renee, on the first full day that she was here I brought her to the crazy surgeon's office, to accompany me to my first Indian surgery.

Not really the greatest welcome, Rae! Hello!

She has already completely baffled me by claiming to be cold. Cold! My husband tells me that I'm the one who is hot all the time. It's true that I have a furnace attached to me, one that is fully engaged. In birth speak, that means that the baby is in position and ready to be born. I'm thirty-seven weeks along now, so it could happen any time. However, my babies always seem to get ready waaaaay before they come. And I have to walk like a cowboy, because there is a skull in my pelvis.

Now this little family hunkers down, waits for this baby, and tries to keep dry. (Ha!)

By the way, the lice are done and gone, thank goodness. The kids never got them, which is amazing, but we have no sofa or soft chairs or stuff like that, so I guess it was just the Superstar Husband and myself, sharing them back and forth on our pillows.

July 29, 2008

I don't know what it is with me and ending up in the hospital or at the doctor's office for strange reasons, but somehow the other day I found myself lying on my back (not comfortable, these days) staring up at that funny floral arrangement of lights that shows up in operating rooms. It was not really where I had expected to be.

But I had this arm thing. ARM THING, it cried out. It started out as an innocent looking little broken blood vessel. Some strange pregnancy deal, like the fact that my face is covered in brown blotches, known as the pregnancy mask.

But then it opened up and bled copious amounts of blood. When it healed, it formed a strange ARM THING, and it seemed to be growing daily, right alongside Muffin. I didn't need to have a baby on my arm as well as a baby in my womb, so I sought medical help.

(Strangers had begun to point it out, and Chinua had once or twice tried to give it orders. "Lump," he said, "Go get us some ice cream." Or something like that, I can't remember what it was. But I realized that my shiny red growth was acquiring a little too much *personality*. Maybe I was jealous, I don't know. All I knew is that it

47

had to go.)

My midwife told me about a doctor that her husband had visited and liked. The doctor's office was in the nearby town, above a restaurant that I knew, so I set up an appointment, talking to the doctor directly. "I'm in the office from 9:00 to 12:00 and 5:00 to 7:00," he said. "Come around 5:00 and I can take a look."

If we're going to talk about differences between the way I've grown up and the way things go here, well, there's one thing. I don't usually go to the doctor at 5:00, but one thing we've learned about Goa is that midday, there is a big long siesta. Nobody calls it a siesta —they call it "lunch"— but *everything* closes. And if it so happens that it is one of the two businesses that don't close, you'll often find some people snoozing on the floor or in a chair or curled up on one of the sofas they are selling. I'm not sure if it's the Portuguese influence, or whether I'm completely blanking out on this aspect of life being present in the other parts of India. I do know that life is a lot more laid back in Goa than it is in north India.

So the next day, off I went to the doctor's office. When I got there, I saw that he specializes in diabetes, foot problems, general surgery, and dental care: a regular jack of all trades. Renee came with me, since we were gathering some things at the market for her, and it only made sense (in my strange, scrambled mind) to combine the two trips. You know: welcome to the neighborhood, here's the toilet paper, here's the general surgeon.

"Sit," I was told. So I sat.

"Wait," I was told. So I waited.

"Come," I was told. So I came. First I went to talk to the doctor, who squeezed and prodded and held a flashlight up to my arm thing.

"Ouch," said I.

"We can take care of this today, if you want," said he.

"Sure," said I, ever mindful of my due date drawing nearer. I'm trying to wrap up as many loose ends as I can, and my arm thing qualified as a loose end.

So the nurse said, "Come." She brought me back out to the waiting room. Renee looked up from her book.

"I could have sworn I saw you go in there," she said.

"I did." I sat for a while longer, and then the nurse commanded me to come with her again.

And she led me to another room, an empty room with two World War II hospital beds in it, and one lone toe bandage left forgotten on the floor. Whoops, I thought, someone's shedding bandages and they don't even know it. I tried to avert my eyes, feeling a little queasy.

But there were brown splashes all over the walls. I looked at my hands. The nurse came in and gave me a robe to put on. "Over my clothes?" I asked. She looked at me quizzically and shook her head yes.

So I put it on and waited a while longer, still looking at my hands. In a while the nurse came back in. She was wearing World War II nurse gear, white and buttoned up, with a white nurse's hat on, baggy white stockings and flip flops. She said, "Come." I obeyed.

In the hallway, we entered a door that said "Operating Stage." Hmmmm. That sounded a little strange. The two nurses stopped me at this point and took my robe off. They turned it around so that it fit like a bathrobe, rather than like a doctor's visit robe in North America, with the back open. Can you just imagine what they were thinking? I put my robe on so that it was open at the back! Not only does this not make sense anywhere, whether it is custom or not, but it must have seemed really strange to people who haven't seen this before.

"Oh, ha ha," I said.

Weirdo, they thought hard at each other.

The doctor apologized when I came into the room. The power was off and there was no air conditioning. Since it was a sterile room, there were no open windows or fans either. "No problem," I replied.

I was too busy eyeing the bowl of discarded bloody cloths and bandages that was sitting on the floor. No time to worry about air conditioning! I took a deep breath. Okay. Trust. Things are different here.

I got on the table and found myself in a stare-down with that circle of surgical lights. And then I remembered that I get really nervous at things like this! Ha ha ha. And they began washing my arm with iodine, from wrist to elbow, back and forth, like washing a window. "Any allergies to medication?" the doctor asked.

"No," I said. He poked me with the needle in reply. Oh dear. Suddenly my life flashed before my eyes, along with that toe bandage and the bowl of cloths on the floor. They revolved before me, my life, the toe bandage, the bowl of bloody cloths, over and over. I started to breathe deeply. I was about to pass out.

"Don't be so scared, don't be so scared!" yelped the doctor. "Hello!"

"Ooohhhhh," I said. "I don't want to..." I couldn't finish the sentence.

After I finished nearly passing out, things looked up. I was very hot, and sweating, but it was okay. I didn't die of an infection, my arm thing is gone, and it looks like I won't even have a scar.

Medical care is interesting here. There are so many things that are so simple, like walking into an office and having something taken care of immediately and without great damage to the wallet. (The operation, including invisible stitches, cost about $40.) But there are simple things that we take for granted, some of us, like the fact that the remains of the last few operations will be cleared out of the room before we enter. And there are strange rituals, like sitting in that room beforehand, and then sitting there again after for awhile, just waiting for clearance to get up and go.

At the end of the day, well, I never did get the courage to tell them about the toe bandage.

July 30, 2008

Today the humidity is at 90%.

The floor is *sweating*. Seriously. The *floor* is sweating.

It has been rather funny watching the dog skid around on the wet floor. Funny until I fall down, like I did on our algae-covered front walk the other day. Moans and bruises.

I feel a little like I am swimming, but I am only walking around. I constantly wipe my upper lip, where the beads of sweat form.

If I keep living in this climate, I bet I'll have really great skin when I'm older, that's all I can say.

July 31, 2008

Conversations

At the store looking for milk.

"Do you have fresh milk?"

"Yes, here, take one."

"I need four packets, can you give me four?" (Milk here is sold in small plastic bags, 500ml each.)

"No, only two."

I look in the fridge. There are at least ten packets.

"You can't give me four?"

"No, someone is coming who needs a lot of milk, this evening.

(Thinks for a minute.) Do you want three?"

"Sure. Three is fine. Okay... Do you have a packet of pencils and an eraser?"

"Yes, yes. Just here." (Hands me the pencils and eraser.)

I reach to pay. "How much?"

"You want four packets of milk?"

"Um, yes."

"Okay, okay. Take four." (Walks all the way back to the fridge to get another packet of milk.)

***

On a date with Chinua, talking to the waiter at a coffee chain here.

"What do you want to drink?"

"Can I have a strawberry shake?"

"No!" (Looks, as Chinua described, as if he has smelled something bad.)

"Oh. Okay. Is there anything else that I can't order?"

"Cold."

"No cold drinks. Only hot?"

"Chocolate?"

"What? Okay, I totally don't understand." (I look at Chinua, at a loss.)

"Can we order samosas?"

"No!" (Same bad smell look.) "Samosa is finished."

"Uh... Can I get a cold coffee?"

"Yes, yes, of course. Do you want ice cream on top?"

"Um, yes."

***

Talking to Chinua on the scooter on the way home from our date.

"I still want to get pillows."

"I think we should just get some fabric and have them

made." (Talking about cushions for our new chairs.)

"No... not that kind, real pillows."

"You want bigger pillows for the chairs?"

"No, no no, *pillows*... for your head sleeping."

We both laugh for a long time about my strange form of communication, but I ask you... is it any wonder?

august

August 5, 2008

Dear Kenya,

Yesterday you asked one of the sweetest questions I've ever heard.

"Where did we start?" you asked, and then furrowed your brow and thought a little.

"Where were you when Kai came out?"

Where did we start? Such a rich question. We talked for a long time about how Kai was born in a little town far north in California, and how you were born when we lived with lots of people in San Francisco, and how Leafy was born when we lived at the Land.

You love to talk about this.

I'm writing this letter just because that question struck my heart, and because of what shone out of you today.

I had to go on some silly bank errand which involved going from bank to bank searching for the right services. You wanted to come with me, even though it was raining. It's not raining very MUCH, you told me, putting your raincoat on. Even the fact that we were going by scooter did not deter you.

And I think I've never been happier. Riding along in the rain with my girl child on the scooter, both of us getting soaked, you turned to look up at me and grinned, not at all perturbed by the rain. You kept me company in each bank, you were polite to all the people who wanted to talk to you, and you kissed me a few hundred times, just to remind me that you were there, that you love me.

I see a lot of me in you. You are always searching for beauty, and when you point small things out to me I see the way that my eyes are often scanning the hillsides, looking for those elusive wildflowers. You find beauty everywhere. You love the gaudy tinselly things hanging from the ceilings of most of the places of business here. "OH, I LOVE that pink one," you sigh, eyes locked on a burped up metallic explosion dangling from a ceiling tile.

When we walk outside, stepping around a few strewn pieces of trash and over some steel rebar lying in the road, you look up. "Flowers!" you call, exhaling happily and pointing at some wilting garland looped over the doorway.

Later, when we're home, you collapse in tears over the prospect of walking on the floor in the bathroom, damp from someone taking a shower. (The bathrooms here have an open space for showers, no separation.) What will you happily overlook and what will cause you to melt down?

I think of you happily looking up at me, your face covered in rain, and think that I will never fully understand you. I don't think I have to. I'm so glad to be riding around with a small girl on my bike, I'm bursting with pride over you. I'm glad that this little clan started somewhere, in a small town in the far North of California, not so long ago.

I love you.

Your Mama.

August 6, 2008

So, what's new with us?

Well, we are not so successfully beating the jungle back. There were hundreds of thousands of army ants in the kitchen the other morning. They bit us as we tried to get them out.

I have bites all over my legs. Bed bugs. Hmmmm.

My cowboy hat has gone on to glory. I tried and tried, but couldn't keep the fungus off of it.

And the biggest deal? Our most important camera lens, the 24 −70 2.8 L, the very first lens we bought for our camera, has fungus inside of it. This is not good. We try to take very good care of our camera gear, but we didn't know that we were moving onto the set of a National Geographic documentary.

However, we are learning about how you deal with this climate, step by step, and none too soon. Because I can't be down about the cowboy hat or the bedbugs or the spider bite on my arm when our things arrived today! Our shipment, but as Kai said, "Can't we just call it our stuff now, since it's not on the ship anymore?" So, our stuff. It's here! It may seem silly to be so, so excited over some books and toys and instruments, but we are silly folks.

Now we need to try to take good care of our stuff in the jungle. Books need to be flipped through and aired out, a couple of times a week. The pages get soft and easy to tear, so you need to be very careful of them. I can't say that it doesn't make me feel sad, to think of my books getting smelly and soft and wilty, but things are things, right?

We will protect the guitar with our lives. The mattress is like the very clouds of the heavens. I'm really happy with the few toys I chose to ship. Lego, K'Nex, PlayMobil, Puzzles, and model dinosaurs and animals. Great stuff. And after three months of playing with about five beanie babies and a plastic monkey and polar bear, the kids are thrilled. THRILLED. Leafy can't believe his luck. He was very sad to stop playing and take a nap this afternoon.

Renee may come up for air eventually, but she has dug into the Lord of the Rings Trilogy for the first time (the books, of course) and so I doubt it. There is nothing sadder than Chinua for four months without a guitar, and I was amazed to hear him play and realize that's what the itchy feeling at the small of my back has been, all these long music-less days. Today I went to look through the drawer for that one steak knife, the one that we usually use to cut everything, before realizing that our knife set is here. *Our knife set is here.* And the homeschool stuff. Ahhhhhh. I'm such a nerd, but I could just stroke the books and smell the paper forever.

In short, we are very, very blessed to have our things.

And I would like to have a moment of silence for some stolen goods. For the computer box, which came to us empty. For the guitar strings and peg winder and wire cutter. We are very glad that they were they only things taken out of the guitar case, and not the guitar itself. Thankfully the computer (a laptop) was empty (of documents or important files). It was broken and we brought it to fix, to use as a back up and as something for the kids to work on. Somehow it never made its way to us. Stuff is stuff, right?

August 11, 2008

A Poem

Somewhere a man walks through a desert
With sand in the folds of his skin
Looking for water

Somewhere there is a high mountain
With thin, dry air
Eagles cry and soar beneath men who stand and watch them
Aware of the great distance below
Aware of how easy it would be to fall

Somewhere a river is running slowly
Small and tame and green
Hot rocks and smooth stones,
A child floats by on a raft

Somewhere there is a house
Almost rocking in the wind
Above a grey ocean- there are gulls and maybe terns
It is colder than normal for this season

Somewhere, somewhere, I sit at my open window
Sheets of rain fall, the spray fierce on my face
Everything is wet, everywhere, everywhere
Everything is wet.

August 12, 2008

Where have I been for nine months?

I think I forgot, somewhere along the line, that I am pregnant. Or maybe I forgot that pregnancy ends with birth. Doesn't that hurt? Right? I'm scared. And then after you don't get to sleep a lot, right? And there's milk, I remember the milk. Lots of milk. Oh yes, and the newborn cheeks and the sweet smelling breath and the kissable forehead. And there are those little grunting scritching noises. And the lack of heartburn. And the curled up bug on your chest.

I guess I can do this birth thing again.

August 15, 2008

No baby yet.

Just because I know that's the first thing on your mind. Don't you think about anything else? Me? I've moved on. Just because this baby prefers the inside doesn't mean that I have to think about the birth every day, hope for labor to start, jump up and down a little, complain unceasingly about how uncomfortable I am, look at my new stretch marks every day to see whether they've grown...

See how composed I am?

Composed enough to tell you about the fact that the water hasn't come for three days now, and we are hauling water out of the well, and I know you'll sigh and sympathize. (Maybe. Maybe you'll say, "buck up, woman, what did you expect when you moved to India?" And then you'll say, "*we're* hauling? Don't you mean, *Chinua's* hauling? He's the one who needs our sympathy. And you should be glad that you have a well." And then I'll say, "See- that's exactly the kind of thing that I needed to hear! Now I'm going to go kiss Chinua- or the Well Man, as I've begun calling him.")

That's all. Have a lovely day and think of me when you turn your tap on.

August 16, 2008

We've been having a little problem with our laundry.

Because it is so very rare that we have enough sun or even dry weather to dry our clothes outside, we let them dry in the kids' room, under the fastest fan, for approximately 48 hours, after which they still haven't been dry and they smell like the dog's tonsils. I'm not kidding. The other day the recorded humidity here was 98%.

We were coping. Then the rains started in earnest again, and it was taking 72 hours to dry the clothes, and at one point all the clothes in the house were in the washer waiting to be dried or on the line, waiting to dry. Waiting and waiting. And Leafy was underwear-less because there was not a single pair of dry undies.

I have a bed-wetter. I have a potty-trainer. And I have an older kid who still, at times, simply *cannot tear himself away* from whatever he is doing in time to make it to the toilet. You know what I mean if you have boys.

The idea of adding a bunch of baby clothing and cloth diapers, nursing wear and the overall generosity of fluids that accompanies Newborn Land into our drying kerfuffle simply overwhelmed me. There is no way around a lot of newborn laundry. We looked at dryers, and they were all very expensive. For us. (I was actually shocked to see a dryer in India at all. I had never seen one before.)

I was talking to my mom about this stuff, and she happened to be sitting next to my grandfather. My parents and grandpa were sitting and perhaps looking at the ocean at my parents' new house in Victoria, B.C., the one that I can't wait to visit. And I got on the phone with my dad and part way through our conversation he said, "Here's some news. Grandpa's going to buy you a dryer." And my dear wonderful Grandpa did it. He sent the money. Which is why we have our very own dryer.

The first time Chinua pulled *dry* sheets out of the dryer, he wept. And then Renee began to dance.

August 17, 2008

We have tentative water. Hooray! The water is tentative because not as much has been coming as usual, so we are being conservative with it. Which is always a good thing.

Yesterday I was very proud of myself for using a tiny bucket of water to wash Kenya's (plentiful) hair. The hair that now fits into a ponytail *without* her complaining about it being too tight, and looks so lovely in the ponytail, because it shows off the way her face is made, that I want to cry? Almost? Or just kiss her. There is no denying that she is a lovely girl. There is also no denying that I am the only person in my family with barely-there eyelashes. Everyone else has scads of eyelashes, enough eyelashes for several people.

So, if we are conservative, the water comes out of the taps to flush the toilet and go through the Aquaguard, our water filter. The Aquaguard is my favorite thing about this house. Imagine fresh, clean water just coming out of the wall. Or maybe it's not hard for you to imagine that, if you've never spent ten months hand-pumping every drop of water you drank through a stubborn carbon filter.

August 19, 2008

After a whopping 39 hours of labor, we have a boy named Solomon, born on August 19th, at 1:00 in the afternoon, weighing 9 lbs 4oz. I'm tired and happy. So, so happy to be done with that labor. Oh gosh.

He looks a lot like Leafy did, with Kenya's color of complexion. He fits right into our family perfectly. We are in love.

I promise to tell you more about the labor, but right now I have to nurse a wee one.

August 22, 2008

What wonderful creatures newborns are. The grunty squeaks, the rooting, the little frantic passes at your nose and lips. And then a wonderful stillness, almost a listening, before their digestive systems overtake them and overwhelm them and an explosive poop echoes into the peace of your bed.

Kai has this absolute horror of Solo's spit up. He loves to hold him and he is the sweetest older brother, but he gags if his baby brother spits up while he is anywhere near him. It makes me laugh.

We all love baby Solo. I am taking every single second that I can to stare at him. Chinua and I trip out on how much he looks like the others. He looks almost exactly like Leafy did, but from some angles I am strongly reminded of Kai as a newborn. And then it's Kenya. And then I am telling Chinua that I need to nurse Leafy, and he's all, *you need to nurse who?* It seems that there is a certain way that we make babies, and they don't stray far from the mold.

I'm a wonderful milky mess, with curves for approximately the fourth time in my life, curves that I show off to Renee and Chinua whenever I get the chance. "Check me out," I say. "My belly is gone and it has moved upward."

I'm weepy. "Do you hate me?" I asked Chinua this morning, tears pitifully flowing down my cheeks. "Do you think I'm a failure?" He lay beside me for awhile and reminded me of these hormone things that happen. It's the third day. Now is the time for tears, and milk, and then the baby pees on me and we are all soaking. And there is so much love, everywhere.

I love to eat. Kind people bring me food. Normally I make breakfast every morning, and lunch as well, but Jaya has been watching me and she brings me the very breakfast I would have made... fruit and muesli and yogurt and honey, even though I haven't asked her to. Now that I'm not pregnant, I don't feel nauseous anymore in the morning, I don't have to eat bite by bite, slowly, so that I don't throw up. I can chug back a glass of water if I want to, first thing in the morning, without having an upset stomach. Renee made me lunch and I had no heartburn after I ate it. I don't have a little tiny stomach that doesn't want to take in food.

That lunch was the best thing I have ever tasted in my whole entire life.

I am weak. Sometimes I feel like I will faint when I stand up. I walk around like an old lady, still exhausted from the birth. I am processing all that happened. I am writing it out slowly. I am recovering.

The kids sit on my bed and watch me nurse. They watch me change the baby, they hold him, they kiss him. I have three boys. I can't believe I have three boys. Leafy seems a little disturbed, although I think it is more from my absence than from the new baby, whom he loves. He sits on my lap and holds him on his lap, with that proud shy look he gets when he thinks he's doing something pretty cool. I'm so glad that Leafy fits on my lap again.

I stare at the baby, I smell him, I kiss him relentlessly. This is how it goes.

August 26, 2008

Some completely scattered thoughts:

Oh, I like him. Baby Solo is just the sweetest thing. Each time I've had a baby I've wondered if I'm up to it. But then there is the baby, with his smell (it really is all about the smell—God knew what he was doing) and sounds and warmth. It's totally okay to wake up every few hours.

Chinua and I have black plastic bags on our heads, with rubbing alcohol and apple cider vinegar steeping in our dreadlocks. We call this Lice kill, Stage Four. Don't even ask. Just feel sorry for us. Thanks. This is so not what I need right now. But I'm going to shut up about it.

Today Leafy started crying at noon, went to his bed, cried some more, refused to tell us why, and then put himself to sleep. He slept for four hours and then woke up in a perfect mood. (?) We are all feeling a little under the weather.

I made the chapati tonight, with Jaya hovering over my shoulder (under my shoulder, really, since she's about five feet tall) muttering under her breath about how not-round they were.

I can't keep myself from cleaning. I'm going to be in this house for a long time, but we're going to be house-hunting soon. The strangest things occur to me when I'm feeding the baby at night. Like last night, I was sitting there thinking about how much I loved it when our plane landed in Israel and everyone on board started to applaud.

We have some new friends, Brendan and Leaf, with us now, friends that we have known about for a long time but have only just now met. They are leaving tomorrow and I wish they didn't have to go. They have the sweetest little boy and he and Kenya have been like peas in a pod while they've been here. And they're Aussies and I love Aussies.

Everyone in this house makes chai differently. Did I mention that I have a garbage bag on my head right now? Did I mention that somehow the kids have managed to escape the lice? Did I mention that the last time I had lice I was in India? Seven and a half years ago? Tomorrow we are putting olive oil on our heads. Just so you know. My back is pretty sore. I'm actually pretty knackered. (Aussie.) Too much chapati making and lice treatment. Kenya has one of the most delightful laughs I've ever heard.

I was really happy about spending some time alone with Leafy after that gigantic nap, while Chinua had the other two kids out with him. I put the baby to bed and was telling Renee how good it felt, and she said, "Do you realize that you still have two kids home with you right now?" It's amazing, how mothers adjust to having a lot of kids.

The weather has made a change, but we sure do need that dryer still. I hope it will rain some more because everyone says it didn't rain enough this year. The sun has been nice, though. And the humidity has been much lower.

I'm pretty sure that I love my Superstar Husband more than I ever have before.

And I'm praying for friends everywhere. That's all for now.

August 28, 2008

My mom called the other day, wanting to know what on earth I was blathering about in my last post, when I said that I would be in this house for a long time, while in the very next breath I was talking about house-hunting.

I'm confusing, I know. That's what comes of writing while sleep-deprived and slightly delirious. You'll notice that I was rambling about lice, too. Ha ha. Who has lice? Not us!

Well, we do. Or we did. Hopefully. But enough about that.

What I meant about being in the house for a long time was that in a sense, I'm in confinement. There is a custom that a woman doesn't leave the house for forty days or more after birth, here in India, in China, and in who knows how many other countries. As soon as I moved here, I understood. Because if I leave, the baby comes with me, and really, Little Solo needs to be home, where it's safe and clean and (fairly, well okay, not all that) quiet.

So I'll be here for a few more weeks, and even after that, I don't think we'll be doing huge marketing trips in Solo's newborn stage of life. There simply aren't family rooms at the mall where we can sit and nurse. There isn't even a *mall*. I tend to be a girl who likes to be out and about, at least a little. I like the conquest of the market, the breeze rushing by me when I'm on the scooter. My creativity is fueled by motion, usually driving, sometimes walking.

That said, I'm looking forward to these next few months or

65

weeks. It is a far cry from Kai's infanthood, otherwise known as the time I stood in bank queues with him in the sling when he was five days old, feeling like my uterus was about to *fall out*.

Now we're more likely to be doing baby massage and more nursing. One of my favorite things about the birthing center here is their postnatal care. During this first week, one of the midwives has come to the house every day; to help take care of the cord, (so good in this climate—it took longer to fall off, and I would probably have worried over it without the help) just to talk, and to demonstrate the massage and bath. Of course I have massaged my babies before, but it is still nice to have a refresher.

So, yes, we'll be massaging and bathing and feeding and doing laundry and checking out the insect life and reading and doing math pages and workbook stuff and drawing and writing stories and Solo and I will be home together. While the others run around doing their run-around things, I will sink into home.

August 29, 2008

A giant moth came to visit us the other day, landing on my friend's skirt and then flitting over to a nearby curtain, where he sat and took a rest. His wing span was almost as long as my hand.

I have sick kids. They're not too bad, but the weather has changed again and it seems that when the weather changes, flu comes. At least that's what Jaya told me. But she also told me that snails are poisonous and I shouldn't let Kenya play with them. (Not true.) Anyway, whatever the reason, the poor Superstar Husband and the three older kids are sick. The kids don't let it bother them all that much. They're just a little more clingy and they don't want to eat.

Kenya woke up last night to go to the bathroom. Let me say that again. *Last night Kenya woke up out of her sleep all by her own self to go to the bathroom.* Except she did come to get me. But she WOKE UP. This has never happened. I remember bragging about what a good sleeper she was, back when she was a small toddler, and how someone said dolefully, "Those are the kids who have problems with bedwetting," (imagine Eeyore's voice) and how I thought, *Well gee, Puddleglum, thanks for bursting my bubble.* But then he was right.

I blame Haight Street, in San Francisco. I blame our bedroom over the street and the alley where we lived when she was a baby, where everything sounded as though hundreds of people were yelling outside at all hours of the night, and where the bouncer kicked everyone out of the club across the street at 2:30 every night and then stood on the street yelling, "Go, GO, GO" in a booming voice to get them to disperse, presumably so they wouldn't bother the neighbors. (!) Where she had to learn to sleep like a sleepy sloth just for self-preservation.

I think this "waking up" speaks well of days ahead, although I am only tentatively thinking this.

Of course, Leafy took his turn and wet the bed last night (he doesn't usually) and the baby was of course soaking in his cloth diapers, but two out of four isn't bad, right?! Right.

september

September 3, 2008

I'm trying to figure out how my own conscience meets the culture here—how the two can get along.

When Jaya first started working with us, or, when we first started living with her, when we moved into this house, I was never sure of myself. I knew that her last employer, an Indian woman, had completely different methods of dealing with a "servant" than I would ever be comfortable with.

In the West, cleaners and cooks are professionals, and are treated as such. I'm sure there are exceptions, but I've never personally come across a household that lived with such a hierarchy as exists here between castes. Castes, or what family you are born into, are categories that define your position in the workforce and dictate almost everything else about you, including who you can marry, what position you have in society, and how you are treated.

In my house, caste has no place. I don't believe in a caste system —it is as simple as that. I believe that people are brothers and sisters;

that we don't step down to reach one another, that we don't look up with cricks in our necks. But I struggled with treating Jaya differently than she was used to being treated. Would she feel uncomfortable? Would it mess with who she was in her society? I wanted to be sensitive, but I really didn't want her to feel servile towards my family.

We felt our way through it. I'm sure it was uncomfortable for her at times, getting used to us crazy Westerners when we were always doing things like jumping around and dancing in the living room. It was uncomfortable for me at times, trying to decide whether I should carry Jaya's chai to her when I made it, even knowing it made her flinch a little. But the chai was done, I wanted to give it to her. For me, acts of service are something we do for everyone. For her, it put me in her role, which, at first, made her uncomfortable.

But over the last couple of months, we've figured things out. Some of it has come from being really clear. *These are the things we'd like you to do.* And kindness is good for her, really, she flourishes. She laughs a lot now. She jokes with us all the time. I've come to love Jaya a lot. It's good to see that kindness can motivate someone to do their best just as much, if not more, than keeping someone "in their place."

And then there are other ways of being clear. Because the situation is strange right now, being as Jaya lives with us, there is never a time that she isn't here. I was uncomfortable because often when I tried to do something, Jaya would tell me that she could do it. But I like to do things. I like to do lots of things. So being clear really helped.

I make breakfast and lunch. Jaya makes dinner. I organize and tidy and put things away. Jaya does laundry and sweeps and mops. She does the dishes. We both put dishes away. Renee and Jaya and

I all alternate between making chai. (Although Jaya's is best.) Renee and I make the yogurt daily. Jaya and I both clean the bathroom. I take the trash to someone who can take it to the dumpster. I burn the bathroom trash. Jaya goes to the market to buy vegetables.

In a way, it's a lot like any community, although strangely, one of us is getting paid to be here and keep things clean. But the roles need to be defined so that everyone feels, "I can live here, I can make this my home." And that's what my conscience dictates to me. Although this is our house—my family's and Renee's, it is everybody's home.

September 5, 2008

This morning was rough. Mornings have been, lately.

Enter the dancing rhinoceros waving his palm fronds: Impossible to ignore, with the annoying whiny singsong voice singing the "Failure" song. I try to keep my chin up, to walk around him as politely as possible. I try to wake up with deep breaths in my lungs, shoulders back, to smile and be kind and be above it all. Above the breakfast traffic in the kitchen, Leafy on the floor crying because I can't get anything quick enough to suit him, Kai and his strong breakfast opinions. I try to be the older one, the calm one, the tallest.

Always ignoring the lumpy rhino sitting on my living room floor, smirking at me.

Sometimes the blogs I read are inspiring to me. There are lovely photos, beautiful images. And sometimes I wonder: do their kids ever drive them to use sharp words? Do their lives ever feel like chaos? Are there days when they sit and stare at the wall, willing themselves to get up and leap in, even though they just felt their last shreds of determination fizzle away in their stomachs?

You guys, it's really not the poo that gets to me. It's the squabbling. The complaining. The shrieking which is happening even right now, as I write this. This is what makes me feel that, try as hard as I might, I'm outnumbered. The atmosphere of my home is not really up to me. And they are winning.

They are children. They need to be helped through and over and above their emotions. But there are so many of them, and only one smiling me. (Actually, Chinua and Renee have been known to smile too, but they're not here ALL the time, and besides, screaming is *louder* than smiling.)

This weekend marks the fourth week that I have been only in the house, except for going to the birth center pregnant and coming home with a baby. (I was home for a week before the baby was born, since the scooter was too uncomfortable for me.)

Today my midwife came over and gave me the all clear to get on the scooter again, so today, in the late afternoon sun, I left the house, by myself, to get ingredients for a cake that I am making for Kai tomorrow. It's been four weeks. FOUR WEEKS.

I can't even tell you what it meant to me. I didn't have music playing, but it seemed to me that the loveliest songs were echoing over the rice fields. I have never seen anything so beautiful. The sun, the new flowers. The jungle seems friendly now, in the post-monsoon sun, not oppressive anymore. Leaves were burning with a beautiful fragrance. Down the road a bit, everything everywhere smelled fresh and new. I smiled at everyone I saw.

And when I got home, the rhinoceros was gone. Or rather, he was out in the yard, but I think I can keep him at bay.

September 7, 2008

Here's a story that goes back to another time and another place. It starts far from here, far from jungles, unless you consider the

71

jungle of the City a true jungle. In any case, the beginning of this story smells like eucalyptus trees in San Francisco.

It's where we met.

Chinua had already been living there for some time when I came along, but the point of *this* story (I could go on and on about how we met, and how we fell in love and how he fell down laughing when I made a joke and that's how I knew I loved him, but I won't) is that we lived with some of the truest and most beautiful people in the world, and we grew addicted to a certain kind of lifestyle.

It's a lifestyle of community. And community not in a myopic, insular sort of sense, but a community of people working together and living together with a purpose; to welcome other people in, to be rest for the weary, a family for the lonely, a soft place for a tired head.

Back then, we all busted it out to help out homeless kids (young folk, not children) who needed food and maybe a shower. Oh— those were fun days. I'll never forget them. I have memories that are like jewels to me, and I take them out and polish them whenever I can. I'm telling you, there is nothing like working together for bonding people and creating sweet and strong friendships. I believe this is what is called church, only it is easier to be together more often when you live close together and know each other really well.

So, we all lived in this big ol' house for a time, and then some of us decided to take a trip to India.

That was crazy. And fun. And life changing. And crazy. And we found that we loved not only the traveling kids and Rainbows in America, but the international traveling community. In fact, some of us, who seemed to have been born with wings on our heels, found that we really really loved the international traveling community.

And we went back to California. And then we came back to

India with even more friends. On our second journey, Chinua and I got engaged. And many other things happened. We saw the Kumbh Mela—a huge Hindu festival, the largest religious festival in the world. We rode on a ship and slept in hammocks. We got sick. We saw naked sadhus. We met many, many delightful travelers from around the world and had beautiful conversations over dinner in our little house. We talked about all of the important and brilliant things of life; the beginning, the purpose, and the end.

And then we came back to California.

Chinua and I got married in Canada, three days before 9/11. We always planned to head back to India. *We'll wait a few years to have kids*, we said.

And by Christmas we knew that we were expecting Kai. And then when Kai was ten months old, we found out that we were expecting Kenya. And then when she was thirteen months old, we found out that we were expecting Leafy. And through it all I wandered my Canadian self through the tangle of a permanent residency in the U.S. of A.

We were still doing what we've always been doing: Living with other people in our Jesus focused community, inviting people over, and helping where we can. Sometimes we did it more sanely than other times. Actually, we were mostly insane. But we were very, very idealistic. I remember one time, when I was pregnant with Kai, we were trying to help this girl who was perhaps crazy and very paranoid. She was really tripping out. But she was pleading for help. She wasn't sleeping well and she needed to sleep so her body could work better, so to make sure she felt safe, I had her sleep in the bed with me and Chinua slept on the floor at the foot of the bed. Not your average situation. But things like this came to us a lot, and it always seemed like God was asking us, *What do you think you can do to help this girl/boy/man/woman?*

For a while we lived in a little house in a town in the far north of California. (For a time, all our roommates were guys. *Every weekend, Kung Fu movies.*)

And then we moved back to San Francisco, where we lived in a flat on Haight St. with about a hundred people. Well, not a hundred, but it might have been.

And then we moved to the Land, where we lived in a one-room cabin for a year, until a bigger house was ready for us. It was lovely and beautiful, and turned out to be unsustainable for our community. But God was calling our names out in loud ringing tones again! And this country, India, that had been in the back of our minds for so long, well—we were ready to try to make it here again.

To live the way we love to live, we have always needed to live simply. We spend our money on very basic things, in order to have the freedom to be around people, in small spaces and big ones, traveling at times, stationary at times. When the Land was sold, it went into a trust that helps with the set up costs of starting a new community. Chinua and I are also working on becoming sustainable financially from our art, music, and writing. We want to perfect our crafts and truly make them a huge part of our lifestyles. (At times, the needs of people and community have rushed over the things we feel gifted at, like a tidal wave.) And we have several incredibly loving friends who have helped us at various times, believing in what we do.

We're here to do the same things that we've always done. We want to be a haven for the weary traveler, a creative and loving community, devotees of Jesus. We have big dreams! Art, gardens, music, dance. We want to make stuff, we want to be living and vibrant, a community that glows. Tomorrow Chinua and I celebrate our seventh anniversary. Seven, the number of completion, and here we are, with a brand new start, back where we first decided to commit a lifetime to each other. And wow, our four kids are with us. Whew! We are heading into the adventure of the first traveler season, looking for a spot that will be the right place for us, wading in waist deep, continuing- onward and upward!

September 9, 2008

We are by no means tired of each other...

...but we *are* tired.

Yesterday the marriage of myself and my Superstar Husband turned seven.

There was a study done awhile ago about romance being rekindled by embarking in new activities together.

"... several experiments show that novelty — simply doing new things together as a couple — may help bring the butterflies back, recreating the chemical surges of early courtship."

If this is the case; we're onto something with this whole "moving to a country far far away" business. But yesterday we were house hunting. It was my first time out with Solo, and by the time we got home I was so exhausted that I begged to postpone our anniversary dinner until tonight. I didn't want to be falling asleep at the table. Today Chinua has been in bed, suffering from some sort of immune system overload. He's just conked *out*. Poor poor man.

And so, today, we postpone our night of gazing into each other's eyes again. But, you know, I'm so glad that tomorrow we will have another chance. And if that doesn't work out... the day after. And another day and another day after that—because we decided to spend our life elbowing each other while we sleep. Marriage is amazing.

September 11, 2008

I don't know which is sweeter—Kai earnestly trying to show Kenya how to do the trick where Daddy pulls his finger off, or Kenya just as earnestly explaining to Kai that he's not *really* doing it, that he's only *pretending*, and Daddy REALLY TAKES HIS FINGER OFF.

September 12, 2008

Up with the baby at night, I had been lying in bed wondering, "What will we do if we don't get any water tonight?" It had been three days already, and we were all desperate for a shower, needed clean clothes, and needed to treat our heads for lice again.

(Since Chinua and I have dreadlocks, we can't use a lice comb, so we've had to re-treat several times to get rid of any lice that may have hatched. Finally, after several tries, we seem to have found a treatment that really work—the medications didn't—so we're on top of it now and are mainly being careful.)

I knew in the morning that no water had come. Why, why why did we not have any water? Normally we get water from the municipality piped into our huge tank. There had been a problem on our water line which resulted in days without any water coming in, but this was getting ridiculous. Something else had to be wrong.

The first thing I heard that morning was, "Mom! Leafy pooped in the bed!" It was a brilliant start to the day. How do you deal with things like this with no running water? Of course, we have the well. Chinua has so sweetly and uncomplainingly drawn up bucket after bucket of well water for us when the running water has given out.

But this morning was different. Jaya had drawn my attention the night before to a small animal, perched on a ledge corner far down in our Really Big Well. It must have fallen in somehow. It was still

76

alive, but we couldn't keep using the well with it in there. Jaya and I leaned out of the window and tried to figure out what it was. A kitten? Awww, poor kitten! But then it lifted its pointed nose. "Is it a RAT?" I asked. We both jumped in horror. If it was a rat, it was gigantic. Ewwwww.

I got up and cleaned Leafy up somehow, and then turned to making breakfast. Jaya came in. "You need to call this man this morning," she said, and I nodded.

"At eight," I said, stirring the oatmeal and throwing some raisins in. "I'll call him at eight."

The man I needed to call was our landlady's handyman. We wanted to ask him about what on earth was going on with the water, as well as ask him for help with getting this, uh, creature, out of the well. His name is Matthew, but Goan people pronounce it, "Madhue." Madhue obviously thinks we're a little cracked, but since he doesn't speak much English, he only tells Jaya, and she is polite enough not to let on too much. Renee has made the observation that he has a biblical face, and she is right. He'd be the perfect casting to play Joseph, or maybe John the Baptist, if his hair was a little longer and he was snacking on locusts.

Madhue came a little while later. Frustrated and stressed out from trying to do eight things at a time, I had eventually handed the phone to Chinua so he could call him. Madhue took a peek in our well, then asked if we would like a tanker of water to come to fill the tank. This was a new option. We said, "Heck yes we do!" or something of that nature. Madhue left and came back with three people—a couple of men and a young girl—to see about getting the animal out of the well. The house was full of people walking back and forth, I was helping the kids with their math, and it was just chaos.

Renee wandered into the big room where the kids and I were.

"They're going to kill it," she said, and then clapped her hand over her mouth as she realized she had just blurted it out in front of the kids.

Kai looked up.

"They're going to KILL it?"

I explained that sometimes when an animal is hurt, it can't get better, and you need to help it by stopping its suffering. These were new concepts. The people left to get more supplies or something, and Jaya corrected my assumption.

"These people want to eat this animal."

Kai looked up again, his eyes huge.

"They want to EAT it?"

We all wanted to see the little guy survive, so we tried to think of ways to rescue it: Chinua, our friend Cate (who has arrived, hooray!) and Jaya put food in buckets to try to get the little guy to climb in. Meanwhile, the tanker had arrived, and water was being pumped into our tank.

Oh, how stoked we were. Now we could move to the next phase of hair treatment. As people continued to parade through the house, I gave up the school morning entirely, and decided to slather the kids' heads with olive oil. Yum. It needed to be on their heads for the rest of the day, smothering anything that might be on their heads, before we could wash it off. Kai was the only one that we were sure about— treating the other kids was mainly out of paranoia. But olive oil was simple. When we were done, the kids had big black plastic bags on their heads, and we kissed them, because they were oily and adorable.

So far, there was no luck getting the animal out of the well. It seemed doomed.

Jaya came in with bad news. "The pump is broken. And the water is gone."

"WHAT?" We had done two loads of laundry and one sink full of dishes. The water from the tanker, 5000 liters, had leaked out of some hole in the tank. This explained our water problem a little more clearly. There was a tiny bit left, but now the pump that brought the water from the tank outside into the tank in our house was broken. We all groaned.

But the little animal had been climbing! He was part way up, in a little hole in the side of the well.

It was obviously time to tie bedsheets in the well, Rapunzel-style, to help him along.

Madhue came back and made the diagnosis that there was a hole in the tank. Thanks, Madhue. We needed to plaster it. It would take about three days. *This was too much!* (That's a Jack Handey quote, by the way, I just needed to throw that in there.) It was lovely that we also all had olive oil on our heads, lulled into safety by the promise of a tanker full of water.

Our neighbor from across the street, a delightful British hippie guy, came by at about this time. He and Chinua put a ladder into the well to help the animal a little more. By this time, he was only about ten feet from the top.

And he offered his house for showers in the evening. Oh sweet, kind neighbor. He had also filled us in on the fact that what was in our well was a palm civet. They are rare and protected in India. We were glad that we hadn't let the people eat it. Now if only it could climb out! Since they are nocturnal, we hoped it would climb out at night. They eat chikoo fruit, so it had probably fallen out of our chikoo tree and into the well.

We trekked down to our sweet kind neighbor's house to take our showers, rubbing dish soap in our hair to get the olive oil out. Kenya and I were accompanied by a lovely butterfly, who hung out with us in the bathroom while we showered.

79

The next morning? The palm civet was out. One more crazy day here, another small animal out of a well.

(The pump is fixed. Water is sporadic, but we are conserving and making the best of it. We put another pump into the well for emergencies. Life is good.)

September 13, 2008

I'm ex-mausted, as my husband likes to say, and the monsoon, she is back.

We had some weeks of sun. Weeks when I was in the house. But I do not complain, for the rice fields, they need rain.

I need to start doing Pilates. My back, she is killing me.

Chinua and I went out for dinner last night. It was lovely. Solo did well. He loves to be bathed. He's very inquisitive. He's just the best. And he looks like me.

We have put a rent deposit down on a new house. Or, rather, houses, because our friend Cate has arrived. Again, we are stoked. As soon as she walked in the door, Kenya started filling her in on every single thing that has happened since we last saw her, in Israel.

We now are proud renters of two little houses with two bedrooms each, and an adjoining yard. One is for Renee and Cate, and one for us. They are not Portuguese style, like the house we are in now, but regular concrete Indian houses with low ceilings. We are going to make a garden in between them. The house we will live in is still being built.

Have I mentioned that Solo smells really good?

Also that I love him?

But waking up with him at night makes me very, very tired.

Tired enough that I write like this.

And go to bed at half past 8.

September 14, 2008

It's like we were raised during the Depression or something.

(Let me make the disclaimer that this was first thing in the morning, so I was pretty sleepy.)

Renee: "So, did you see my note?"

Me: "Nope."

Renee: "Well, last night when I went to add the starter to the milk to make yogurt, there was a little frog in the milk. Do you think I should throw it out?"

Me: "Did it just jump in and jump out?"

Renee: "No, it was dead. I think it got in when it was hot and couldn't get back out."

Me: "Hmmm. Let me ask Chinua. Chinua, there was a dead frog in the yogurt, do you think we shouldn't eat it?"

Chinua: *"What?"*

Me: "A frog got into the yogurt and died—we shouldn't eat it, right?"

Chinua: "Why are you even *asking* me that? Of COURSE not!"

Rae: "Oh... right."

September 16, 2008

A glimpse into the mind of my youngest son:

Whoa! I'm falling! Oh, false alarm. No, I'm faaaallling! Oh actually, it's okay. I'm not falling.

There's something soft! Maybe there's milk? I think it's milk! Not milk. It was worth a try.

81

Wow, that is the most beautiful line that I've ever seen. That line is ssooooo beautiful. I love that line.

I'm faaaaalllling! Oh, is that milk? Maybe there's milk! Something soft, it might be milk...

Oh my gosh, that is the loveliest shadow that I've ever seen. I've never seen anything as beautiful as that shadow. I think I'll lie here for a while and stare at that shadow.

Oh, I don't like lying at this angle at all. Not at all. Somebody change things quick! This is so uncomfortable I just can't bear it! Why is no one moving me? Oh, softness! Wait, is that milk?

September 22, 2008

Dear Solo,

This morning you smiled right into my eyes for the first time; one of those big gummy smiles with slightly squinched up eyes. Heartbreaking stuff, my boy. I felt another small piece of my insides being filed away in a tiny box with a label. "Love for Solo's smile," it says, in block letters and permanent marker.

(Sometimes I imagine that there is a mosaic of sorts, inside me, and all these little bits are devoted to small parts of my loved ones. Leafy's lips; a blue triangle, Kai's eyes; a square piece of a green plate, Kenya's edible nose; one of those dented glass marbles that you might find in a fish tank. The smell of Chinua's neck; a small, perfect ruby. These form the most beautiful picture, right in the center of me.)

But you, Solo. I don't have much to say. You turned a month old a couple days ago, and we celebrated by cuddling and having milk, just like we celebrate every day. This time around, I am amazed mostly by how physical this all is. You are held and burped and nursed and kissed. And the feelings I have for you are linked irrevocably to your smell, your sounds, the way you nuzzle your head back and forth when you are looking for me. I'm so tired, sometimes, in the middle of the night. I mean, really, it's a nice time to sleep. And there you are, grunting and squeaking and wanting milk. Argh. But then I pick you up and your head is by my cheek and your hair is so soft, and I'd say that I would stay up all night with you every night, if I could.

I'd say that, if only your brothers and sister wouldn't insist on waking up at such a horrific hour.

I love you, Solo. We all do.

Mama

September 25, 2008

On the porch, the jungle night is alive with the vibrations of hundreds of thousands of insects. They have so many different sounds; the clicking, the rubbing, the creaks and rhythmic squeaking.

I sit and think about small regrettable things. Words I should not have spoken, sharp frowns, unkind eyes. My children receive the best of me, but they also are on the other end of my impatience, my fretfulness, my lack of intention. Most of the time they don't even notice when I am grumpy and not fully there. Sometimes, like today, there is something small that has crept inside, something that I have to tiptoe into their room to repair, when they should be already sleeping.

There has been an angry fire inside me, for a few days now.

In the distance I can hear a hundred howling dogs, irate and roused about something or other. Maybe a stranger to the dog clan tried to invade their trash pile.

The truth is that sometimes happiness is boring, obstinate, or old, sometimes the simplest things take too long, sometimes beauty is messy and thoughtless. Tonight I have so many resolves for the days to come. I will open my face, I will play more. I will be more thankful, I will laugh.

In the morning a thousand birds will bring the jungle to life in their own way, singing and chirping and shrieking and rustling. I'm so glad that we get so many mornings. There is one for every day. The darkness of the evening covers our regret, but the morning holds a new song, if we will wake up to hear it.

September 27, 2008

We are moving again, very, very soon. As excited as I am, it makes me tired to think about it. And so I don't. I'm procrastinating nicely.

It's exciting because we will be living smack dab in the center of a little Goan village, full of lovely Goan people and also many, many international travelers. Hippie travelers. The kind that carry didgeridoos and guitars with them, as we saw yesterday when we went to check on our new house.

At the moment we are living in another village that has large houses that are more spaced out. We've only gotten to know a few neighbors. I know this won't be the case in our new village, which is also on the beach. The wonderful beach, filled with kids playing soccer, some trash, many cows looking for friends, the inevitable beach dogs, gypsy women selling things, and tourists who want to take our pictures. I've really never seen anything like it. It's beach culture, but with Indian intensity.

September 29, 2008

Lately there seems to be a closed door in my mind. On the

other side of that door is clear thinking.

On my side there is a lot of wire, some bits of old fabric, a few nails, a pineapple that I forgot to eat before it went bad, and a rhinoceros. *And* a post-it note that says, "In case you were wondering, the water didn't come tonight."

I think it's just that there are so many small holes in the road for me to leap over. They take up all my mind-space and keep me on this side of the door. We need to move. But when? And how? And is Jaya coming? Is she not? What about the dog that we are watching?

I need to go to the market tomorrow. But I need to learn to drive our van, first. (We bought an old van, a tiny Maruti Omni.) I've never driven a car here, on the left hand side of the road, with the stick shift in my left hand. To tell the truth, I'm a little afraid.

But then I'm afraid of a lot of things. And I'm learning that the only way to deal with it is to leap in head first, letting all of you get wet until your feet slip in last, and you are swimming. So tomorrow morning, Chinua and I will go out and drive in circles in the jungle, and I hope I don't ruin another clutch, like I did when I learned to drive stick shift with my dear father.

And here's another thing: When the children of Israel wandered in the desert before they entered the promised land, they were afraid all the time. And years went by, and they forgot that there had always been water in dry places for them. Even water from a rock. Food out of the sky. Their sandals never wore out. In forty years, their sandals never wore out.

Often fear is in forgetfulness. I forget about my life and every jewel, every small cup of water, and I am afraid for the future. But trust doesn't come from looking forward. It comes from remembering, from storing, from searching among pieces of fabric and a few nails and a lot of wire for the things that have always held us up.

September 30, 2008

We have frogs and toads all over. I just saw a few hop past. We also have bats. The jungle is so alive. Kenya plays with the insects for hours, holding caterpillars up to her face to feel their fuzziness. This horrifies Jaya beyond description.

Today I heard Leafy say, as he let a teeny tiny black ant crawl onto his hand, "Come on little ant, I'll give you a ride on my finger!"

Still fighting back the fear here, folks! But as Jesus said, "Each day has enough troubles of its own."

I drove the van this morning! And there were no casualties. It messes me up, worse than I thought it would, to have the gear shift in my left hand. I feel like I'm trying to learn how to drive stick shift, or "standard" as we would say in Canada, all over again.

People laughed at me many times. Because I'm funny looking! And foreign! And driving a van! Not to mention stalling. I take it all in stride. But I was sweating by the end of our marketing episode. There really aren't many road rules. Use your horn a lot, pass when you feel you can, get where you need to go. If say, you're at a traffic circle, feel free to exit from the inside lane or the outside lane. Actually, what am I talking about? There are no lanes!

Thankfully we are all driving fairly slowly.

october

October 2, 2008

It was my Superstar Husband's birthday yesterday. We didn't plan a whole lot. I was rather at a loss. My hands feel quite full, lately. But I made him an omelette for breakfast, with some yogurt and chai on the side. He liked it. He's 35 and I can't imagine that I ever didn't have him beside me.

We decided to be spontaneous. *Let's just drive!* So we got into our little white van and drove to a beach north of here. Right away I spotted purple flowers. My flower loving heart has been in a state of bliss lately. All the flowers and their cousins have come out to see the post-monsoon sun. We laid out our bed sheet and sat down quickly so it wouldn't blow away. The kids ran and played in the sand and the surf, and Chinua and I sang together while he played his little travel guitar.

The beach was not too crowded, but a group of men came by at one point and stood looking at us. We sat and kept singing. We talked a little and then they went on their way. I used my body to shelter Solo from the wind. The kids played tic tac toe in the sand.

When we were hungry we packed up and drove off to find some food. We ate on a little plastic table on the beach in the village where we will be living soon. I was excited to see how many kids there were. We talked about the past year. It has been a momentous one for both of us. Chinua juggled for a while on the beach, and the people at the table next to us broke into applause at a particularly good trick. The kids ran panting and laughing in a circle around him while he juggled.

On our way back to the van, in the dark, we found a shop where the birthday man picked out some clothes. The shopkeeper joked with him and chased the kids through the racks of clothing. The clothes were beautiful and very easy on our budget. Chinua told me, as we kept walking in the dark, that this was one of his favorite birthdays ever. I know that it was one of my favorite *days* ever. What a happy birthday.

October 5, 2008

I'm pretty exhausted right now, due to a gassy-baby Sunday. The child barely slept all day. But he's doing better at night—actually, really great at night, so I'll catch up, I think. This is a tiring time of life for me. And very, very blessed. Do things always come in extremes? I wonder this at night, when I think of all the people who tell me to treasure these moments, but then I forget to treasure them while I'm busy hunting for my keys because my brain exited when my free time did.

Jaya has been gone all weekend, which is good because I need to get back into the swing of things. We move in a week, and she won't be coming with us. I don't regret a single moment of having Jaya work for us. We've learned so much and I've already become SO much more confident about living here, but I'm excited about having a kitchen that is my own. My chapatis have been getting better and better, too.

I'm torn about moving. It will be wonderful, I know, but I don't like change. I believe this is due to my lack of imagination about the real world. I can't fathom how things will turn out. We'll just have to see.

Once again, after having a baby, I'm filling up with creative juices. All these ideas, all these thoughts. They come to me in dreams, I mull over issues and see wonderful things that I would like to write about, or photograph, or paint. My book always calls to me — it almost hurts. I really want to do more visual art again. I feel far from it. All the creativity... but NO TIME. No time.

I make lists. *These are my goals for the month.* They are modest goals, but I don't get them done. Sigh. Big sigh. I will not wish this dear, maddening, sweet time in my life away. Not one minute in delicious baby time, not one long complicated story from a six-year-old boy. I won't will it to pass. I will take the advice of those older and wiser than myself, and not rush it. You can't spend all of your life frustrated, you know? Better to sink into it. I love them, I love them. They are slowly making me into the person who I really want to be.

The book will get written some day. Maybe this will be the month that I make my modest goals. And maybe the pigs we feed with our scraps, down the hill from us, maybe they'll sprout wings also.

It could happen.

October 7, 2008

Today I almost packed it in, curled into a ball, and had a grand old pity party. I mean, really. It was three in the afternoon and I was so tired, and I almost cried. I think I did cry, a little. My eyes were wetter than normal, anyway, although I don't think any tears actually *fell*.

I was just tired. This morning I called a tanker again to get some water because no water had come for a few days, and our tank has a hole in it, so we need water every other day. At least this time I knew that all I needed to do was call the tanker, pay him the equivalent of seven dollars, and have our tank filled with water that would seep out into the jungle. However, the hole is maybe a fifth of the way down the tank, so we have that one fifth left.

While the water seeped, we did everything we could to use it, before it left. Everyone got a shower whether they wanted one or not. Everyone had their hair washed, whether they wanted to or not. And actually, everyone needed all of the above, because, like I said, it had been a few days. But it meant that I spent the morning bathing everyone. Which is great! Except for the crying. And the whining. Do any of you have kids that act as though they are being tortured when REALLY what's going on is someone is pouring lovely *warm water* over their heads and then massaging their scalps gently with *nice-smelling shampoo,* and holding a towel *kindly to their foreheads* every few moments to make sure that no dreaded water gets into their eyes?

I mean, I would pay money for it. I would not stand there, naked and wailing and carrying on. But, I also would not spend half a day delighted by the antics of a caterpillar, so I guess it all evens out.

So. Everyone was washed and all the laundry was done and the dishes were clean and the house somewhat picked up, and Jaya and I were ready to hit the market. I'm getting a lot better at the driving thing. You just have to grit your teeth, honk with the best of them, and drive into the tiniest spaces you've ever seen. Chinua was home with all the kids while we went.

We split up, did our shopping as quick as we could, and then walked around in the sun looking for each other for as long as it took us to shop. I told Jaya where to meet me, but then she wondered if she heard wrong, and we walked back and forth, missing each other.

Anyway, I'm losing my point. My point is, eventually we got home, and I found myself, in the afternoon, trying to help Kai do some math, and realizing, *look, Rae, it's the hottest part of the day, you won't get anyone to do anything now, so don't even try*. So I told the kids to play, put Leafy down for a nap, took the bucket of food scraps down to the neighbor's pigs, and set the bathroom trash on fire in the backyard. Just when I was sitting down with a cup of chai, ready to read for a half hour or so, I heard it. The baby crying.

I still had things to clean, emails to write, faxes to send.

And that is when my eyes got a little wet.

And that is also when I decided to chill the heck out. I picked up Solo, sat down, and hung out with him for an hour. We looked at each other and smiled and talked and I didn't cry. The kids played pretend stuff, and I listened and laughed. And when I finally had put the baby to bed, a sweet Italian/French couple with their two kids stopped by because they had heard about our family and they wanted to meet us. We made arrangements to get together on Saturday.

And oh, I don't hate my life, I love my life. I just need to slow down, sometimes, and look around at who I'm with.

October 9, 2008

I need to tell you that the Leafy Boy calls his forehead his "two head."

While I'm sure that he is not the first two-and-a-half-year-old to think up this great wordplay, (Kenya has a four head, I must have a

91

two head), it would surely break your heart with cuteness to hear it in his husky, slightly lispy voice, coming from such delicious lips.

October 10, 2008

Thinking about depression, I started wondering about what I have forgotten. It's always there in my brain: *I have struggled with postpartum depression with each of my babies,* but then I forget what it was really like, because I have a habit of remembering only the good things.

(The smell of the trees, the light through the leaves, the river talking to us night and day, not the unreliable water, the falling down buildings, the septic tanks that didn't work.)

I dug through some of my old poems and found one that I wrote when we lived in San Francisco after Kenya was born. It's true as true about PPD... the love mingled with darkness. I thought I'd share it.

*

dreams

my infant daughter wakes in the still night
[it is quiet for once on the streets
outside our window.
everyone gone home
or sitting in silent stupor,
having finally run out of things to scream about.]

my infant daughter wakes and I
can tell from her thin sad cry that fear brings her out of
sleep; afraid of what shapes I can't imagine
what nightmares jostle her into wakefulness

[do you dream of being wrapped in
blankets that cannot warm you,
or maybe of being wide eyed but blind?
or do you dream of being alone
under huge pale colorless skies?]

I won't tell you what it is like to be alone,
and what nightmares are like once you have names
for them. I won't tell you of cracked houses falling
and deep sorrows revealed. dreams of betrayal and
adultery, even death. all the nameless unsayable fears that are
haunting in the night, that wake you up crying
with a taste like vinegar in your mouth.

[when you have bad dreams I pick you up and
sing the fear into yesterday. I look down into your eyes
and wait for sleep to carry you back smiling.]

where is the calm for my dreams, both waking and asleep?
who will send the tornadoes into oblivion,
calm the monstrous tigers with gaping mouths?

windows with no glass, roaring wind enters.
wounds and holes and old friends' hurt.
torn clothes, no clothes.

[I will keep you, my worst dreams are of not
having you... my haunting is what might have been
if you never had been born.]

[sometimes, though, dreams bring safety not grief
often there are warm hands for me to hold
I am not alone
and I will shrink into my blankets until sleep comes
to carry me back smiling.]

October 14, 2008

When Kai was just six weeks old, my grandparents drove down from Alberta to California to meet him. I think they were visiting friends as well, but I'm pretty sure a yummy six-week-old baby was a big draw.

I was floundering a little. I was doing okay. Just okay. I had hemorrhaged after Kai was born, so I was very anemic and weak, tired and overwhelmed. I thought, though, that this was just how parenting felt. I was also working and was back in the bank making deposits only five days after Kai was born, not realizing that this was just plain dumb.

Sometimes I look back at myself and think, "You poor girl."

Anyway. My grandparents.

They came and they saw our precious first baby (my Grandma was big on the word precious, and since she just passed away in April, it still hurts me to write 'was') and Grandma cuddled him close, just like I've seen her cuddle us in our old baby pictures. She always had this fierce, possessive look on her face when she was holding us. I feel that face glomming onto my own face, at times, when I look at my kids.

She was holding Kai out, away from her a little, with his head in her hands, looking into his wee face. "Oh the laddie," she said. He started to coo to her.

"Oh yes, tell me a story," she told him. "Tell Grandma Great a story."

94

And this is what I've thought of, every time my kids get to this absolutely incredible stage: Telling stories. The littlest things can be missed. I may never have realized that my babies were telling me stories, if it wasn't for my Grandma. There's nothing like lessons from someone in your life who already had grown up children when *you* were born.

October 15, 2008

This and that:

The moon tonight was a huge orange circle, hovering just over the jungle as I scooted down into town tonight for a little late evening shopping. The day was so crazy that I felt like I was escaping, riding on my scooter through the wafting of smoke from burning trash and the smell of the jungle cooling down after a hot day.

The heat has been intense, this last week. The kids have this strange bumpy heat rash on their fingers and toes. I'm just coasting, as far as school is concerned. Whatever we don't get done before the hot part of the day, doesn't get done. It's a good thing that we are ahead. Goan school is out at 1:00 or 1:30 in the afternoon. I am beginning to see why. Brains shut down from 2:00 to 3:00.

Leafy inexplicably calls geckos "penguins." "I saw a penguin on the wall!" he shouts happily.

Leafy poured a bottle of vanilla (fake) and soy sauce (real) onto the counter today. Yesterday he squeezed half of the tube of toothpaste into the sink. I've explained to him about the global economy, but I think he's intent on sabotage.

The other day Chinua broke down on the scooter. A man (who happened to be a mechanic) stopped, picked him up, and then stayed up all night to fix the scooter because he was leaving for out of town the next day. In the morning he brought the scooter to us

95

and charged us about $35. It was an unbelievably kind thing to do.

On the other hand, the used refrigerator salesman really did try to convince Cate and Renee that the fridge he sold and delivered to them was working, even though it, well, WASN'T. What, they broke it within half a minute?

I am so ready to move. I am ready to have my own house, my own kitchen, my own routines. I am ready to not have a live-in housekeeper. I am ready to feel more free, to not worry so much about my kids making a mess because I can hear her sigh and see her look over at me with frustration even if I'm cleaning it up. I am ready to not have her snapping at Kai.

I love Jaya. And for the season around the birth it was perfect to have her here. Maybe it is just a sign that it is the right time to move on—the fact that I'm dying to do things my way and I'm so glad when she takes a day off and we have the house to ourselves and I can wash my dishes and do my laundry and it's mine ALL MINE!

I'm a freak. A control freak. I've come to think that you have to be, to be a mom.

I need some mental health leave. Halfway through the day I realized that I was having angry conversations with various people in my head. This is never a good sign. Not only is it a waste of energy, it's also a little, you know... nutso.

Today we went to the birthing center for a little group baby check up and Solo was the youngest and largest baby there. He's a whopping 13 pounds and 4 ounces. 6 kg. The giant baby.

Although it may be understood throughout most of the United States and Canada that it is not the nicest thing to walk up to someone and call their baby "whitey," it doesn't seem to be a global understanding. Or at least not with one certain man I know, who comes from a country in Europe. This is one of the startling things about living internationally.

Yesterday we were invited over to the house of some new friends to celebrate her birthday. The Mama kissed me and the little girl told me things in Italian and the Dad gave us all the cake he had magicked up in his small oven.

Kai wanted me to lie down with him to help him go to sleep tonight. He was afraid of beetles dropping on his bed. Personally, I'd be more afraid of cockroaches or centipedes, but to each his own. I tried reasoning with him, asking him what he thought would happen if a beetle *did* fall on his bed. I mean—it would just run away, right? But that didn't work, so I lay beside him and stroked his hair and hummed for a while, and then he turned to me and said sweetly, "There IS a one-legged animal." And by this I knew that he was feeling better.

And I turned over and whispered into the sky, out to that moon, whispered to that Great Papa out there that I'm a little afraid sometimes too, of bugs and the economy and being displaced and angry people and not pleasing people, even the woman who works for me, and would he please sit next to me to help me sleep? And he didn't even try to reason with me. He just lay next to me and stroked my hair.

October 17, 2008

We moved yesterday. I love it here. Our house is smaller and hotter, we are buried away in between the rice paddies and the jungle and the beach, and I love it.

The floor is constantly sandy, and still I love it.

I made very mediocre Indian food tonight, and still I love it.

I spent the day washing the sticker goo off of our stainless steel dishes, and still I love it.

And now I will fall face down on my bed and not get up for a few hours. Right after I give Solo a bath.

October 18, 2008

They have completely rewritten the memory of our major car accident in November.

I eavesdrop on their conversation as they sit perched precariously on the place where the backboard of their bed and the windowsill meet.

"Remember when we got into the car accident?"

"Uh huh... and we went straight down that hill?"

"Yeah, and remember it was SO FUN?!"

"Mmmm and we thought it was so much fun!"

"And I said, 'WHEEEEE' when our car just went right off the cliff and then I said 'Wait, why is everyone crying?'"

"And we all said WHEEEEEE!"

"And then I cried because you were crying."

"But it was so fun, and then we got to go to the DOCTOR! Remember that?"

"And in the ambulance, and that was so fun."

Apparently, I was the only one who was really afraid. The crying was all just a mistake! Seriously, though, it's really good to see that they are not traumatized.

October 21, 2008

My life has changed a lot during the last half of a year. Who am I kidding, though? It's been a full year of change. Now I am adjusting again. Wowsers.

This house is wonderful. Small, simple and deep in a tiny village neighborhood, it is just where I want to be. Our next door neighbors thresh rice on their rooftop and feed our scraps to their pigs. The men in the village come to the well we all share to take their showers. I'm not sure where to look. Of course they are wearing underwear, but should I go inside, if I am sitting on my porch? Is a public bathing time private?

I guess I will find out.

Yesterday was a little bit rough. Our water problems have been solved, largely, by moving here, although we are a little wary of the fact that all our water is well water now. (There are fish and a turtle living in the well.) But yesterday morning we woke up without power and there was no power all day, and eventually the tank on our rooftop ran out of water and there was no power to pump more up. And we had very little food. And it was very hot and because we had no power, we had no fans. I mean, it's HOT. Hot hot hot.

There was a strike throughout all of Goa and I think that explains the power outage. A strike here is different than a strike in North America. Basically an extremist group says, "Close your businesses or we will hurt you." So everyone does.

I did what any mama with four young kids does on a day when there is no power and no water and it's HOT. I let the kids watch a DVD until the battery ran out. There are times when you realize that the day's goal has been simplified to: Get through this in a loving way.

And then we all walked to the beach, where the kids rolled in the surf and I stood there up to my calves in the water, with the baby in the wrap on my chest, and watched my kids laughing. A man came along and wanted to sell me some things, and although I told him I didn't really have money to buy jewelry right now, he told me about his children, and that he had no business. So we sat down in the sand and he laid his livelihood on a sarong for me to rifle through and critique. We settled on a couple of things, and he told me to pay him the next time I see him. I told him to say hello to his wife for me, and he thanked me for the business.

The kids and I walked home and saw what Kenya called a "pile of goats." ("A pile of goats would be goats stacked up on each other," interjected Kai, and I laughed out loud, which embarrassed him because he didn't understand that what he said was genuinely funny.)

And about half an hour after we got home the power came back on and I filled up the tank and ran the filter to fill up the water bottles with stuff to drink and was just glad.

October 23, 2008

Dear Solo,

We made it to two months. All in one piece, too. Actually, let me check. (Counting my fingers and toes...)

Okay, yes, all in one piece. But tired, oh so tired.

Oh, Baba. Solo. You are the best thing that has happened to our family since the Leaf Baby was born. And although many things in my days are driving me to the brink lately, whether it be Kai's absentminded melancholy, Kenya's will of sharp steel and endless arguments, Leafy's perpetual eating and drinking of things which are not meant for him to eat and drink (cooking oil, raw oats, and raw onions), or even your own gassy crying jags during which you instruct me to keep on moving if I ever try to stop walking you across the floor...

Well, it only takes a few minutes of sitting and talking with you to bring me back. You are like a small star in our dark galaxy. While the rest of us are behaving like beasts, galloping and complaining, nagging and slouching around in our underwear, you catch our eyes and make contact and you make us better people.

Leafy will stop pouring the bottle of tea tree oil all over the couch cushion to sit by you and stroke your hair, so, so softly. Kenya tells you that she loves you in her softest, sweetest voice. And Kai holds you and his heart swells when you recognize him. Your dad and I are smitten. I've never been so challenged or so blessed. I want to say your name over and over, just to hear the sound of it, because there was a time before you were here, and I'm so glad I don't have to go back.

Bear with me kid, I'm a mess of a mother, but I do love you so,

Love,
me.

October 24, 2008

Sometimes I get stuck, and I have to write about things until I get unstuck, and that can take awhile. It's probably the adjustment to having another child. Or maybe it's the fact that some of our wild stompings have settled down and we're moving into a chaotic kind of routine, more the shape of what our life will be here. Or maybe it's my poor neglected novel and ungerminated other ideas, gathering dust at the base of my skull, longing for water and sunlight.

Whatever it is, I've been thinking about a certain kind of lifestyle.

It's my pretend world. It's pretty simple. I'm not really one for clothes or parties or shoes. I don't like standing on stage. I could go without watching any more movies in the theater without much regret. I like concerts, but can live without them.

But this is what a day in my pretend world would look like:

I would wake up with the sun of course, after a deep and refreshing sleep. I'd make myself tea or coffee, and make some for someone else, too. I'd wander to some spot outdoors and pray. Then I'd start to write. When I got stumped for the next sentence, I'd pick up my knitting and think for awhile as I threw down some rows, then continue until I had my work done for the day. I'd paint in the afternoons. I'd cook or garden, edit my writing, and then read great and beautiful books with whatever time I had left.

Evening would be soft and purple. Maybe there would be sunsets to watch, maybe there would be firelight and singing.

It's not that my children wouldn't be in my pretend world. They'd be harmoniously working amongst themselves, singing and creating and taking such good care of their things.

They wouldn't be peeing on the floor. Or destroying an entire pack of clothespins that I just bought. Or fighting.

Okay, so life is a little bit different in the real world than in the Pretend World. There is coffee, also tea, but they are often cold before I get to them. I read guiltily when I really should be doing other things. I knit a row and then set my project down. My book is very, very neglected.

But here it is! This is the life I have been given, God came over to me and placed it gently into my hands and now I'm supposed to do something with it. And now that I have it, it's the one I want, really and truly. But how?

Kids are not seamless. They are not convenient, they are not quiet. They are not always harmonious. They are often not careful. What they are is boisterous! Joyful, loving, genuine, hilarious, sweet, adorable, hungry, moody and engaging. I need to find a way to access the bits of me that can work with these traits. I need to find my fun side.

Of course, as always, God knows what we need. Because I am incredibly selfish. Not with stuff, usually, not with money (usually) but with my time. It's mine it's mine it's MINE! And no, it's not. And because I am still a child, too, I will learn these lessons even as I teach them to my children, giving up my way for someone else's, making my boundaries and then relaxing them. Being kind. Being more of an US than a ME. Asking the only important questions: What open road is before us today? Who will we meet? How will we love? (Not: What will my word count be?)

October 29, 2008

The other day Kai lost his first tooth. It was also my first brush with the tooth fairy. We were in a restaurant when the tooth itself came out. Kai waved his little bottom tooth around the table and we all congratulated him. Then Solo started crying very VERY loudly, and I made a quick exit. I think he hates that restaurant. We've been there three times since he was born, for cheap dosas, and he always freaks out.

The day before, Kai and I had started talking about what you do with your tooth once it falls out.

"You put it under your pillow, and then the tooth fairy comes and takes it and gives you money for it!" I told him.

"Is the tooth fairy real?" Kai asked, cutting, as usual, to the heart of the matter.

"I've heard that she is," I said.

He rolled his eyes and cocked his head to one side. "Please don't listen to what you hear on videos, Mama," he said. "Did you hear that on a video?"

"Noooooo... but I've heard that you will get money if you put your tooth under your pillow."

Kai spent his time after that running back and forth between Cate and Renee's house and our house. Cate had some wisdom for him.

"Whether or not the tooth fairy is real," she said, "when you put that tooth under your pillow you will get some money."

But then she started to worry. Maybe we didn't do the whole

103

"tooth fairy" thing. Instead of coming to talk to me about it, she sent Kai over with this message:

"Cate says that you'll need to email the tooth fairy, to let her know that I lost a tooth," he told me confidentially.

"Ohhhhhhhhh," I nodded. "Yep. She's right. Because we're not in California anymore."

And then the tooth came out.

Kai ran around the house with his precious tooth, almost losing it every five minutes, until Chinua convinced him to stash it in a Turkish Precious Box that we have. (That's not its real name, but it's the name I'm giving it for the sake of this post.)

When the time came, at night, the kids were wondering whether the Tooth Fairy was a boy or a girl.

"Maybe you could email her and ask her," Kenya suggested.

Suddenly the Tooth Fairy and I had a regular email correspondence, which came in handy when Kai popped open the Turkish Precious Box and found that it was empty! Oh no!

"It's okay," I said, when tears started to form. "I'll just email her and let her know what happened. It's her job! She'll know what to do."

And I was right. There was a five rupee coin under Kai's pillow the next morning. And, as he told me, she was so strong that he felt her lifting his WHOLE BED from under him when she went to put the money there.

You can imagine my shock.

november

November 1, 2008

It is one of those days with prospects in it that make you grit your teeth, just to get started. When rolling out of bed feels like moving in slow motion.

One of those mornings when you hold the baby and hold the baby, and oh gosh he's just so fussy, and the dishes are piling up and the kids are outside in their underwear again, playing in the sand pile, pretending not to hear you when you call them in.

It is one of those mornings when everyone needs to get ready to go into town to do some errands, town being forty-five minutes away on a drive that curls your toes every time; the potholes, the narrow misses, the cows stepping out in front of the car.

It is one of those mornings when for the life of you, you can't get anyone ready in time to leave so that you won't hit the market in the heat of the day.

It is one of those days when the thought of wrapping the baby onto you like a wonderfully efficient body-heater makes you have to

105

grit your teeth again to force yourself to do it. You tell yourself to get up and go, to be an adult, to get it done.

It is one of those days when you hit everything at the wrong time, so that everyone is prematurely hungry, thirsty, and tired. You walk in the market with the heat draping itself around your shoulders, pressing down on your head, slumping you and making you dull and dusty.

Your children grow flushed and cranky. You eat food, but it is too spicy for the kids. The baby fusses.

It is one of those days when the amount of time and energy it takes to get simple things done like groceries and kids' clothes bought, the time, the dusty time—it seems to spin out in front of you in a never ending loop. You will always be tired and in the midday sun.

It is one of those days when the kids fight in the backseat of the car during the entire ride home, when your husband is exhausted and you start to make dinner but then ask him to finish because it is too late and the baby is wailing and you really want to just put him down and walk away but that is generally frowned upon. The house is still close with the heat.

And all your efforts all day, all the smiling and kindness wear on you, making grooves that are good but not exciting, brave but not sparkling.

And then the tides turn a bit.

You remember when, coming back, you turned onto your tiny jungle road and it felt remarkably like home. Your neighbors were in their coconut trees, harvesting young coconuts, and they asked if you would like any. The climber nimbly climbed back up and chopped a few down for you, then made sure to tell your husband that one of them is "only for your wife." You drank the coconut water and felt refreshed. You remember this and smile.

The children go to sleep. The baby finally drops off. You want to go for a swim in the darkness, but it's not safe to go alone. You ask a friend to come over and do her reading on your porch, so that you and your husband can go together.

It's dark and you cling to him as you walk. You can see the milky way, thousands of stars, and one star falls as you step onto the sand. The ocean is different at night. It is huge and you can't see where it is-the line of sky is gone—there is a solid inky black sheet, everywhere you look. The white breakers are like a roaring mouth to you, and you hesitate before walking in.

But it's warm and glassy and you aren't as afraid now. Suddenly your husband yelps as he drags his hand through the water and at first you think he has been bitten, but then you see what he sees. Thousands of sparks, like the sparks that shoot up when you throw a giant log on a bonfire. They trail after his hand, they are all around you. It is phosphorescent algae, lights upon lights in the dark water. They glow as you move, and there are millions of them.

Now you are laughing and making huge arcs with your hands, lights trailing after. Both of you have turned into children again, and there are stars above you, stars beneath you, stars all around you. When your husband swims away from you, under the water, you see the angel's wings that his arms make; he is glowing as he moves through the dark. When he stands up, there are stars in his dreadlocks, clinging to his beard, running off of his skin.

You stay as long as you dare, before you head back home to the kids, thanking God inside and out loud, glad for this cooling, for this beauty, so much beauty, so much of what you need, above, below, and all around.

November 3, 2008

I think there is a moment when as a writer you finally get it.

So that's why I'm always watching, you whisper for your own ears. *It's the sharing that makes it all more real, all more true and beautiful.*

And now, in the spirit of sharing, I have some advice:

If ants get into your sugar (and they will, because they can walk up to a sealed plastic bag and somehow end up on the inside without any visible entrance), relax! Don't be sad, you can still use the sugar for your coffee. Just put it in, and then pick the small floating ants off the top. (Another hint: It's easier to see them if you add cream. If you are too proud to add cream, well, it's not *my* fault if it takes you a long time to pick your ants out.)

Also, you can avoid the whole problem altogether if you store the sugar in the freezer to begin with.

November 7, 2008

The other day I made lunch, and it was pretty good. It was some kind of leftover redo, some flip and flap creation that I had tossed together, but it tasted good and had vegetables and protein, hooray!

Kai ate a few bites and then said, "*Mama.* This isn't good!" You'd have to hear his tone. His tone rhymed with "Mama. I've got more toys than you!" Sort of a sing-songy-I-just-thought-you-should-know-so-I'm-telling-you tone.

I said, "Kai, just eat your food."

He scrunched up his forehead and rolled his eyes and yelped, "It tastes like Monster Food!"

So I had no choice but to say, "Kai! That's a terrible thing to say to someone who just cooked lunch for you."

My tone rhymed with "You *ungrateful wretch,* I cook and I clean and I rock the baby and I slave away, and all you do is play and talk about Monster Food!" It's a tone I reserve for small children and baby animals.

(I find it's good to use this tone to make empty threats that you know you will never in a thousand years carry out. Like, "If you talk about my food like this again, I'm going to stop feeding you." Effective.)

Anyway, Kai pondered this for awhile, and then he asked me a perfectly reasonable question.

"Mama? What *is* a nice way to tell someone that you don't like something that they made?"

I was stumped. I had to say, "I don't know." Is there a nice way? It's something to think about.

November 8, 2008

10 Beautiful Things on a Day When I'd Rather Not Admit That Anything is Beautiful:

1. My husband is juggling and passing with a new friend from New York who is here for a short while. New friends are beautiful. Especially guy friends for my dear husband who is the only guy in our little community. He's hanging out a lot with Cate, Renee, and me, lately.

2. Solo's smiles.

3. Leafy being a brave boy even though he has a skin infection; a form of staph which is common in young kids in developing countries.

4. My house is clean. Somewhat.

5. We're heading out tonight to have dinner and watch the sunset.

6. Laundry hanging out on a neighbor's roof.

7. The little Russian boy next door learning English from my kids, as well as how sweet and patient they are with him. *"What is this is?"* he asks, over and over again as they look through books. And they tell him. *"Speed boat... police car... caboose... taxi... truck...*

tractor..." He definitely has thematic inquiries.

8. Cold water when I'm thirsty.

9. A headache easing with a nap.

10. There is a certain beauty to loneliness, isn't there? It lets you know you are a person, you are real, and you need others.

November 11, 2008

Have I told you about the parrot? The dead one?

The other day there was a dead parrot in our yard. Not a blue jay, or a sparrow, but a parrot. A brilliant green parrot. It just fell out of the sky for an unknown reason.

It's the kind of thing that reminds me that I moved *really far from home*, even when I'm getting so used to it here.

But that's not what I wanted to write about. Things have been crazy in our little home here, but they're getting better. The baby had some rough days when it seemed like all I could do was hold him and watch my other kids quarrel with each other. An exaggeration, but only just.

The days are slanting upwards, however, and I re-examine my goals again. My ideals have come to a pinpoint: writing takes the back seat. The daily goal shrinks to *peace*. Let us have peace and let us be kind. Kind to each other and to everyone in this jungle village/metropolis. The begging women who come to the door, the peddlers who pester me, the wonderful neighbors, the little boy next door who pounds into my house at 9:00 PM and wakes Solo. I have emails to catch up on, I have thoughts that beg to be shared and expressed and colored over oceans and skies, but we will have peace this day and the next.

November 13, 2008

She had a Normal Day.

She said, *I want you to get some clothes on before you go outside, Leafy.*

She called and she asked, *Did I leave my mobile phone there yesterday? I can't seem to find it.*

She said, *That's alright. I'm sure it will turn up.*

She ran into the house and she said, *Guess what, Chin! It was stuck behind the seat of the car.*

She said, *I need some pomegranates, some oranges, some bananas and some spinach.*

She said, *I know you can finish your work, Kai. I've seen you do it before. Just focus and keep trying.*

She said, *Leave it on my desktop for me, Cate, and I'll try to proofread it for you.*

She said, *No climbing on the windows, Leafy.*

She said to herself, *On 56 different occasions yesterday, I was so homesick that I could have cried. Today is better. Today home is here. It's the business of moving, this back and forth dance.*

She said, *Sure, you can take this sheet into your fort. Just try not to drag it through the dirt.*

She said, *Don't go over to the neighbors' house again without telling me. Otherwise you'll have to stay in the house tomorrow.*

She said, *Goodbye my love. Have fun in Amsterdam. I'll miss you. I love you. If you see anything nice, get me one!*

She said, *Only a few days now until UNCLE MATTY gets here, kids!*

She said to Renee, *Sure, you can borrow the scooter. Oh- actually- where are the keys?*

She said, *Chinua took the keys but he's going to send them back with the taxi driver.*

She said, *Should we turn on some music, Leafy? Do you want to dance?*

She said, *Sure she can walk to the veggie stall with you, Renee.*

She said, *The cat liked you, Kenya? Really? Did he follow you home?*

She said, *Will you get me a dozen eggs and two packets of milk, Kai? Here's 100 Rupees. You should get 29 back.*

She said, *He laughed for the first time, today.*

She said, *Oh beautiful beautiful beautiful beautiful baby.*

She said, PLEASE GO TO SLEEP.

She said, *Can I call you back?*

She said, *Dinner's going to be a little late, kids. I have to help Solo get to sleep.*

She said, *What day is her birthday again? Is there anywhere here that we can buy a cake?*

She said, *Yes, you're singing. Oh yes you are. Oh yes you ARE. Oh you are a* GOOD *singer, singie wingie singer yesyouare.*

She said, *Renee, there's a lot of soup if you want any.*

She said, *Also, this question might be a little pointed, but do you feel like walking to the store to get yourself a lime soda? Because if you do, I wouldn't mind having one too.*

She said to Kai, *No, I'm not mad at you. But I want you to know that you cannot take anything of ours and decide to throw it away, okay? That's a rule. No throwing stuff out.*

She said to her Russian neighbors, *Can I borrow your bottle opener? My son threw mine into a trash pile.*

She said, *That man bathing at the well is completely stark naked, Renee.*

She said (about twenty times) *Get back in your bed, Leafy.*

At night, just before she went to sleep, she said, *Oh thank You thank You thank You. Thank You for all of them and for peace and for grace like the sea.*

November 15, 2008

I found my camera battery charger. It's only taken me a month of looking for it to find it, which really means a month of telling myself to look for it, and then finally finding it right where it should be; buried in my computer bag.

I've been rather busy. But you already know that.

(I hope that underneath all my exhaustion you can read the pure and joyous love that I have for my family. You can? Good.)

Chinua is in Amsterdam for a week, and judging from his emails, he likes Goa better. He used the word "grey" a lot in his description of landing in the cold city. Whenever Chinua is away, I shove down that lost child inside of me, the one who wants to wail and carry on, and I become my strongest self. I need to. Of course, it's all just preparation for the meltdown that occurs as soon as his travel-weary feet cross the threshold again. That lost child is now very well aware that it was left alone for a long time and she is mad. Kind of like when your kids are playing nicely with some other adults, but as soon as you reappear, they all start crying and running toward you and clutching at your clothes in misery, and the other adults are all "Wha? They were doing so well!"

The other adults don't understand the power of suggestion. The mere sight of their mother suggests to children that they probably need something, *what could it be?* And for me, after trips when my Superstar Husband is gone, the mere sight of him suggests to me that I'M SO TIRED I WORK SO HARD NO ONE KNOWS NO ONE UNDERSTANDS.

Unfortunately.

But, I know well enough by now that this meltdown is inevitable. All I can hope is that my Superstar Husband will be patient enough to shake his head sympathetically and click his tongue in disbelief (while I'm regurgitating small grievances at him) and it will be quickly over and then we can hug and kiss and dance around like fools. Because? I actually just really oh really miss him.

November 17, 2008

One of the greatest events of Autumn has occurred here in our little village.

UNCLE MATTY is here!

Oh, Uncle Matty, my beloved younger brother.

Uncle Matty has already dealt with poopy undies in a public restaurant in a bathroom that had no toilet paper, only a bucket of water and a pitcher. Uncle Matty has already been tickled and punched by the older kids and had his hair pulled numerous times by Solo. Uncle Matty has already been pooped on by Solo. And has spent a lot of time searching for one lost shoe in the aforementioned restaurant while Open Mic went on around him and all the kids were losing their minds with exhaustion.

He has certainly entered our chaotic world. And with this chaotic world being at the moment "Daddy-less" what better man than an uncle to step in and SAVE MY MIND.

They don't call him Uncle Jesus Matty for nothing.

(Actually, I think it's the long hair and beard that does it. That was Kai's name for him when Kai was a wee lad and couldn't tell the difference between Jesus and his uncle.)

November 20, 2008

(You would have laughed too.)

"Leafy. I'm VERY serious. You need to look at me in the eyes. Okay. I want you to BEHAVE at the table."

...

...

"Leafy? What do you say?"

...

"Mama, I'm NOT *have*. (Pronounced to rhyme with "pave") I'm LEAFY."

November 23, 2008

I had no idea, when Matty and I left the house with Kai's hand wrapped up in a bloody cloth diaper, his arm held up with a tourniquet tied around it, that we would be gone for almost twenty-four hours.

It explains why I didn't bring a book, my phone charger, a change of clothes, a toothbrush, or enough diapers for sleeping Solo, coming with us because he always needs to be with me.

I had no idea that we would be sent from one hospital to another. No idea that I would wear a labyrinth into the floor with my aching feet, there in the trauma ward with people in varying degrees of pain all around me. Broken leg, broken arm, someone hurt enough to need oxygen, all on small hard hospital cots. I was thankful that Kai's hand was only cut, not broken.

I had no idea how angry I could become, feeling trapped and marginalized in a hospital where no one was nice to me or my brother or my son. Or how angry I would feel when too many doctors (no less than eight) prodded his deep cut, where he had severed his tendon, and hurt him, already hurting. Matty stayed with us, and I was so grateful for him as I sat, woozy and exhausted. Eventually one of us had to go home, and Kai wanted me to stay. So Matty reluctantly left.

I had no idea what love I would feel, what great shining love, as I lay with my two sons on one of the cots, finally able to rest, waiting for the operation to repair Kai's tendon. Solo lay between Kai and I, my hand rested on Kai's curly little boy head, and my love swelled up like a great shining bubble, golden and filling the room, blocking out the dirty ceiling, the terrible hospital smell, the hunger that I was feeling, the exhaustion. I waited until after he was asleep to cry.

(They gave him some anesthesia, and he spoke sweetly to me as he drifted off: "When you smile with your lips closed, you look like a stranger with lips... you have three eyes...")

I padded out of the cot every half hour or so, asking when he would be operated on. Finally, at 4:00 AM, they told me to put him on the gurney. It had been twelve hours since he cut himself playing with a glass bottle, something that threatened to flood me with guilt every time my brain skittered back to the moment that he ran up to me screaming, covered in blood.

I was asked to wheel him to the place where he would be taken into the operating room, and it was not a nice place—it looked like a cellar, or a parking garage, with uncovered concrete walls. Unfortunately, he woke up, and he was afraid. I kissed him and prayed for him and then they wheeled him away from me as he wailed for me. It was my least favorite night so far. Give me childbirth anytime.

I returned to my labyrinth, walking quietly in circles past sleeping forms on beds who were still and quiet. *Jesus, Son of God, have mercy on me. Jesus, Son of God, have mercy on me.* The Jesus prayer seemed to be all that I had brain power for, that and the occasional, *Oh God, help. My boy my boy*, which really means the same thing. It was enough.

We had ended up at the wrong hospital, sent there because there might have been a plastic surgeon there who could do a better job than the one at the children's hospital. I have since been told by an Indian man who has lived here in Goa with his family for ten years that he would NEVER take his children to that hospital. The

116

question is not of the work that they do, but the way that they treat the patients. It is a world away from how I would suggest treating hurt people, but I was the foreigner at the hospital. It was not my place. I was lying beside the fish bowl, gills quivering in futility.

Eventually I lay down, again, beside Solo, and I think I drifted off a bit, because the next thing I knew was Kai being wheeled out to me. He was naked under a blanket, and I lifted him from the gurney to the bed. He smelled, incredibly, like his newborn self. We were all reborn.

The morning was old and tired, but we made it through. I ran back and forth trying to find food, carrying Solo in my baby carrier which made everyone stare, occasionally crying which made everyone stare, sitting in silence which made everyone stare. Staring is a way of life here, which I don't usually mind. But everything is different at the hospital.

I have never hated any place as much as that hospital, with its hardness and mosquitoes, the abandoned IV next to the sink on the floor in a bathroom that smelled like the bathroom at the Delhi train station. I don't usually rant about hygiene in India—I understand that things are different and I can adjust. But this was a *hospital*.

He was groggy and didn't want to eat. After hours and hours of sitting (trying anything to keep myself occupied, even reading the scraps of newspaper that were used to wrap my food) I decided to get us sprung. He was coming out of the anesthesia just fine, I told the nurses. We needed to be discharged. It was a teary process, the tears coming from me. They wouldn't send for a doctor to discharge us.

"But I have children at home. I've been up all night. I'm so very tired."

"You'll just have to wait."

"I'm going to pick him up and take him out of here."

"I'll call the doctor."

Finally the doctor came and we were all set free, like birds. The taxi that took us home had carpet on the ceiling and fake fur on the dash, as well as a very glitzy queen of heaven display on the console. It seemed heavenly, and the trees had never been so green. I didn't even mind the heat that pounded down on the roads and the roof of our taxi.

Kai will be fine. He has a cast to wear for six weeks, to keep his thumb still while the tendon heals. He has analyzed it all to little microns, and as usual, his analysis is surprisingly accurate and intuitive. I like to see him solving problems, figuring out how to eat, whether or not he can play cricket, how to get dressed. When to ask for help and when he would prefer to do it himself.

Chinua arrived home yesterday and got caught up on all the news. We spent some time just being together, and then all seven of us walked home last night along the dark beach, our feet in the water, tired and yet content.

November 24, 2008

We are all okay! Kai is doing remarkably well. He's annoyed, as well he might be, by a big white heavy arm, but he's playing cricket in the yard with his left arm, so I'd say he's doing okay. I don't have a computer at home. It's frustrating and a mini-unplugged blessing all at once.

We have lots of new neighbors in this international neighborhood. Our next door neighbors are Russian, kitty-corner are two Israeli women, across the way is an Irish-French couple, and down the street are some more French friends and some British friends. We are getting to know everyone, and it is fun and challenging, all at once.

Kenya is a great lover of all animals and insects and reptiles and amphibians. Her love for them is so strong that I sometimes fear for her. "I draw the line at spiders," I told her once, as she ran up to me to show me the jumping spider that she was playing with.

The other day she said to me, "It's like the mosquito was telling me a secret. He got all close to my ear and said mmmmmmmm."

The curiously horrifying whine of a mosquito, in my daughter's world, is cuddly and cozy and kind. If that's not beautiful, what is?

November 28, 2008

Many lovely things have happened, things that I haven't written about because I haven't had time. I'm still waiting to get my at-home Internet back. But really, there are wondrous things every day. Kenya tells Uncle Matty that I am the most beautiful girl in the world. Solo kicks and kicks, a little kicking machine. Kai reads to his brother and sister for an hour while I try to get the baby to sleep. My husband and brother joke around as easily as if they were born brothers.

And then there are things that seem too sad to be.

It's not my story. I'll just share a little because it seems to be occupying a lot of the space that I have inside me, these last few days.

The last thing she told us was that she was going off to eat a curry, to see whether she could get her labor jump-started. She was laughing. Just the day before, we had talked about doing portraits of her and her baby when he was born. A couple of days before that, her husband pushed my stroller kindly through the deep sand, the part that I always have trouble getting through. We walked along in the early evening, and she held Solo's hand while he began to fuss. She wanted her baby more than anything in the world.

I was afraid, when Renee came into the house the morning after

119

I had been away for a day and told me something bad had happened. I was afraid that something had happened to the baby.

Nothing in my experience told me that a woman could still die in childbirth. That she could have her baby just fine, but then die afterward. In so many ways it seems that it was preventable. I have so many questions, so much anger. I am hurting for her husband, for her tiny son, for her mother. It's impossible. It is so heavy. *Maybe if we were there?* I think. *We would have carried her away to the hospital. We wouldn't have waited for the ambulance. We would have flown with wings, we would have stopped the rush, we would have saved her.*

I should have known something was going to happen. The thoughts lead me into trails out and down and down and down.

But who were we? Only new friends, in the neighborhood, sharing an experience, walking to the beach, planning to get together soon.

It was preventable. I am angry. It is not my story. I saw her son today, tiny and perfect with no breasts to turn his rooting mouth towards. Solo looked like a giant, when I got home. I looked in the mirror and there I was. The mother of my children. Still here, despite terrorists in Mumbai, despite the train ticket that I still have, the one we didn't use, which would have taken us there just one day before the attacks started. Still here, and not quite deserving.

I am so sorry.

december

December 1, 2008

Yesterday we went to the ceremony for the woman who died, and I have moved a little farther on in the cycle. I realize that I wanted something or someone to blame, *sure* that it must be somebody's fault, but it seems that everything happened so fast that even in a hospital it is unlikely that they would have been able to save her. Something just went terribly wrong.

You would have to smile and cry to see how strong and earnest her husband is, just full, *full*, of love for his little boy. He is planning to stick around for a while, so hopefully we will be able to spend time together. I'm trying to be respectful, at the same time as wanting to rush in and glom all over everything. Several women have offered their milk, but it is being discouraged because of health issues. Which is understandable. I know that the milk in milk banks in the U.S. undergoes strict testing, which we couldn't do here.

I am doing okay. There is a lot of sorrow in me, so many sad

121

things have fallen like rain.

(My mother's brother passed away suddenly the other day, also at a young age.)

I realize that I'm still fighting PPD. It's mild, just that thing where nothing sounds enjoyable in the slightest, and you are faking having fun a lot. You know. But we will walk right through this. There are tools that I've always used. Writing is one, and taking photos that tell a sweet story is another. Both of these have fallen to the wayside as I have become more and more busy, but Chinua and I are trying to see what we can do about that.

I have calmed and quieted my soul. Like a weaned child is my soul within me. *

Uncle Matty made dinner tonight. Now he and Chinua are juggling fire. In the morning I have a date with a Russian woman to hang out with our kids. My bed calls me. Life is blessed, sweetly blessed.

Psalm 131:2

December 9, 2008

Cate and I are sharing a small room as a studio, and I can't even tell you how much I love it. I went for the first time today, and spent an hour and a half writing. It felt like an hour and a half of pure heaven. No interruptions in a quiet, sunny, yellow room. Cate was painting on the other side of the room, and the oil paints smelled like my muse's wings. She tiptoed over (my muse, not Cate) and kissed me on the forehead, rattling back to the windowsill when I looked up at her, smiling.

There is a bathroom in the space, which is nice and practical.

I wrote a list of the projects I want to work on right now. There are nine things on the list. A little giddy with all the freedom?

Tonight we went out to a fire performance show on the beach. I didn't end up seeing it, since the baby was extremely fussy and I drove myself home. But Leafy entertained us for half an hour by dancing with his crazy moves in the spotlight area in the sand. He couldn't see that people were watching him, because of the lights, so he just went for it. It was awesome.

Today we lingered on part of Psalm 119. We chewed on it, crunchy and sweet.

I will meditate on your precepts, and contemplate your paths.

His paths: Straight, lined with trees, filled with kindness, not littered with bitterness or worry. Lovely, lovely, lovely.

December 15, 2008

Some things:

1. I spent two glorious sessions in the studio and have not been back since. I forget why. Guests, or something. Oh yes, dear visiting friends and frolics and gallops and wriggles. But those days were so life-giving to me that they must become part of my daily routine, by hook or by crook. It's funny how much I can get done in an hour and a half with no interruptions or unfolded laundry staring at me.

I WILL write this book.

2. We seem to be under terrorist threat after the Mumbai attacks. The two big bazaars have been shut down, here in Goa. There is a Saturday Night Bazaar and the Anjuna Flea Market, and both are on hold until after New Year's. Bummer. When things are shut down, it feels like the terrorists are winning. A lot of people count on those markets for their income.

I'm horrified to imagine Goan people (some of the kindest, sweetest people in the world) or other Indian people or Westerners getting hurt. But I'm not afraid. This is because of the lessons I received last year. Tomorrow I will write about the lessons. They bear repeating.

3. Though I can't claim a super amount of empathy for the masterminds behind terrorism, my heart always bleeds for the gunmen/suicide bombers/whateverwhatevers. These poor young guys with no jobs, who are picked up and brainwashed and sent out with weapons. And then boom and flash and it's over.

4. I am bringing Kai to see a plastic surgeon on Tuesday. He may need another operation to get the use of his thumb back. Where? When? These are the great mysteries. I don't know how to communicate how I feel about the way my son's little hand was worked on in that terrible hospital, but angry and sad and guilty are some words that I could use. When his cast came off we could see what a hack job they did, how they opened up a long line on his wrist, messily, to find the tendon and reattach it. It has healed, but it was unnecessary. However, life goes on and so do we and he is brilliant and blossoming, so all is well. We'll fix this, but we need prayer.

5. Yesterday Matty helped us take a family photo. Ha ha ha. You have: six-year-olds and their funny face tics, four-year-olds and their lack of understanding about what "smile" means, two-year-olds and unnatural seriousness, a baby whose head wobbles every which way, and a Mama and Daddy who are opposite in coloring. Not easy.

6. Matty leaves today. Oh, the pain. It has been the best visit we have ever had, which is a special gift that I did not expect of moving to India. Lara, Matty's amazing wife, did a good and unselfish thing by giving him up for a month.

7. Sometimes, in the midst of the dust and heat and work here, there are moments so crystalline, so lovely, so breathtaking, that I almost sit down and cry. I love it here. Sometimes missing my friends and family gets to be unbearable, but in that moment the

breeze brings me the fragrance of jasmine, or I walk out into the waves holding my daughter and she turns her wet, salty face up to me and tells me she loves me.

8. My other studio is my kitchen, and I've been cooking up a storm. Yesterday I walked down to the beach first thing in the morning and bought prawns from one of the fishermen who was folding his nets. The gentleness of the early sun on his face was exquisite. My husband brought me a coconut, and I spent the morning making a prawn curry with rice and chapati and we had people over to eat it with us.

December 17, 2008

Well, I did cry pretty hard before Matty left. I sort of fell apart. But then I got in the taxi to go with him to the airport. We talked along the way. I have a good brother.

On the way home I thought a lot about life, and how we find ourselves in places that are unexpected. I thought about moving. I thought about quiet, and peace, and about joyous chaos, which seems to be the state of my life, lately. I thought about how isolated it makes me feel when people react as though I have two heads when they see how many children I have. And then I thought about how much I love my brother—how it felt like a part of me was going to sleep again when he went away, and I thought about Kenya feeling that way about Kai or Leafy or Solo when she's older.

Suddenly everything seemed right again. The shape of the sun's light inspired me, and I worked on my book a bit, in the quiet car as we drove the long drive to get home.

We meditated on this verse yesterday morning:
You will keep him in perfect peace,
whose mind is stayed on You,
because he trusts in You.

Trust in the Lord forever,
for in YAH, the Lord, is everlasting strength. *
I could sit and let these words sing through me all day long.

Isaiah 26:3 and 4

December 19, 2008

She *still* doesn't have the Christmas thing together at all. Year after year, it's messed up.

I think she's doing a pretty good job, really, all things considered.

A good job of what? She hasn't prepared anything.

Well, how would you do, trying to prepare for a holiday when you're in a new country and you don't even know where to get the things you need?

It's not really just that, though. Have you noticed how she's dropping all the balls? The thin strands that she grasps to hold her relationships together, the emails going unreplied, the way she knows the phone calls that she should be making—but still doesn't make them.

Is unreplied even a word?

You know what I mean. Don't pretend you haven't seen it. She doesn't send photos out, she hasn't done Christmas cards this year. She's just irresponsible. I saw dirt in her baby's ear the other day.

She's so young, though.

Not that young. Wasn't she supposed to publish a book by twenty-five? HA! How's that going for her?

Wasn't that your stupid idea? You told her that youth was some sort of competition. She's too smart for that now. She knows about the body of work that she will gradually add to, all of her life. There is no need to be a prodigy, no need for fame. Just page after page, added to a pile, like leaves in an old book, crumbling slightly because they've been read so many precious times.

126

It's a pretty small pile, at this point.

But zoom out, and all of her children are part of her body of work, and zoom out again, and all of those relationships (which are not held together by anything as flimsy as threads, regardless of what you mistakenly believe) are part of the body of work, and then come back even farther and you can see that every dish washed clean in a late night sink, every old smile held on by sheer willpower, all of these are a part of a majestic body of work. By the time she dies it will be higher than the tallest trees.

But she can never keep up! All of those late night dishes are in danger of falling over and crushing her, and her laundry is never clean and there are all of those emails that go unanswered. She knows that she needs to do these things, but she's always failing, she's always so far behind. I saw her lying in bed this morning, when she knew she should get up and start working.

She was watching the wind move the trees.

She knew she should get up, though.

Yes, but isn't there a lot more to life than your to-do lists? You always talk about owing—she owes a lot more than work. She owes delight, she owes noticing, she owes attention and laughter and listening to that rustling of the wind in the coconut trees and sitting on the floor memorizing the faces of her children.

I've lost you.

That's because you're losing her. She won't let you mess with her forever. She won't listen to you anymore. She'd rather watch the wind.

December 26, 2008

There are some definite perks to having a family that right now is a bit like Romper Room, and there are some definite drawbacks. One drawback about having four children, the oldest of whom is six, and being a homeschooler to boot, is that the moment you turn your head from the dear darling angels, they turn into beasts.

127

You turn back to them, in shock, unable to comprehend that in four minutes of your inattention they have poured sand into everyone's hair and spread mashed potatoes over the floor, but it's true. They really have. Or they have gone and slapped each other and everyone is crying.

Leafy is doing this screamy thing lately, mostly to protect himself and his things from his sweet, strong, and controlling older sister, and his sweet, strong, and domineering older brother, and the sound that he makes causes me to immediately walk out of the room so that I can flush my head down the toilet.

I can't bear the screamy thing.

The worst form of inattention in my house seems to be Mama's computer time. Can I get an amen? Because the minute, the very second, that my eyeballs focus themselves on the screen, all of Pompeii erupts in my house and I'm too fragile for Pompeii.

So, I've limited computer time to 1) The two seconds that I'm awake before the children are, and I'm thinking, YES, I'm up! They're not! I'm UP! They're NO... Oh dang. 2) The two seconds that I manage to stay awake after they go to bed, and 3) Studio time, which is for my novel, and occasionally a blog post. Occasionally. Also 4) the very occasional Internet glut, which happens when Chinua asks me if I'd like some time off and I don't feel the ticker going, telling me to write, write, write. This is the time that I read blog posts, when I get to read them at all.

And when large holidays loom up before us like wildebeests coming out of the mud, those four seconds before the day and after the day are taken up by wrapping and cleaning. Nothing for it, wrapping and cleaning must occur. That means a long Internet break.

What's been going on is Christmas, and giving, and the reading of Christmas stories, and celebrating, and the requisite Christmas cry (I have to cry on Christmas Day, it's a tradition) and a Christmas party in our backyard which is a little farther along from looking like a construction site, and paper stars with lights in them, Goan style, and wow- we've been busy.

I know. I'm all, *poor me*, I'm forced to actually *interact* with my children and *play games* with them, rather than do fun *grown-up* things like obsess about the yarns I cannot buy and stalk knitters on the Internet. Also crafters, although I've decided to stop imagining that I am a crafter.

I had to drive to the capital, Panjim, to do my Christmas shopping, which I did for the kids in a tiny toy store with approximately four hundred people who were packed shoulder to shoulder. I sweated and wept, because I hate buying things that are cheap and I had very few choices, but in the end I'm happy with what we got.

Then, yesterday, I decided to make samosas for our Christmas Party, and ended up finishing with a pan of delicious samosas and a vow to never enter the kitchen again in my life. That's my M.O. Burn yourself out with silly pastry-type foods for large parties.

january

January 2, 2009

I'm exhausted. My brain fluid is leaking out through my elbows, that's how exhausted I am. Did you know that it could do that? Neither did I. Also, there's something underneath my left shift key. I'm pretty sure it's a dead ant. And I don't use my right shift key, which my ~~eighth grade~~ Grade Eight (Canada, yo!) computer teacher would hate. It makes writing a bit annoying. Also, there are people bathing at the well outside my window. Sometimes my life feels very strange.

Why am I exhausted, you ask? (Thanks for asking, by the way.) It's because teething has begun, and last night by the time I got to sleep the bread wallah was already riding by on his bicycle. Which means it was about 6:00 AM. Not good, my friends, not good. But I'm hoping to sleep better tonight, because of the Tylenol I gave my hurting son. My philosophy on baby meds is this: Sanity. Let me repeat that. Sanity. For both of us. It is for the greater good that we remain sane.

We spent the night at the house of some friends, and wow, these friends are beautiful. The husband is French and the wife is Italian, and they have kids that match Kenya and Leafy in age. So sweet. The woman, I'll call her Annette, is one of the loveliest and most joyful people that I've had the privilege of knowing. The kids all slept in a row in the great room, and Annette threw them each a flower before they went to sleep. I watched as her daughter spread the petals of her flower all over her bed and then lay down on them to go to sleep. (!)

The last eight months have been a study in cultural adjustment for me, and since the community here is so international, it's like a UN study of culture adjustment or something. I've met people from Slovenia, from the Ukraine, from Portugal, Korea, Iraq, Iran, of course Israel, countless Russians, people from Denmark and Belgium and Finland and Germany, people from all the corners of the UK, and the other day I met a couple from Luxembourg. They spoke Luxembourgish. It's a recognized language now, though it used to be considered a dialect—a particular mix of German and French.

But get this. 200,000 people speak it. 200,000. That's like Kelowna, BC; Yonkers, New York; Providence, Rhode Island; Huntsville, Alabama; OR Dayton, Ohio deciding to speak their own language. Just one of those cities. The world is a cool place.

So there we were with our European friends, and we had decided to wait until after the kids had eaten to eat our own food. We do this because we like to enjoy our food, just one out of a hundred times. But Kenya didn't want to eat her fish, so I picked up her plate and polished it off for her. Annette entered the room and said, "Oh no no, Rachelle! Not like this!" Because we were setting the table with champagne and candles, not eating our children's leftovers for dinner.

131

And once again I made the great North American gaffe of being overly casual. Like waving goodbye (K, Bye!) instead of kissing. Or standing when you eat. Or shutting the lights off while you say to your kids, "Goodnight! If I hear any noise out of there I'm coming in and smacking people indiscriminately!" (Not that I ever say that.)

I mean, who's to say that my way of putting my kids to bed isn't just as sweet as throwing flowers at your children? Ahem. (Cough.) Well? Who's to say?

Oh dang. Maybe if I'm really good, one day I'll get to be European. But then who will make potty jokes with Chinua? I guess I'll just stay me.

January 4, 2009

Snippets with exclamations

Teething. Oy vey.

Lots of crying from older kids who maybe are a little under the weather? Man, oh man.

Deep, sweet, and difficult conversation with a friend on the beach, watching the light turn from yellow to gold to bronze on her face as the sun makes its way down. Hurting for her. Jeez oh Pete.

More teething. Great Scot!

Missing my Dad on his 60th birthday. For crying out loud in the sink.

Putting off laundry and the other things on my to do list, thus making my morning just a little more chaotic tomorrow. Jeepers.

Three ice cream bars. Oh, snap.

The pomegranate was perfect. Hallelujah.

Goodnight all. Tomorrow is new forever.

January 10, 2009

Grumpy as the grumpiest grumper, (sometimes I like to talk like this: "Fussers fussing," I say to the baby, when he's whining and grizzling. "Chubbers chubbing," I say as I poke at his knees) I slouch along down our little street. I hate my life right now, I say, ungratefully, disregarding the moon and the light spilling from everywhere, the food in my belly, all the blessings piled up in heaps.

I'm tired of shallow new friendships and forever trying to go deeper, I say, as I smile and stop to talk with my neighbors, disregarding the thousands of small kindnesses that I receive every day.

"Weren't you supposed to find that out for me?" I say to my husband.

"Did you realize that you put them to bed a half hour early? No wonder they're not tired."

"Do you think you can remember?"

This kind of talk is not kind talk, if you know what I mean.

Meaner than the meanest meany, I slouch along our village street, which is the width of a single car. It's also made of dirt. Red dirt which is in my house and in my bed and we bathe all the time and clean all the time and I'm up to my neck in laundry and so tired of dirt. I'm tired of wondering about how to pay for things, tired of sorting out squabbles, tired, just tired.

And then I stop to watch some pre-wedding celebrations. Three men are sitting in front of a Catholic shrine, and the middle one is covered in milk and flour and water. The other two are also quite drenched, but he is sopping.

Wow.

"He's the groom?" I ask the man who was closest to me. Funny. I had talked to this sodden man three times today, and had no idea that he was getting married tomorrow.

It reminds me of being in Thailand, so long ago, for Song Kran. Everyone in the streets ends up as sodden as the soon to be married man, since the custom is to throw colored flour paste and water on each other. Gunky, messy, sticky, fun. Apt descriptions of my life right now.

I can't say that I feel any less grumpy (though I do apologize to my Superstar Husband and kiss him on the forehead a few times) but at least I feel inspired to sit down and write this. I love it here, where they throw flour and water on soon-to-be-married men on the front porches of houses in the village.

January 15, 2009

Recently someone who reads this blog told me that they thought I would be more productive somewhere else because things obviously weren't working out for me here. It made me think. I wouldn't say that I'm less happy than I've been in other places.

I think that when you do challenging things, you make a trade. You trade one thing for another, and you may trade something like convenience or the public library for color and the rustle of coconut trees. Or deep times with friends over coffee for voices in many languages. But the circumstances that you have found yourself in cannot define who you are.

Everyone has to decide what they will spend their life looking for. I learned a few years back that happiness is a shifty creature. Happiness is not easily found, or when found, is as elusive as a jellyfish. You can't hold onto it. My emotions are all over the place, folks. Blame it on artistic temperament, genes, or maybe I'm just sulky, but I know that I cannot count on feeling a certain way for any length of time. Happiness. It's something that happens to you and then whoops! There it goes.

No, I can't follow after that. My life must take a more

intentional path.

My tagline is *Cultivating Joy*. We all have many things that we can cultivate, things that don't happen to us, but that we go out and water every day, things that wrap their little shoots around their neighbors and need to be staked and cared for and checked for bugs. Like joy. Like love, thankfulness, kindness, honesty, choosing not to be offended, choosing to see the best in others, refraining from ill wishes or gossip.

What I mean is that I wouldn't use the word *happy* to define my life. Neither would I say that I am more productive when I am happy. I know that I am the most productive when I embrace and fully receive the truth of the unfailing love of God who made me. (Because when I do, I am not telling myself the evil mantra: *you're no good, it's your fault, you will fail,* and I can shut those voices out and just have fun making stuff and loving people.) I know that the words that define my life are *loved, blessed, supported, sure, steady, secure, at peace, content, broken, thankful, hopeful and waiting*. There are probably many more.

So then, the question of where we live? There are many things that are hard. Language barriers can be hard, especially when I would like to get to know someone a little bit more, but find that I can't because we can only speak to each other as children do. Dust can be hard, but in a silly way. (Like pine needles were hard, back at the Land.) Being away from family and dear friends is very hard. The poverty in India and trying to figure out what to do about it is hard.

But there are things that *wow!* stun me. Like the Iranian friends who showed up on my porch yesterday, friends we had met in Turkey. Now, here in India, we can have them over for our meditation time and lunch together. One of them, a woman named Fazeah, wants to make lunch for us on Saturday. And let me tell you,

Persian food is *good*. So it's beautiful for my stomach, too. Or meeting a friend from San Francisco who owned the restaurant downstairs from us and now happens to be staying in the very same village that we are. This international community is why we moved here. As well as our community and our meditation space, which is budding like the lime tree in my yard is budding.

Then there are the kids, growing and learning and so happy and trying my patience. Like they would be anywhere. They can find Turkey and Israel and India on an unmarked map, as well as Canada and the States, so geography is big on the learning front. And normal things, like knowing the guys at my vegetable stall, or swimming, or the lovely cows everywhere, or the herd of goats which runs through our village twice a day.

And my book, which is coming along. I am not only blessed, I am happy. At least, some of the time, when I don't look at it hard enough to find out what it is, this happiness thing. I think we'll stay.

January 22, 2009

<u>Open Letters</u>

Dear Kenya,

Next time, dearest daughter, if you're feeling a little churning in your tummy, turn your head *away* from Daddy's computer.

Hope you feel better soon, sweetie!

Love,
Mama

*

Dear Me,

Yes you. Next time, don't use your husband's computer to keep the kids occupied with a DVD. Dummie. No, just kidding, I don't talk to you that way anymore, remember?

Okay, bye. (Just *kidding*, I'm still here!)

You

*

Dear Chinua,

I'm so, so sorry. I hope it can be fixed. If not, I'll auction off my left liver on my blog and make us some money for a new one. I only have one liver? Bummer.

Love,
Your Wife

*

Dear Weather in Goa,

You call this a winter? Serious, though? This is all we get?

Listen, if you need some tips, I'm here. I hail from the True North Strong and Free. So just let me know, because you are losing in the winter department. This is like a weak autumn, even. Heck, Goa, this is SUMMER. Alright.

Glad we are clear,

Rae

*

Dear Well Water,

I'd appreciate a little more effort in the category of "making the laundered clothes smell fresh instead of like they've been left under a junkyard couch."

Thanks,
Rae

*

Dear Goan neighbors,

I *am* wearing pigtails. It's true. No, your eyes do not deceive you. And yes, it is funny! I'm laughing too. I'm even a bit startled. And yes, my head looks incredibly big with these giant branches sprouting from above my ears. But it was just that kind of day.

Love,
Your neighbor, the one with the four kids

*

Dear Kai,

You can never know how much it means to me that you laughed at my corny jokes tonight. Your smile makes me want to sing.

Love,
Mama

*

Dear Person who Wrote in the Dust on the Back of my Van,

I don't read Konkani!
But what did it say? I'm curious. Wash me? Don't park here? Just married?

Just wondering,
A friend in the village

*

Dear Bow-tie pasta,

I believe that you taste good anytime, anywhere.

Love,
A true fan

*

Dear Superstar Husband,

Oh, and I'm also sorry about the bad choice in eating that samosa in the market the other day, and then convincing you to eat one too! Heh heh...

Maybe if they had actually tasted *edible*, we would have been able to overlook the bowel problems that have ensued, huh? No?

Ha ha, whoops!

Love,
Your adventurous wife

*

Dear Sand,

The beach is your designated space. Not the sheets.

Thankssomuch,
A Housewife

*

Dear Beach,

See you at sunset tomorrow!

Love,
This happy traveler

*

Dear Northern California,

I think that heaven will be a little bit like you.

Signed,
A little homesick

January 24, 2009

Here are three passages that are inspiring me today:

"But whatever his weight in pounds,
shillings, and ounces,
He always seems bigger
because of his bounces
'And that's the whole poem,' he said. 'Do you like it, Piglet?'
'All except the shillings' said Piglet. 'I don't think they ought to be there.'
'They wanted to come in after the pounds,' explained Pooh, 'so I let
them. It is the best way to write poetry, letting things come.'
'Oh, I didn't know,' said Piglet."
The House on Pooh Corner, by A.A. Milne

*

"If the landscape reveals one certainty, it is that the extravagant gesture
is the very stuff of creation. After the one extravagant gesture of creation in
the first place, the universe has continued to deal exclusively in
extravagances, flinging intricacies and colossi down aeons of emptiness,
heaping profusions on profligacies with ever-fresh vigor.

The whole show has been on fire from the word go. I come down to the
water to cool my eyes. But everywhere I look I see fire; that which isn't flint
is tinder, and the whole world sparks and flames."
Pilgrim At Tinker Creek, by Annie Dillard
*

"As we walk home we often realize how long the way is. But let us not be discouraged. Jesus walks with us and speaks to us on the road. When we listen carefully we discover that we are already home while on the way."
Bread for the Journey, by Henri Nouwen

January 30, 2009

Leafy had one of his two front teeth knocked out. The good news is that it's a baby tooth.

The bad news is that it will be three to five years before it grows back in.

The good news is that he's cuter than ever.

But still... I have this wistfulness that comes from knowing that his appearance is changed permanently, now that there was pushing going on in the shower and he slipped and fell and he cried for about five minutes and then was better, now he will never look the same. I wasn't ready for that baby tooth to be gone yet. Sigh.

     *

I have added new layers of BUSY to busy. We are beginning a meditation center in the Christian tradition at our house, and construction is commencing right now on our rooftop. (Eventually we may get a building, but, as they say here in India, slowly slowly.) The construction has nothing to do with me—Cate is designing and overseeing the building, but what does have to do with me is the week of teaching and workshops taking place right now.

Our friend has come to do some lectures and expand our knowledge of meditation: Eastern, Western, and all the middle bits. He leads a monastic life with his wife, the type of life where one prays in a cell and builds buildings with rocks that one has quarried, and one bakes bread with wheat that one has not only ground, but grown, harvested, and threshed. And one has no electricity.

His knowledge is of the doctorate variety, and his presence with

142

us is of the fun and fresh variety. We're enjoying the lectures, the meditations, and the conversation.

(Kai: I had a conversation with Evan the other night.

Me: I noticed. What did you talk about?

Kai: Oh... *almost grownup* things.)

But we have been busy, meeting until almost eleven every night, and then starting over in the morning. Yesterday everyone drove off to look at churches and ruins in Old Goa, and I stayed home because, as I told everyone, it wouldn't be fun *for them or us*, to drag the kids around for the day.

Staying home looked like this:

-Watering the garden. (I'm obsessed. I touch and whisper to the new growth on our plants every day.)

-Walking to the painting for kids workshop.

(Me: If you can't behave, Kai, I won't bring you back.

Kai: That's okay—I don't really like painting.

It's true—he never has.

Me: Sigh.

Kai: Do you know what my real job is? (Announcing to the class.)

Elaborate pause.

Kai: STUDYING DOLPHINS.)

I refrained from telling the teacher that once upon a time I was a painter too. I just let her tell me about colors and mixing and sat with my baby, laughing into his face, in my *new* life.

-The kids bringing a little friend home for the afternoon. There is a coffee house here which is run by the friend of a friend, a man from Manali. His daughter came to the painting workshop with us and then spent the day at our house, braving socially inept attempts to impress her by the boys. (Kai, painting on his face and spraying others with the spray bottle while at the workshop.)

143

-Having a Belgian friend who is here studying massage give me a free *two hour massage*. Wow. It was the nicest thing that has happened to me in a long time. What was happening with the kids? *Ratatouille*. The movie, not the food.

-Eating the kimchi that our Korean friend made. He is going to teach Chinua how to make it, and then I will be in heaven, sitting on the floor cross-legged, throwing it into my mouth. I love kimchi.

-Having the surprise delight of Cate volunteering to sit with the kids after I put them to bed so that I could go to one of Chinua's concerts. I sat and dreamily remembered the day that I first heard those songs. I watched his every move from the front row, singing along, clapping loudly. I was his biggest fan. It was wonderful.

february

February 4, 2009

A few weeks ago, the kids and Renee and I got in our little white van with a friend and her daughters. We set off to travel in the sun to a nearby banyan tree. A banyan is a strangler fig which covers another tree and then sends shoots and roots up throughout a large area, many of which look like more trees, but are in fact all part of the same tree.

My friend was from Devon, England, with daughters so round and brown-eyed and freckled that I wanted to scoop them up and keep them forever. (Not to mention their accents: "It's all rather *muddled*, isn't it?") She's gone back to England since, so this was a special farewell trip, to see the tree that another friend had told us about.

"The canopy is as big as this whole *restaurant*," he said, throwing his arms out expansively.

We drove along, our directions limited to: "When you pass the petrol station and then look off and to the left, you'll see it out

145

there, in the middle of a big field."

I passed it without meaning to and got myself into a bit of a pickle trying to turn around, while small British voices in the back called, "I want to go back to the tree!"

We parked. As we approached the tree, about twenty huge langur monkeys departed, swinging down effortlessly and loping away to a distant spot. They watched our invasion of their perch impassively.

I thought the tree would be kinda neat, but it was not merely neat. It was majestic. It was peaceful, it was shady, it was a perfect play place in a hot field. Perfect for monkeys, perfect for people. The banyan is quickly becoming one of my favorite trees. Like the madrone, or the sequoia. Or the oak. Well, I could go on and on. I guess I just like trees. Big surprise.

At the end of our time we all joined hands and wove in and out of the branches singing, "The banyan tree, the banyan tree, God made the banyan tree, the banyan tree, the banyan tree, lots of shade for you and me..." And there were other verses, but I won't trouble you with them here.

February 8, 2009

a tangle of thoughts—i
always doubt myself, chewing my
nails, no matter how many signs there are
that they are thriving/growing/happy/kind.
tonight kai made friends with a man
who had a telescope. while the rest of us
were listening to his father's music
he was looking at the moon. *the craters were this big,*
he said, gesturing with his thumb and forefinger.
i was glad for him—first dolphins, now the moon

146

his six-year-old self sees so many things.

February 13, 2009

Dear Solo,

Logically I know that we don't usually remember our lives at three and four and five months.

But I still wonder, little one, whether you will remember. When I am walking with you under the deep black of the night, singing softly along with the sea and your eyes close and then open, close and then open, I wonder whether this will stay humming inside you. When you are a man and you journey to the water, will you feel as though it catches you up and rocks you to sleep?

You have never felt grass on the bottoms of your feet. But you stand in the shallow surf, and I hold your hands so you can lurch around on the sand.

I love you. This goes without saying, but I'm sure I love you now more than I did before, and not only because you cry less now, or because sometimes you co-operate now, and when it is time for bed you are reasonable and understand that screaming doesn't help you get to sleepy land. We are not as often trapped in a sweaty circle of insomnia, staring each other to tears.

This is good progress, my boy, but I love you because I see more of you every day. Like the the way you were hitting yourself on the forehead with your hand today because it had just occurred to you. *My hand! My head! My hand! My head! A circular motion and they connect! My hand!* And so on and so forth with the mildest expression of surprise and experimentation on your face. This is you!

Or when you are tired, and you forget that you are far too old and dignified now to root; to mistake a cheek for a breast, and you

147

turn your mouth to my face patiently. It is not the grunty frantic rooting of a newborn, but more of a step of faith. You are confident that if you form your lips into that perfect little kissable oval, the milk will somehow be there to meet you.

Sometimes these days there are real kisses, though, not only the search for milk. Real open mouthed baby kisses. You kiss me and then look at me saying, *I got that right? This is the way we do it?* with the most heartbreaking question in your eyes.

I kiss you back to say *you got it perfectly right*, and what I say out loud is a little sing song, "Oh, *thank* you," which is reserved for kisses. I said it to your brother, and your sister before him, and your oldest brother before her.

What so often occurs to me, King Solo, is how "same" this all is— all my babies of the past and present melding together in one plump heap.

But then you are different, too. You are you.

All my love,

Mama

February 16, 2009

"This is our house, and this is the path, and this is the Blue Pyramids," Kenya told me. "Do you like it?" She asks because she knows what I'll say and she wants to hear it.

"I love it," I said. She's always building something. She takes paper and scissors and constructs animals with tape. She takes markers and draws worlds of people, houses, snakes, worms, and birds. Sometimes there are planes, sometimes the people have babies strapped to their chests.

Today she built with Lego. She built our house, with our garden, and a path, and the Blue Pyramids, a beach shack restaurant nearby.

148

She builds the things that are around us.

Some people build houses for other people. Right now we have construction going on on our rooftop, where men are building a meditation space for us and people we meet.

I am building a story, and a book, and a body of work. I am building a family, and I am building a home with fresh flowers and tablecloths and curtains.

My husband is building songs from rhythms and notes that come to him, it seems to me, out of the blue.

Leafy builds towers, then knocks them down.

Kai builds Star Wars ships from K'nex.

Sometimes we build sand castles, and then the tide comes and carries them off. We can't build ourselves a wall big enough to keep us safe, but we are always building a community to love and to love us back.

We are all building something.

February 21, 2009

I find myself with no words, after they've finally stopped kicking their little legs and have let go of the day. Other than the occasional sleep twitches, they are still.

I think to myself, "I should write." Then I second-guess myself. "But what would I write?"

I am a woman who should never run out of things to write. I have one million and a half things to write about, all around me. But I don't seem to have a lot of chances to collect my thoughts, lately. Here are some things that I've thought of writing about.

*Leafy turned three.

*A man thought that I was screeching to a halt on my scooter and then reversing just to say hello to him, and was understandably flattered.

*Kenya's art amazes me every. single. day. She draws a new animal every day, in worlds that are filled with laughing people with crinkled-shut eyes, a mommy elephant and a baby elephant on top of ground that has a mommy worm and a baby worm in it, but then no! The mommy worm has turned into a mommy elephant-worm and the baby worm has turned into an elephant baby worm! And here's a giraffe, in the rain, with a person on his back, laughing, and there's a rainbow. And a house with a bird standing on top, singing. And a person singing with a wide pink mouth, notes floating up into the sky.

No one shows her how to draw like this. I could look at her drawings forever. You'd better be glad you don't live next door, or I'd be running over every day with my daughter's INCREDIBLE DRAWINGS! (If Cate read my blog she'd be thinking, *But wait, I do live next door... so that's why she's always running over here with her daughter's Incredible Drawings.*)

*Speaking of Cate, she is going through a labor of love, designing and overseeing the construction of our rooftop meditation space. She's so amazing at designing and putting together things like this space. I feel lucky that it's on my rooftop.

*Speaking of meditations, I led one last week. It was an imagination meditation based on the story of the woman at Jesus' feet, the one who wept and kissed his feet, and wiped them with her hair. It was incredible to really sink into the story. But the memorable part of the day was the attempt to sabotage which is a longtime bad habit of mine. Just get me leading something or speaking somewhere, or I don't know—taking a day off, and I'll sabotage it as quick as you can say *I'm about to eat a purple cabbage raw.*

(Here's a hint. I do it because I'm afraid of failing.)

This particular sabotage was the always-effective fight with

Chinua. It doesn't matter what you fight about, any argument will do. This one was rather ridiculous. Here's a little taste for you, since I'm shameless and it's funny:

Rachel: "Weren't you supposed to be helping me have time to prepare for tonight's meditation?"

Chinua: "I *am* helping you. I'm watching the baby."

Rachel: "That's not helping. I can still hear him."

Chinua: "But he's not fussing."

Rachel: "But if he does start fussing, I won't be able to concentrate."

Chinua: "So you want me to leave the house altogether?"

Rachel: "Yes."

Chinua: "How about this? If he starts fussing, I'll leave the house."

Rachel: "But then I'll KNOW that he's fussing, and I'll be thinking about him fussing..." (Pause.) "Plus, it's bothering me that you're just sitting there. I can't concentrate."

Chinua: "I'm not even talking to you. You're the one talking to me!"

And there you are.

But the meditation actually went really well. There are reasons why I mostly choose to write, though, and they have something to do with the fact that you can just sit down and go tappity tappity on the keyboard and there isn't a lot of time to sabotage anything. I think.

*I just pulled a really big beetle out of my hair.

*And with that, I'm off to bed, because my *sister* is arriving tomorrow and I have to get up at 4:00 to go and get her.

February 24, 2009

This was going to be a different kind of post, but before I got

151

back to the computer, my husband talked me down out of my tree. I don't call him a Superstar for nothing. Superstar Husbands can talk their wives who are suffering even out of banyan trees, even with vines so vast and branchlike that almost a wife could just disappear. Or turn into a Langur monkey and go loping off into the distance.

I'll just say that postpartum depression sucks. And it's so much better now than it was with the other sweet babies, so really I am so, so blessed. But life has lost a lot of its taste, and the space from peace to stress is small and puny. I'm biding my time. I know it can't last.

Meanwhile, I'm reading *The Lion the Witch and the Wardrobe* to Kai and Kenya and they hang on every word. There's not much that's more rewarding to me than reading a book that I love to my kids. We've also been admiring the art of Bill Peet. Sometimes I think that what I'd really like to be when I grow up is an illustrator.

We are awash with Canadian girls in this community. Two wonderful whippersnappers arrived a couple of weeks back, and my sister, Becca, arrived a couple of days ago, so now there are four of us Canucks hanging out with three Americans (six, if you count the kids, only six because who knows what Solo's nationality really is) and our friend Miriam, who is German. Our community and meditation practices are taking shape more and more, a pool that is so fun to splash around in.

Solo's thighs are delicious.

Renee teaches West African dance on the beach on Wednesdays and it's so fun.

And my irritation and dryness and itchiness when I have to sit anywhere for any length of time, my lack of enthusiasm, my lines of sadness. They can't last.

February 25, 2009

152

Inspired by a fellow blogger, Elan Morgan at www.schmutzie.com — I'm writing Grace in Small Things every day.

Here goes: (The rules are: list five positive things every day. Simple, eh?)

1. I was having a stern talk with Kai this morning about the need to be kind to his little brother, the Leafy Boy, and to think about his brother rather than just doing whatever he wants and ending up hurting him. All the while Leafy was piping in with, "Hugging is kind, right Mama? Kissing is kind, right?"

2. Tonight after I got the baby to sleep, my Superstar Husband put the kids to bed so that I could head back out on the scooter to join the girls at their favorite coffee shop. (The only coffee shop.)

3. While we were there, we were discussing the differences in age between siblings in my family, and I said that my younger sister and brother are exactly two years apart. My sister, the ever zesty Becca, shot me a look and said, "Two years and one day," and then mouthed threateningly, "*Not EXACTLY two years!*" I collapsed in giggles, something I haven't done in a while.

4. After our community lunch today, a few of us sat and created some things together. I worked on a drawing and wrote a letter to someone who is leaving tomorrow. The kids painted on paper, the floor, and themselves, Renee mixed colors and kept exclaiming, "I *love* painting. I *love* painting!" And we all played at art and listened to music for a couple of hours. It was nice.

5. I didn't make it down to the beach in time to dance, but I did watch the dancers in the late afternoon sun and the water in front of them. The kids drew in the sand with sticks. I met some new people. I invited some people over for dinner tomorrow. I will make pesto and attempt to use cashews. We'll see how it goes.

February 26, 2009

1. Pesto with cashews is really really good. (There are no pine nuts that I know of in India, and if there were, they'd probably be too expensive.)

2. Our friends who came over for dinner showed us pictures of where they live on the Isle of Mull in Scotland. We have one more place on our map of Must Visit.

3. Renee and the Canadian girls (Becca, Cat, and Jocelyn) took the kids to their house for a few hours of fun this afternoon. They played games (Leafy invented a version of Duck Duck Goose called Cake Cake GHOST!) and ate yummy stuff. I stayed home and...

4. Worked on my book, which I fell in love with all over again. I think I love it. I love the characters.

5. Now that we have government water, the laundry smells nice again! (The water in the well had all sorts of stink.)

February 27, 2009

1. People in the village have this thing about brushing their teeth outside, so that in the morning you can look any which way and see someone brushing his or her teeth. Today I was out on the scooter on the way to the veggie stall and I saw a man on his scooter with a toothbrush sticking out of his mouth, which was taking it to a whole other level. It made me smile.

2. Speaking of the veggie stall, I was buying veggies there today, since it was my day for cooking lunch. (We eat lunch together every day and alternate with the cooking. People often join us, so there is always a different crowd around the circle.)

As I was about to leave with my potatoes, tomatoes, spinach, onions, and chillies, one of the guys who works there said, "Wait. Oranges?" Because I hadn't got my daily dose of mandarins to keep my children supplied for their orange habit. And I love to buy food from people who remember my children's orange habit.

3. One of my guests brought me some strudel last night, and we didn't end up eating it together, so I had some for breakfast. Strudel for breakfast is delicious.

Except that the ants had got to it, and there were dozens of them, so I had ant strudel. I put it in the fridge to stun them first, and then got as many as I could off, then just closed my eyes to eat the rest.

And now I am explaining how I stun ants by refrigerating them, then eat them. Just when you thought it couldn't get any stranger here.

The point is strudel for breakfast. Yum.

4. My neighbor told me that I can use the curry leaves from her plant anytime that I need them. Fresh curry leaves from just over the wall.

5. We had hummus for dinner that wasn't quite creamy enough, but still delicious.

February 28, 2009

1. Since there were power cuts last night that had the kids up and crying at 3:00 AM, (they hate the dark) they slept in until 8:30 this morning, giving me tons of time to write before they woke up. Beautiful.

(Sidenote: I don't know if you grow tired of hearing about my book and my writing life, but I will blather on. It occurred to me today that it is taking me precisely the right amount of time to write this book. I have moved past loving the book for the sake of being a writer or hopefully being published and now love it for the story's sake. I feel that I have to finish it because I love the story and the characters, and I don't want to give up on them before their story is told—these fictional people in this fictional world where I spend a lot of my time. I wasn't here two years ago. I was still thinking too

155

much about what a writing life should look like. I am now a bit more practical, and so I commence writing in the morning when it is just me and the ants, and there is not a candle to be seen, nor a flowing pen, nor a cabin in the mountains. Just dishes from last night.)

2. A beautiful woman who came over for lunch yesterday took the time to doodle on the kids with henna, and now they have mendhi on their hands and whiskers on their faces.

3. I've been taking Saturday mornings to go off by myself, sometimes for a ride on the scooter, and sometimes for a walk on the beach. I need it after a week of school and community life and work. Today Becca and I went for a swim together and then we lay on the beach for awhile, which I've never actually done here. It was like heaven.

4. Jocelyn, a girl from Canada who has been with us for three weeks and now is going back to her home, sang a duet with Chinua at a concert tonight. There were people sitting on pillows and lanterns everywhere, dim light that lit the faces up all around. I love Jocelyn's voice and her music and the two of them sounded beautiful together. (By far the most talented people there... cough cough, did I say that out loud?)

5. And then, at the point in the concert when Leafy was so tired that he was dropping, and Solo was wide awake in the sling for a few too many hours, banging his little head against my chest, I called my landlord, who is a taxi driver, to see if he could get me home. I walked to the concert, but didn't feel like I could make it back with the sleepies. He came, and drove us home, and then he didn't charge me. Grace!

march

March 1, 2009

More Grace in Small Things:

1. Cat and Becca making crêpes in my kitchen for a goodbye brunch for Jocelyn. Strawberries, mango, and cream on top.

2. Fresh basil in eggs. (Hey, this is turning out to be about food again!)

3. Leafy saying, "I'm a CUDDO monster!" (cuddle monster) in his best monster voice.

4. Singing together.

5. That moment when the fans come back on after being off all day because of a planned power cut. It's a hallelujah moment, a blissful sigh as we turn our faces up and the moving air helps the sweat on our upper lips to dry.

*

This will not be the only way I write forever and ever, but right now it is helping me to write here daily, something I haven't done for quite some time. Maybe that's number six.

March 3, 2009

1. There are a few drops at the very top of a wave, just as it crests, that seem to want to leap straight into the sky, shining. I love those drops.

2. Yesterday we used our new rooftop space for the very first time. Outside, above everything, in the shade, surrounded by the rustle of coconut trees. Beautiful.

3. Leafy would like us all to know that crabs like to dance, and that they dance backwards. Also, that they scare him, but not really, because the small ones don't bite, but the big ones do, but a small one ate a part of his foot once. (Not really.)

And I would like you to know that although it is tiring to carry this great big boy down the beach just because he is afraid (but not afraid, not really) of the crabs that scuttle into their holes as we pass —I love his soft face nuzzled into my neck.

4. The bread wallah waits for me now, honking his horn on his bicycle, instead of whizzing past like he used to. I run out and ask for das pao (ten rolls) and then I wave and say thank you, and he nods gravely and rides off until tomorrow afternoon, when he will wait for me again.

5. I kissed Kenya's cheeks and her forehead before she fell asleep, and she kissed me back, even after an evening of her high emotions, of crying, of being unreasonable, of wailing loudly and inconsolably about things that don't seem to make any sense. I kissed her and she kissed me back, and there was grace for both of us.

March 4, 2009

1. Here's another fact about the sea: Sometimes a cloud covers most of the water except a glimmering bar throwing sheets of gold

back at the sky, way out there. That way-out-there gold gives me the most exquisite yearning that I've ever felt.

2. There were many things that I ticked off of my to-do list today. I bought watercolors for my kids, picked up cushions for our rooftop space, bought tea cups, brought my van in to have the clutch fixed, visited an older Indian auntie, and bought a 50 lb bag of rice. All in the heat of the market in the nearby town. I'm very proud.

3. The aforesaid Indian auntie cooked food for my sister and I, and continued to feed us throughout our visit. She fed us aloo tomato curry, chapati, pulao, cookies, tea, and cake. We sat and gobbled food, and she gobbled up our appreciation.

4. I spent a day marketing with my sister. A treasure.

5. The hot season is breaking in on us like a sweaty tide. We are making plans to move to the Himalayas for a few months, and while we prepare, I have declared a school vacation. The grace part? Hope for cool weather ahead? Remind me of this post when I actually put on a long-sleeved shirt for the first time in ten months.

March 5, 2009

1. I missed paying the electric bill by half an hour yesterday, I was supposed to pick up my van and some stepping stones for the garden today but I forgot, and I am supposed to be booking train tickets, but I never do.

Wait. I think I forgot the point of this exercise. Let me start over.

1. Fresh Lime Soda. Club soda, a squeeze of lemon or lime, and some sweetener. It fizzes! It's cold.

2. It cooled off today.

3. Leafy: "I'm just giving my baby a snuggle." (His baby is a

stuffed cow that our friend left here for the kids.)

4. I am hand-sewing my daughter a skirt out of an old t-shirt of mine, because I like to do something with my hands while I talk, and it is too sticky for knitting. (When the yarn won't slide through my fingers it just makes me mad.)

5. There was a girl who came over today for lunch. I think I had pegged her in a different light than I saw her in today. She was difficult for me to understand, but today she seemed so soft, so needy of friendship and people to love her. I was glad to see that in her, glad to not think of her as just a party girl. I was reminded about not being hasty, even if someone is drunk the first time you meet them.

*

Grace is always around me, but I have been grizzling along to myself today. Poor me. Poor, poor me. I'm sooooo tired. Who will take care of me?

Wealthy woman! Stand up and sing, already! The treasures in your house may loudly demand a lot of attention, but they are clustered around you like stars.

March 7, 2009

1. Today I saw a photo of Kai and Baby Kenya, sitting in their highchairs, eating salad at the Land. It was right after we moved there. A part of me feels so sad, looking at them. Because those people are gone, and in their place are the wiry brown children that we now know, the ones who read, the ones who say things like, "I would like a scooter with only two wheels because it would be a lot more challenging for me. Challenging means harder, that's why I say *more challenging*."

I know that somewhere deep within them, though, the chubby cheeks remain. And we wouldn't want them to have to eat in

160

highchairs for the rest of their lives, would we? (*Yes we would!*) No, we wouldn't.

2. There is always Solo, the cheeks and thighs of whom none have ever equaled.

3. Yesterday I booked train tickets for the beginning of April. There are still kinks to work out with our trip, (there are ALWAYS kinks. And high jinks.) but we are getting there. We will keep this house for when we come back to Goa in September or October.

4. Today I opted for not walking through the deep sand with the stroller, and decided (instead of going to the beach) to wander over to the house where Aunty Becca and Cat live, walking through the village, with the kids. They weren't at their house. (Where *were* they? And why didn't they have a consultation with me before they left?) So their house owner invited me over to her place, a little stone Goan style house with a tiled roof and a cow dung floor. She fetched us all Maaza, and we sat and talked for a while.

Her mother-in-law, a wizened woman with the huge black-framed glasses so ubiquitous with elderly people here, kept indicating that I should give Solo some Maaza too. I probably shouldn't give any of my kids Maaza, since it is a "mango flavored drink" containing "some fruit" (we all know what that means, and it begins with an "S" and ends with a "ugar") but especially not Solo. Then she started joking in the way that I've noticed is common here, when you have a baby and older kids.

"I'll keep your baba, you won't have him anymore." The answer from my kids is always a vehement shaking of the head, not quite a contradiction in a rude way, but firm enough. Apparently they're fond of him.

It was nice to sit and visit.

5. And then we had ice cream cones, (packaged ones) and we sat on the steps in front of the shop to eat them. Leafy was ice cream

face monster, Kai scarfed his back with incredible speed, and Kenya made hers last for two hours. Solo didn't get any ice cream, either. Just typical, you know? A good Saturday.

March 9, 2009

When I was in France the year before last with friends, we noted that there seemed to be no rhyme or reason to the kissing. Sometimes when greeting, someone would kiss us once, on both cheeks. But then sometimes there was a *return* to the first cheek thrown in there, and we were all, WHa-whoA-well-Okay. And then, sometimes. Four. Two for each cheek.

As my Italian friend said to me here, *This is just too much.*

But we kiss a lot here. North Americans tend to be huggers, but here in our international community, there is such a conglomeration of Indians, Europeans, North Americans, Aussies, Russians, and people from the Middle East, not to mention Koreans and Japanese, that, well, the consensus seems to be kissing. Unfortunately for us, we are the least practiced. Maybe Korean people are less practiced, I don't know. A lot of Indian people kiss, and a lot simply smile, and some shake hands.

The thing is, when you say hello or goodbye with kisses, and you happen to be Not Practiced, *any number of awkwardnesses* can befall you. Here are some examples.

1. The duck and collide. You go for a hug, they go for a kiss, and you end up smashing them in the nose with your pointy shoulder. It's not only awkward, it's a little aggressive, you.

2. The h-h-h-hello. You second guess yourself so many times that you do a little hen dance, trying to decide which cheek to aim for. Then you are embarrassed, so you end up saying, "Awwww..." in your cute awkward lovey voice.

162

3. The ear explosion. This happens when you aim too far back, and end up making a lip smacking noise at the exact angle perfect for puncture of the ear drum. You know you've done this when the person backs away from you with a look of surprised injury. They are wondering why you hurt them like this.

4. The accidental lippist. Perhaps the worst of the bunch, this is what happens when angles are all wrong, again, except that when you go to make your move, you overcorrect and end up catching the corner of the person's mouth. At this point you back away without meeting their eyes.

5. Then there are all manner of awkward ducks and dodges, beard rubbings and half hugs and the question of two? three? Oh, are we going for another? Okay!

I've compiled a few tips that you may find helpful.

1. Air kissing is so superficial. Make contact, at least with your cheeks.

2. Sound helps. You need a nice MWAH.

3. Greeting kisses are not meant to be wet. Keep it dry and quick. You'll know if you have lips that are too moist if you catch people surreptitiously wiping their cheeks with the back of their hands after you kiss them.

4. I'd say that your best bet is two. Don't second guess, just go for a smooth swooping motion. Aim midway, definitely not too far back. Be the leader. Your kissing mate will follow your lead. Only go for three if the person you are kissing is French, or Dutch, or... well, better off sticking with two.

If you are really good friends, a little hug at the same time is always sweet. But trying to combine sideways hugs and greeting kisses is the SUREST path to awkwardness. Avoid this at all costs.

Over time, with practice, you may get to a point where you can keep from embarrassing yourself too much.

March 11, 2009

Today I had many good intentions but the day picked me up and started swinging me around by the seat of my pants. Swing swing swing. Somebody please tell me that this is just a phase. I am so tired.

Grace abounds. Small and big.

1. Yesterday a beautiful couple gave me a new baby carrier. It is more comfy than my baby wrap right now, as Solo continues to morph into a toddler at the age of six months. It was so sweet of them to give it to me.

2. There is a field by my house that is covered in flowering bushes. Every color of butterfly imaginable is attracted to these bushes, so walking through the field is like walking through butterfly heaven.

3. I didn't have to gut fish today. Every day, since the day when I was around eleven and my parents bought several gallons of herring and we stayed up all night cleaning them, I am thankful that I didn't have to gut fish today.

4. I didn't have to eat any herring today.

5. Leafy is a hugging monster, the chai was good in the afternoon, I made the bomb soup for lunch, Solo said Dada, we danced on the beach (it's Wednesday), *someday* I will have our train tickets figured out, there are more things in life than having a clean house, and maybe I will be able to get up earlier than the kids at some point, so as to have some solitude before it's all oatmeal and mashed bananas up in my face.

One can always hope.

March 13, 2009

Let's just jump in, shall we?

1. I stopped my oldest son today, (oldest is a deceptive word; I shall endeavor to remember that he still is only six) because he was obviously trying to hide something from me as he went into the bathroom. When he reluctantly opened his hand to show me what was inside, there was a kidney bean nestled on his palm. (!) Later I found the little family of peas that he was bringing the kidney bean to join, on the bathroom floor, in a bowl, floating in water, surrounded by peas and salt.

(He's trying to make things grow. A little futile with the peas, since they were roasted masala peas. He may have fared better with the bean.)

When things like this happen, I:

a) Remember that he is a blossoming scientist and that I only need to encourage him to wait for a cue to begin the experiments involving beans and water and peas all over the bathroom floor.

b) Find it hysterical when I demand to see what is in his hand and see something as meek as a solitary pink kidney bean. So harmless! So bean-like!

c) Wonder how on earth I landed the job of mother. I'm still twelve.

2. Whew! Points within points! I cut my sister's hair tonight and it gave me creative joy like ice sculpting would if I had ever actually tried it. (I haven't.)

3. There are two things that I am not permitted to do, now that I am married to my Superstar Husband, who never puts his foot down about anything. They are:

a) Cut myself a mullet. (I don't want a big one, just a little tiny short-hair space at the front of my head.)

b) Wear leggings.

Tattoos, ear-stretching, body-building, tap-dancing. All would be fine. No mullets and no leggings, no negotiating. I can handle that.

4. My neighbor gave me a bag of cashew fruit. I have NO idea what to do with it. It seems to be inedible, while still being the juiciest fruit ever (in Renee's words). I'm also quite flabbergasted to see that each piece of fruit, while being the size of a small green pepper, contains ONE cashew nut. *How do they get so many cashews all the time?* Seriously, the world must be full of cashew trees.

5. Leafy walked over to me while I was working on an email today, holding a plate with three cups balancing on it.

"I got you some water-milk!" he said, handing me one of the cups that was precariously sliding around on his "tray".

I looked into the cup. It appeared to be water with a few drops of milk inside. "Wow," I said. "Thanks so much!" And then I took a sip.

March 14, 2009

You should have known what kind of day it was going to be when the tears sprang into your eyes at the sight of a man losing his shoe.

He was walking on the side of the road and his sandal slipped off. When he turned to retrieve it, the motion felt like falling. It felt like sighing, like shaking your head as you stare at the pebbly ground, like being just a person, after all, a person with feet that sometimes let a shoe fly, so carelessly.

Days like this are particularly vivid, when a rooster scurries across the road in front of your scooter, and he is not merely someone's future lunch, out for a jaunt, he is all of creation in a small flightless bird.

The trees are your brothers, every leaf made by God just as every

166

cell of you is quivering with his breath. You are called out of your body by fields, by gardens and water drops flying, by haystacks so casually symmetrical and golden.

Flowers are almost your undoing, on this kind of day. You almost can't look. It's not decent to be that beautiful.

An old man with glasses sits on a wall in his undershirt and slacks, belt hitched to a comfortable place above his waist. He looks up as you pass, his wrist, roped with veins and tendons, resting on his knee. Jackfruit slowly ripening, palm groves as tall as a cathedral that calls you to come and worship, a woman threshing her rice, clouds of chaff flying out from her. She is the center.

The women at the well, drawing water.

You remember that there was a time when you wondered if anything would ever be as beautiful to you here as home was.

Not every day is exquisite, most days end up having too many pees on the floor, but today is unspeakable. In the cool of the early morning, you drive on and on, wondering if at some point your wheels will leave the pavement completely and you will be in the sky.

March 17, 2009

Grace is everywhere.

1. This morning my gas can (for my stove) ran out. Two beautiful things: My dear neighbors in the back allowed me to run over with my porridge pot to finish cooking breakfast. And my landlord brought another gas can by, just in time for me to start cooking lunch. "I knew you would want it for cooking," he said.

2. Miriam had a cooking evening with the kids today and made puri in the shape of dogs and hearts and flowers. They were so proud to host a little dinner for us with food that they made themselves.

3. I swam with Chinua today, something we have done together

167

three times in the last five months of living by the sea. It was wonderful.

4. Chinua and I like to pretend we are Wall E and Eve.

5. Kenya told that I'm the most beautiful girl in the whole world. Just me, she said. But don't feel bad, you are the second, I'm sure. And another one thrown in there- today we took Kai's second cast off and everything seems fine and we are *done* with the cast. Hooray, because a six year old with no use of his right hand is about the same as a three year old, with dressing and eating and stuff like that. Maybe a two year old.

March 18, 2009

There are times when I am very upset with Chinua, and Just Plain Mad, but then I look deeper and by golly, it's not about Chinua. It's about my book.

I started writing a book four years ago. At the time I was twenty-four and thinking, "I'd better get on it! Anne Tyler's first book was published when she was twenty-four." Now I hold my sides while I laugh, thinking of little twenty-four year old me a) comparing myself to Anne Tyler in any size shape form or age, b) imagining myself finishing anything quickly, ever c) imagining that the book I was writing then was anything but rubbish.

Because, of course, that book is long gone, and another has taken its place. This one I really believe in. This one is my precious.

Whoops, did I just say that out loud?

So sometimes, Chinua, when I return from driving on the scooter to the ATM which is half an hour away and it's time to run out for drum and dance lessons and I have to get the baby up and walk down the beach with him and one of the kids to meet you there, but first I have to make sandwiches for us to eat for dinner and the kitchen's a bit of a mess and it looks like I will miss dance class again, but you have to go because you are the drummer and suddenly nothing seems fair and I let you know so, loudly, while you drive off... well. It may be more about the book than about you. Or than it is about the kitchen. Or the cut up pieces of papers on the floor. Because sometimes chores are simply a representation of more time spent away from my writing.

And *Rae, you may say, Reader, you smart person, you. People who will move to India, and who will live in communities, and who will keep having babies and who will have a meditation center at their house and who will have people over every single day, may not always find the time to write.*

You are so, so right. But four years later, still trying, I find that I still want it all.

March 24, 2009

It is now almost 1:00 in the morning, (I never, ever stay up this late) and the post that I was planning to write has been squeezed out of my day. So here is some of what I read at a creative gathering we held tonight. I wrote it today, and I read it tonight on our rooftop. Everyone shared something. Renee danced and Cate showed one of her paintings, Becca and Cat did performance painting, and Chinua sang. Miriam performed as a mime, and our guests sang and played the flute and told jokes.

It was such a wonderful evening. Here's what I read:

*

This is what I want to tell you. There is a kind of attention that is not bad-breathed or oppressive, not angry or amused or derogatory.

One day when I was young, which is about eight or nine or ten, I pretended that I had fallen into a frozen creek. In reality, I was walking on the thick, thick white ice, and I sort of purposefully slid myself into the bitterly cold water. And then I flailed and shrieked and all that.

It was for attention.

So that winter evening I walked home with jeans that were soaked with icy water, shoes sloshing with it, small icicles forming on the frayed edges. I'm pretty sure it didn't work. I got in the tub, and I don't think I even got a cold. So much for pneumonia which would have everyone crying by my bedside.

There are many ways to look for eye contact. You can steal cars or magazines. You can start a band. You can write a Pulitzer Prize-winning novel. You can work for a car dealership and sell fancy cars. You can smoke behind the shed, you can hurt yourself, starve yourself or set things on fire. You can be mean or provoke abuse. You can sleep with people or make funny jokes about how you're sort of an idiot.

Some of these things will get you good attention, admiring attention, and sometimes even money. (Money is its own kind of attention, and with money you can pay for attention.) Some will get you nothing but hurt and aching insides, some will get you a slap on the face or a jail sentence.

But there is a gaze which is as gentle as the wings of a butterfly, and that is what I found, once I had finally stopped stealing magazines, going through trashcans, and making jokes about how I was sort of an idiot. There is breath that is sweeter than plumeria avenues, softer than wind kisses from the seashore. There is a kind of attention which you don't even draw to yourself. It was there in the beginning. This is what I found.

Imagine yourself standing on a wooden floor, with beams all crisscrossed with light because of the bright open window and dust motes floating like tiny golden people. You are barefoot and the air is warm and smells like old wood and plants. Green things. You are old and sad, but you are standing here still, singing an old hymn, maybe an old spiritual about Jesus. And then there he is, and he leans towards you, puts one of each of his warm and strong hands on either side of your face, and looks into your eyes. I can tell you from experience that what you see in his eyes will not make you blush, or run away, or shake your head, saying 'Stupid stupid stupid, what did you expect?'

You may begin to cry.

Have you ever played that trust game where you fall back into someone's arms? Dumb game. How are you supposed to fall? Like a block of wood? Everyone knows that humans are not made of wood. When we fall, we fall like a bird, plummeting to the ground. There is a heart beating in there, after all.

I needed someone to tell me that I didn't have to justify my existence, to be so spectacular that it would be okay that I was here. I needed someone to be sad that I was dying. To let me know that I would be missed, or that I wasn't just taking up space.

To say "I made you because I like your shape and the patterns you make in the air around you. I like the air that comes off of you. I like your voice when you start to sing and you haven't talked in a while, so it is all rusty and pleghmy, and then you get embarrassed and quietly clear your throat and start over." There are many ways of praying, some are just acknowledging that someone made you, that there are feet that you can bow before, and let that love roll over you. This is what it means to be a created being, to be in the presence of someone so good that it fills all the spaces inside of you. You may feel like running, but it would be to your benefit if you stayed.

You stand barely breathing, with your feet on that wooden floor, and he is still looking at you, and you realize your clothes are wet from falling in the creek, and for the first time in your whole life you feel like someone is really, really paying attention.

March 28, 2009

Yesterday we had a birthday party for our five year old princess. I made a little scavenger hunt for her, so she had to find some of her presents and I loved her so much when she got the first clue.

You'll find your first gift if you look on top of the cold food house.

Kai read it aloud for her, and she stood for a minute before exclaiming, "I think I really know where that is!" and off she went, jubilantly, her little five-year-old legs carrying her away.

At moments like this I can barely stand how my heart feels.

I have to say that this was a good kid party, and it is proof that old dogs really can learn new tricks. The new tricks being: 1) asking for help and 2) calmly going about getting the necessary party players together.

It's my new approach to life: The Players. In Indian cooking, you have the players, the basis for almost every meal. No one told me that they were the players, but I just started thinking of them this way: onions, tomatoes, cumin seeds, mustard seeds, garlic, ginger, chillies. The concept of the players also includes the way you prepare them. So, when I think of a recipe, I think, start with the players.

I think it's the same with party planning. Start with the players. The players seem to be: Something to eat, something to drink, something to do (with kids—games), music, decorations.

It's the same with making a home. You need something to sit on, something that moves (plants or curtains), something on the walls, something to smell, fresh flowers, something to place your coffee cup on... and so on. It helps me, because these things don't come naturally to me.

We are getting on a train in four and a half days. I have many things to prepare, many many things. And I've been having Indian

172

post office adventures, which adds a lot of insanity to a busy life.

HIMALAYAS

Part of our lifestyle in India included traveling with the other travelers, following the seasons. This meant that we had the privilege of moving our family up to the Himalayan mountain range of India for five months—one of the best things we ever did. We still look back on those times with love and longing. They were certainly not without their challenges, but there were days full of stunning views and the fresh air of the mountain ranges. There were animals and people from around the world, new friends and a new house. There were also struggles, from loneliness, lack of water, and difficulties traversing the mountains. But the Himalayas! Oh, what beautiful, beautiful mountains.

Of course, first we had to get there. And that was an adventure all in itself.

april

April 3, 2009

Traveling scenes

Maria, my Goan next-door neighbor, kisses me on both cheeks with tears in her eyes as we prepare to get in the van taxi. All of our things are loaded and the heat presses down on all of us. I say goodbye to Miriam, knowing that I will see her again in October after her trip home to Germany, but six months is a long way away. We wave goodbye to our house.

*

We stand on the train platform with our numerous bags and boxes around us. We are thirsty and it is very, very hot. All around are the coconut palms and cashew trees of Goa, as well as the red earth. It is the sleepy middle of the day, and we count fifteen bags, including Renee's. Becca and Cat will board the train in Mumbai. We are no longer exactly backpackers with our fifteen bags, but we are doing pretty well for a family of six. We discuss strategy: One

175

person will board the train with the kids, one will stand on the platform passing bags to a person standing on the train. The train will only stop briefly, we will need to get everything on in a hurry.

*

We have been told the wrong platform. When the train stops we need to run four cars down, but we can't carry all our stuff at once. "Just go!" Chinua yells, as I hesitate with the kids. We run, and Kenya asks, "Is Daddy going to be left behind?"

I sincerely hope not as I board the train and watch Renee loading our bags. Chinua is running back and forth and I try to keep the kids out of the way in the narrow corridor. Not much help, I find us a place to sit, and we wait. After Chinua and Renee get everything on, the train sits for another fifteen minutes. So much for the rush. It was by far our most panicky moment of the trip.

*

The air conditioning in our car feels heavenly. Our seats are a little scattered, and there doesn't seem to be enough room for all of our bags. I am exhausted already, and I sit with Leafy and Solo, waiting. My Superstar Husband does the bulk of the arranging. My mind feels tied up with my baby.

*

I whisper goodbye to Goa, as we pass by stunningly beautiful rivers and palm groves.

*

We drink our first of many, many cups of chai that are making their way through the train car. Lunch is served and we attack it like the ravenous beasts that we are. The light outside is soft. I walk down the train car and stand by the open door for a minute. The hot, humid air strokes my face. The color of the air here is always orange, or red, or golden. We pass through tunnels and I muse about the endless lines of people who have dug these tunnels, carrying the dirt out on their heads.

*

I have a six-year-old boy who is incredibly hyper in a small compartment. We will be here for thirty more hours. Will we survive? He jiggles his arms up and down and hops on both feet. He literally shakes from the energy that wants to rip through his body. I close my eyes.

*

I will be holding my baby for a long time. I try to get him to settle down for a nap. I am not successful.

*

Kenya makes friends with a little girl in the next compartment. They play with stuffed animals together. Leafy knowingly tells the girl's parents that the elephant is a rhinoceros. They don't know that he is just messing with them.

*

The snack wallahs pass by every three minutes or so with their calls of "paneer pakora," "samosa," "chai," "tea bag chai," "Nes-coffee," and one that we think is "hard cheese sandwich," but sounds like "Awwww... cheese sandwich," For the rest of the trip, every time the hard cheese sandwich man passes by, I say "Awwww," under my breath and Chinua laughs.

*

Time for bed. We get the kids situated on their small bunks. This class provides blankets and sheets. They are hyper and have been climbing up and down the ladders all day. "Lie down and go to sleep," we say. Kenya says goodbye to her new friend, who will get off the train in the night.

*

Chinua waits for Becca and Cat's station in Bombay. I am

177

trying to sleep, but am too wired because of the possibility that we won't find them. They get on, and relief washes over me. I am sleepily listening to their description of their adventure as extras in a Bollywood Film; the dance scene, the costumes. It all feels a little unreal, and I drift off...

*

The family in the booth next to me wakes up to get off of the train and they behave as though it is the middle of the day and we should all be up. Solo wakes up beside me and believes them. I spend three hours trying to get him to go back to sleep, but the loud talking and laughing and bright lights interfere. At 5:00 in the morning he finally falls back asleep.

*

At 7:00, my kids wake up. Argggh. My hips are bruised from the iron bar that was the joint where the two seats became my bed. Have I slept at all? Thankfully, the chai wallah is ready and prepared.

*

Kenya is climbing off the walls. I cannot believe that I am on this train with these four children. We are supposed to board another train when we reach Delhi this evening. I'm not sure that I will make it.

*

By the landscape, it appears that we are in Rajasthan. Now there are sloping desert-like hills. Men squat in dhotis and turbans. We see many flocks of goats and water buffalo.

*

The train food is really good. I feed Solo bits of curried potatoes. He loves them. I've been holding him for so long that I feel like my arms will break off. Chinua takes turns, and Becca takes him for a while, but he always wants me when he sees me.

*

There are wheat fields all around us, and people are harvesting the wheat by hand. We see the sheaves lying tied on the ground, we see bundles of sheaves, and we even see golden stacks of grain. All done by hand. It's incredible, and I stare, fascinated, at the colorful people bending and swaying in the fields as we pass.

*

Monkeys are lined up along the tracks. We catch sight of them and then they are gone.

*

We discuss a change in strategy. We will stay the night in Delhi if we can find a good hotel. We take many, many trips to the bathroom. Kenya is a pro at squatting now. Everyone is fascinated by the fact that the toilets simply open onto the tracks. Poo on the tracks!

*

More chai. More veg pakora. More samosas. More bouncing off the walls. The kids in the next booth have become very tired of the train. The littlest one cries and I see his exhausted mother walking with him as I try to bounce Solo to sleep. She is Indian and wearing salwar kameez, I am Canadian and wearing a shirt and a skirt, but we could be sisters.

*

We call hotels and make a reservation, a little ways out of the busiest part of Delhi. I know now not to book two train journeys back to back, even if it seems convenient. 30 hours at a time is plenty.

*

Porters board the train and help with some of our things. Each kid grabs the hand of a grownup in our group. I have Solo in the carrier and Leafy in the stroller and bags to boot. Everyone has something and we make our slow way through the crowded station. There are people sitting everywhere on the platforms. I meet a set of stairs and am stumped. Leafy gets out of the stroller and tries to pick up the front to help me carry it up, but it is weighed down with too many bags in the back and we can't make it. I could almost cry from the sweetness of his gesture. One of the porters leaps down the stairs and picks up the stroller to carry it up. We follow.

*

We haggle with the taxi drivers. This is the India I remember, far from the softness of Goa. Chinua bursts out laughing at the high prices they start out with. Everyone is yelling, but no one means anything bad by it.

*

I head back in to get our money back for the tickets we will cancel. While I'm gone, Kenya needs to pee, and at a loss, Chinua helps her to squat by a wall (this is how it is done here). While she is doing her business, a giant rat scurries past her, two inches from her feet. "A mousie!" she cries. "A mousie, did you see the mousie? Kai, I saw a mousie, so close to me!" she tells her brother excitedly as they rejoin everyone else.

*

After we get to the hotel, after we climb the flights of stairs and order some food and get everyone in the shower and put the mats on the floor and I finally succeed in bouncing an over-tired and over-stimulated baby to sleep, I look around and take stock. There are cupboards in our room. ("A wardrobe, Kai!" Kenya shouted, thinking of Narnia.) Our children have fallen asleep in their jammies, and there are so many of them. We put them on mattresses on the floor, Leafy goes on the couch, Solo is in the bed with us.

"I'm so proud of them," I tell Chinua in a whisper. He nods and

180

tells me the rat story. We look at our treasures and love them. Travel with them is tiring, but it has never been so magical.

April 5, 2009

Climb every mountain. At least, that's what Kai wants to do. His suggestion, with every mountain he sees, is, "Maybe I should get out of the van and climb it!"

I can't even believe it is Sunday. We started traveling on Wednesday, and we are *almost there*.

Our last day is ahead of us, and it promises to be a doozy.

But I left you in Delhi, in our hotel room, and so I should bring you up to speed. I have always loathed being in Delhi, but I had a whole new outlook after living in India for ten months already. Delhi went from being the horribly crowded and polluted place where we first landed to... a big city! With shops and everything! We spent part of the day looking around at the different shops. I wanted to go to the Government Khadi Emporium—I've been jonesing to go for a long time. However, we managed to land in Delhi on a Government Holiday (a festival of some sort—there are so many, I can't keep track. However, there were parades) so it was closed.

And then we spent a big part of the day trying to figure out our travel plans for the rest of our journey. There is no easy way to get where we are going.

a) Night train boarding at 10:35, then taxi for the rest of the 100 kilometers.

b) Night bus, then taxi. (Horrific option, really. There is nothing more terrifying than being on a night bus on switchbacks in the Himalayan foothills with a crazy driver, swinging from side to side in your bunk, not sleeping, seeing nothing but headlights coming *right toward you*.

c) Hiring a car for the entire journey. This is the option we chose, and I am so glad we did. The cost ended up being only about $40 for each person, with plenty of space for our stuff and all of the people. It was more expensive than the other options, but also more sane. Sanity is good.

A pause here for a small miracle.

When we reached Connaught Place; a large market in Delhi that spans several kilometers, Chinua jumped out of the tiny auto rickshaw with his camera, spying a photo opportunity across the street where a dozen men were rolling out snacks together. I herded the kids to the sidewalk, and we stood watching Chinua framing shots until he turned around, clapped his hand to his head, and said, "My camera backpack!" We both whirled and looked. The rickshaw was gone.

Three lenses. Much worth.

It was like one of those movies with a helicopter zoom out, and I saw the city crawling with rickshaws like green and yellow bugs, thousands of them, all of them exactly the same, all of them possibly containing contents which could earn their struggling drivers some much needed wealth. Wow.

I sat down in the shade on the sidewalk with the kids and we prayed for a minute. Then the beautiful things started happening. Some kind men wanted to know what was wrong, as Chinua walked around asking questions, and he told them.

"No problem no problem," they assured him, and went to work to help, asking questions, making phone calls. There is no radio system in the rickshaws, but they called the head of the network of auto rickshaws. I have no idea how they found our driver, but they did.

And he brought it right back. It was incredible. A small miracle.

I've never realized before how incredibly helpful the people in Delhi are. At every step there is someone ready to offer assistance, advice, help with getting a rickshaw or directions (right or wrong ones). Delhi is also heartbreaking with its plethora of beggars and rows of slum housing. One man approached us asking for help to buy him some medicine from a chemist, since he had been in some kind of accident and had a large wound on his arm. At the same time, Leafy decided to pee in his pants, and we danced back and forth between figuring out what to do with pee boy on the street and buying the man the medicine and then following another man who was trying to lead us to the tourist office. It was chaos.

I eventually booked our van and yesterday morning we were off, through more and more fields of grain, helping the kids to pee on the side of the road innumerable times, taking snack breaks and driving past truckloads of people.

When we reached the foothills, we hit the switchbacks. The air coming into our van was suddenly fresh and cool, the first air like it that I have felt since we left Israel ten months ago. All of it was amazingly nostalgic. There were flowers springing out of the hillsides and the kids nearly fell over each other pointing out the monkeys. At one point we got out for a pee break and below us was a red toy train, an old wooden one, making its way around the mountainside. The kids jumped up and down with glee.

I loved hearing Kai and Kenya playing 20 questions together, of their own volition. Here's an example of Kenya's questions:

Does it crawl?

Yes.

Does it have a mouth?

Yes.

Is it alive?

I love how generously she splashes out her questions, not hoarding them or keeping them sensible. (The answer ended up being a mouse, but I think Kai gave her a lot of hints.)

Anyway, we reached Shimla, our halfway point, last night, after our 12 hour journey. And now we will hop into the van for another day of switchbacks. Another day of stunning views and terraced mountainsides and Himalayan people in their sweater vests and toques.

April 8, 2009

We are here, in Bhagsu, Himachal Pradesh in the Himalayan mountains of northern India. I woke up a few hours ago and dug through my backpack to find my clean underwear and toothbrush, then braved the cold and went outside to the small outbuilding where there are two toilet rooms and a shower. I turned the hot water tank on and waited for it to heat up.

I had initially decided to hold off on showering until it got warmer, since I am practically showering outside. But today is rainy again, and *cold*, with no sign of it letting up. So I stood outside the shower door and reluctantly pulled off my shoes and socks, then huddled under the thin stream of warm water for only as long as it took to get wet and soapy and rinse of. My dreads can wait for a sunny day.

It's a good thing that I washed the kids yesterday, when we had the guest house with the attached bathroom.

Ugh.

Being here so far has been a combination of frustration and breathtaking beauty. We are looking for a house, and it is not so easy to find one. So far we have found two rooms in a guest house, side by side, with a kitchen that we can use downstairs. It's hard to believe that we were so hot, just a few days ago. We have changed climates drastically and now we are cold, cold!

I had forgotten just how beautiful it is here, so stunningly, wonderfully beautiful. Impossible steps cut into the side of steep mountains, boulders cradled in lush ravines, flowers on the hillsides. Yesterday I flinched a little, seeing what looked like pollen drifting through the valley. My allergies make pollen a scary sight. But then I realized that they were actually small white butterflies. Clouds of them.

We are cold, but keeping warm. We bundle together under thick blankets at night, or even in the day, to warm up, because there is no indoor heat anywhere here. It isn't normally this cold at this time of year. Soon the sun will come back and we will run around in T-shirts in the middle of the day.

I had also forgotten just how friendly and caring the people are. The Tibetan and Himalayan people are astoundingly kind. We are happy to be here, trying to work out the kinks, shivering in the shower for now.

April 9, 2009

With all of the Tibetan community talk, I didn't exactly describe the place we have come to, so I'll tell you a little bit now. We are living (soon we will move into our new little house, where we will really be "living" instead of "guesting") in a small village to the north of McLeod Ganj, far north in India. McLeod Ganj is the home of the Dalai Lama and the Tibetan Government in Exile. There is a huge Tibetan refugee community here. So although we are still in India, we are surrounded by a combination of Tibetan women, men, and children, Buddhist monks, and of course the local Himalayan Indian people.

Our thoughts are to remain with the international traveling community, and our experience of India is always an international one, at once getting to know the local people but also spending much of our time with travelers. It is not always the most comfortable place to be, but we are always thankful for all the

185

friendships we have with people here. Shekina means "the Divine Presence" and my friend Cate wrote something recently which describes Shekina Meditation as follows:

"By use of the Holy Scriptures and other Christ centered literature, we intend to create a safe place for the Divine Presence to speak to the individual heart, while also speaking to us as a group seeking the Divine Presence."

For the next few months, which are the hot season in Goa (hot? I feel like I was hot the whole time I was there!) as well as the monsoon, we plan to be up north here, feeling out what kind of meditation gathering we could have in this area.

Kenya's attitude toward the food here has done a 180° turn since we've been in India. It's good therapy for picky kids. Also, the bathroom therapy has been successful. She will now use any kind of toilet in any bathroom, with only a mild amount of complaint. She still doesn't like it when she has to use the bathroom after someone takes a shower, though.

Back on the train she was shoveling the food *down*, while saying, "Wasn't that dahl SO GOOD, Mama?" Here's a tip, though. Don't assume that train food is included in your ticket if someone doesn't *specifically* tell you that it is. Otherwise, when the train food wallah comes around for payment, you'll be giving each other blank looks while patting your empty pockets.

April 18, 2009

Well, I live on the side of a mountain. It's bold of me.

I have this friend, you see, who is one of the boldest people I know. When I was younger and depressed and unsure of how on earth I was supposed to live life, I used to go to her house and sit on her sofa and sit with my mouth open, taking in all of the boldness. Because it's bold to put an antique birdcage in your living room; you

186

have to be able to say, "I really like that birdcage. I think I'll buy it and put it in my living room." Or, "I'll buy this carved screen here in Thailand, because I know that I'll be able to convince the flight attendants to carry it on the airplane, even though it's six feet tall."

Making decisions about what to eat was very hard for me at that point. So I was the type of person that would see a carved wooden screen in Thailand and say, "That's nice. Too bad it's too big to carry on the plane and I couldn't get it home."

And I would be the type of person who would look at a house and say, "That's nice, so beautiful, and the kids will have so much space to play and so many rocks to climb on. Too bad it's a twenty minute hike up the mountain."

That's what I would have said. And then I changed, somewhere along the line. Now I can do things like get up in the morning and soak garbanzo beans for hummus, because I know that I like it, and I can learn to cook in an Indian way, and I can decide to move onto a mountain with no road close to the house.

Of course, it was Chinua who figured out the part about hiring the pack donkeys to move our things up the mountain. We swiftly realized that bringing the stroller was a bad idea after we saw it strapped upside down on the back of one of the donkeys, but we found the cutest little house way up high, after I had almost given up. Giving up is never a good idea. Now we have a two bedroom apartment on the rooftop of some other apartments, and the view is stunning. If you take away the fact that we have no water today it is pretty near perfect.

April 22, 2009

Now that we have a house, we have thrown ourselves back into school. I love school at home, it's such great fun, and it makes for a disciplined life. We need to move along in a rhythm, whatever the

187

rhythm may be, so that we are learning and creating. And of course we need to take time to rest and sit on rocks.

I'm also diving back into the creation of my book, and, contrary woman that I am, rather than being happy about writing, I am riddled with anxiety.

I'm hard on myself. Sweating and gritching and flicking small pieces of dust across the desk. I forget to play, to be a child.

Sounds like it's time for another batch of Grace In Small Things. Time to be thankful, to write lists, and to take a break from hardcore writing so I can find solace in the simple.

Unfortunately, it will have to wait—our Internet is not working right now, so I'm down in the village and I need to get some groceries and start the trek back up to the house. My family is hungry and all that. Selfish of them.

Hopefully the Internet will be back on tonight. The man on the phone said 2 hours, which means a full day in India.

(Indian time chart:

5 minutes= 15 minutes

15 minutes= 1 hour,

half hour = 2 hours,

1 to 2 hours = all day

1 to 2 days = a month or more)

I'll be thinking about my list.

April 23, 2009

Every time I leave my house and trip down the stones and along the path between the wheat terraces, I see

1. A Tibetan Buddhist monk or two

2. A Hasidic Jew with black hat, beard and jacket.

3. A number of small Hindu shrines.

Conclusion: This is a very interesting place.

April 24, 2009

Here's some Grace in Small Things:

1. I climbed up the hill to get home with Leafy and Solo the other night; Solo snuggled into my chest, Leafy's little hand in mine. Looking up, Leafy said, "Mama! The stars are coming with us!"

2. Today I stopped thinking about whether my writing is any good and just listened to the characters. It was nice, like creative eavesdropping. They were having a husband and wife spat.

3. In this town there is peanut butter made by the women from the Gaddi people, the Himalayan tribe of the region. They make it and sell it in old jam jars and honey jars. I love to buy it. I love to buy things that are carefully made. I was making peanut butter in Goa, to save plastic, but this is even better (and easier!)

4. Having a water crisis (it has been a week of little to no water, in the morning we have enough to flush toilets and maybe do some dishes, and I filter what I can before it is gone) makes me so thankful for the water privileges that I've had over my life. It also makes me much more conscious of how precious water is. They rely on run off in this village, and there was no snow this winter. However, the village across the gorge has plenty of water because they pipe it from a different source.

5. Bread does not come to my door here, but milk does, and a small boy delivers it in reused water bottles, before school. I hand him back the previous bottles solemnly, he accepts them just as solemnly. Today I will make yogurt.

And a bonus:

Yesterday I was a little concerned about the old man apparently throwing small rocks down the hill, dancing and shouting inanities while I was passing by. Was he about to attack me? But then I noticed his goats, sluggishly moving down the hillside, pausing to gracefully extract leaves from the wicked thorn bushes. His antics were not aimed at me. Grace indeed.

April 26, 2009

1. Tired from too many night wakings, I slept in for a couple of extra hours this bright morning, rising when the sun and the calls of my children refused to let me lay abed any longer.

2. We walked for a long time today and the kids skidded over rocks and up hills and picked up a baby goat. Mountains were brilliant in the distance.

3. One time, nine years ago, Chinua and I were lost in a valley and spent eight hours trying to orient ourselves. Today we visited the spot and we had four children with us, miracle of miracles. We gave each other smitten looks, retold the story, remembered the thorns that we fought our way through, trying to be found again. We remembered the tiny jeep that took us home, Chinua's legs not quite fitting in the jeep and his knee switching off the headlights repeatedly, always right as we would take a wild corner in the dark. It could only be called careening. The adventure continues.

4. I love the potatoes here.

5. There are these sweet moments when I am not tired, and not irritated, and I realize just how blessed I am with these children and their endless enthusiasm, the way we spend time at a small, bare-bones playground and they find 101 ways to propel themselves up and down a slide. We eat falafel and drink chai and meet people and pose for pictures with Indian tourists. I come up with a new reality TV show idea which is based on the wild fashion of one tourist attraction street here. Tibetan fashion, pop Indian fashion, Sikh gangster style, the many ways one can sport a scarf, the hippies, the monks, the simple grace of fabric. I am thankful.

190

April 29, 2009

1. Yesterday I put the kids to bed after Chinua had gone out to play music with some people in the area. When the kids were finally settled with the eighth glass of water and hug and prayer and bathroom jaunt, I walked out onto the rooftop and sat with my back against the wall of our house. (It is the rooftop and veranda at the same time; the rooftop of the apartments below, our veranda.)

For a while I just sat, with a book, kind of reading it, and kind of listening to the moths bonk their heads repeatedly against the bare bulb above me. Slowly, a sound separated itself from the sound of the moths and their bonking heads, and floated towards me. It was unmistakably the sound of my Superstar Husband playing guitar on another rooftop across the valley. I sat and listened to him, from rooftop to rooftop, glad to be a part of the evening.

2. So I already told you that Chinua was out playing music last night. Today I met up with a woman that I know from Goa and she told me that he had played a new song that he wrote for me, a song called "Weave." She said many women were getting tears in their eyes at the thought of a man who was so vocal about his love for his wife and his commitment to her. It is rare, it seems, in the world these days.

One woman called out, "Lucky girl!" when he finished, and he shot back with "No, lucky me!" I am extremely blessed to be married to this man.

3. Renee, Becca and Cat are supposed to come back from their trip to Darjeeling and Assam tomorrow. WOOOO! Oh, how I've missed them.

4. Yesterday I choked back all my fears and thoughts of my crushing lack of ability, and scouted the nearby big town for fabric for the kids' clothes. We've been having most of their clothes made

in India, and I found a tailor nearby who threw together the cutest little elastic waisted pants for Leafy a couple of weeks ago. Kenya and Kai desperately need pants, since they won't stop growing inches each day, and so off to the cloth shops I went. I entangled myself in a few polyester and sequined booby traps before making swift getaways, and finding my jackpot in a shop staffed by a lovely woman who let me know which bolts of fabric were 100% cotton. There were many. There was also a man staffing the shop who was an Indian Mark Ruffalo look-alike, his Indian twin. And I emerged triumphant! Cloth for pants and shirts and one dress. Lovely.

PS: It may sound strange or excessive to have your clothes handmade by a tailor, but it's the way things are done here. The other way things are done here is with large cartoon graphics on the front of extremely ugly and poorly made clothing, so we'll take the tailor route, thanks. Tailors here are also very affordable. I paid 430 rupees for three pairs of pants for Leafy last time (about $9.00) and I was all, "Man, that was expensive." Because I'm frugal. Chinua says I'm a cheapskate and I need to examine my priorities. He continues to insist that clothing the children is a priority. Huh.

5. And on that note, on the acquiring things note, may I say that my blender (known here as a mixer-grinder) that I bought in Dharamsala, works at least fifty times better than the one I had in Goa. It is like a brilliant dream of a blender, actually making the hummus creamy, the lassi frothy, the baby food good for the toothless. I may try to find a way to get it on the train and bring it back to Goa.

PS: It cost 1000 rupees less than the crap-meister we bought in Goa, the blender that believes we are asking it to tickle the spinach, rather than purée it.

may

May 2, 2009

Today I emerged from the cave of my soul in the worst funk of the era.

I tried all my tricks, friends. I made coffee. I cleaned. I picked up my knitting and stared at it and then frowned at it and contemplated throwing it across the room. I lay and cuddled small people, because sometimes that works. And then sometimes I just feel angry that I am responsible for people and no one is responsible for me.

It was a funk.

I moved to confession.

I confess that I am jealous of those with plenty of time to spare.

I confess that I am ungrateful.

I confess that I'm a jerk. (That's not a real confession! That's like when you were in the sixth grade and you used to say, "Well, SorryforLIVING," but you weren't actually sorry for living, you just wanted someone to tell you that you didn't need to be sorry for living.)

I confess that I'm being selfish and childish. (That's more like it, Love.)

This is opposite day. No grace in small things here. Just a mum who threw her hands up this very evening and said, "I need a grownup here!" (You are a grownup.) "No, I need a different grownup. A more grownup grownup."

I do have a cute story for you, though. Two cute stories.

I was lying down with Solo and Leafy today, asking Leafy for definitions of things, which I do occasionally, ever since I discovered that I love his definitions. I thought his definitions might de-funkify me.

It started with fog : "A kind of smoky cloud."

Smoke? "Something that touches the ground and the sky."

A sweater? "Something we put on our heads and our bellies and it makes us warm."

A brick? "Something that is heavy."

A Mama? "A shark mama? Or a guy mama?" A guy mama. "A guy mama is someone... who lives in a house.... and plays... and cooks and snuggles."

Exactly. Sort of. So what is the problem?

*

Becca, Cat, and Renee are back from their trip to a wildlife reserve and other stuff. They arrived dirty and tired and we hugged them. And they told us about Becca in the night, chilly in Delhi, scrounging around in that half asleep way for something to cover herself with. They were all sleeping in one bed.

She grabbed ahold of the lungi that was on Cat and pulled. Cat said, understandably, "Hey, that's mine." Becca shot her a wild-eyed look, then took a small corner of it and smoothed it gently over her knee. In the morning when they all woke up, Becca was wearing

194

pants on her arms.

"Why do I have pants on my arms?" she must have wondered.

It makes me laugh.

*

Oh friends. Am I content with my lot? Or am I just faking it? Does it matter? Does anything matter?

Apparently it is time for bed. Time for oblivion and no more questions and plenty of hours between here and the space I will occupy in the morning. Plenty of time to be made new again.

All my love. Goodnight.

May 7, 2009

The good thing about getting a swift roundhouse kick of stomach flu is that you recognize once again that you are married to a Superstar. A SUPERHERO.

We all fell prey to it on the same day. First Kai did his math, then halfway through reading to me started to complain of being tired, then started holding his head and crying, then curled up in my bed and went to sleep. *In the middle of the day.* He has not slept in the daytime since he was two. I started feeling a little "off" right around then, and by nightfall there were chills and vomiting and all that goes with a stomach virus. (I think you'll thank me for sparing you the details.)

Miraculously, wonderfully, Chinua did not get sick. He spent the night trying to get enough blankets on me and revolving kids to the bathroom where they threw up and cried. And then the next day he took care of us as well, alternating with me because I was still not in great shape. The peak of my appreciation came when three of the kids were in my bed with me, all of us sitting up and eating broth, Chinua spooning it into both Kenya and Leafy's mouths.

We're all much better today. And I'm so thankful that our water

195

came back just before that endless fluid trial. Can you imagine us trying to deal with it with no water?

May 10, 2009

I woke up that day and knew right away that it was pointless to get out of bed. I turned to my husband.

"I just want to die," I said.

"That's a bit of an extreme reaction, don't you think, Rae?" he said, mildly.

"No. No, I don't think."

*

When the time came, we all assembled on the rooftop/veranda, against a stunning backdrop of blue sky and green hills with one little lone wooden house tucked in an impossibly vertical location. (Every day I look at that house with awe—the climbing required, to get to it. The climbing!) There were boulders strewn over the hillside like the seeds of mountain peaks, and we were armed with a large plastic bucket, several plastic bags, (black market items here, since plastic bags are outlawed) and many towels.

Renee, who, quite honestly, was behaving as though this was a party, told me she liked my outfit.

I frowned.

"I'm going to start wearing only black and grey," I replied. I was morose.

Becca, Renee, and Cat all smiled indulgently. My head felt like it would pop off. And good riddance if it did.

*

Chinua poured the special solution made of half vinegar and half rubbing alcohol over the hair of the first victims. He moved from a hairdresser routine for the girls to vomiting sounds for the kids. "I'm a blue whale and I just ate but.... blleheheeeheheheh," he

196

said, pouring the solution over their hair while everyone giggled uncontrollably.

I may have cracked a smile.

*

With the plastic bags on our heads and towels and scarves draped over the bags, we had a collective style reminiscent of a headgear cult. Leafy was sporting a red checked towel, very Arab in style, Renee had the look of a woman smoking a cigarette beside the garden gnomes and baby deer on the veranda of her trailer, Cat had a glazed cult follower look, and Becca had rosy cheeks and looked beautiful. I tied Chinua's plastic bag in a Tupac style, and me?

My hair has the incredible ability to soak up a lot of fluid, which leaked slowly into my bag, creating a puddle in the bag which I hung over my shoulder. It nestled just over my collarbone. Like a small pet draped around my neck. Or a breast implant, gone horrifically awry and fleeing north. As the day went on, I began to feel protective of my lump, speaking softly to it to comfort it.

*

We huddled in my bedroom, watching shows on the computer and eating ice cream, while we waited the requisite three hours before we could wash the stuff out of our hair. It was not a bad way to pass an afternoon, all of us lined up and glazing over at a stand up comic who was quipping his way unintelligibly around the computer screen.

And then the Internet guys showed up to help us connect to the new wireless signal that has been installed. A man from Israel and a Tibetan man born in India. It was interesting timing, to say the least, all of us huddled and turbaned. They needed to come into the back bedroom to work on the computer there. I tried to hide in the bathroom.

*

When I realized that hiding in the bathroom probably wouldn't work, I decided that talking about it was the next best thing.

"Lice."

We all commiserated. Little jerks, chomping on your head. The Israeli man was sitting at the computer, while the Tibetan man was sitting cross-legged on my bedroom floor, typing away at his laptop. The girls and I were still all slouched against the wall, and kids trickled in and out with their curiously large heads. I mimed the cult mother behind the man on the computer, talking to my bag of water and listening to the instructions it gave me.

The Israeli man had grown up on a kibbutz. "We used to use kerosene," he said. Our lot looked better.

Okay fine. I decided to be a good hostess.

"Chai, anyone?" I asked.

May 13, 2009

We have not been abandoned here.

We plan our steps down the mountainside very carefully, always looking for the next stone to land on.

Stone, stone, stone. We could make a pile and name it. Call it the hill of our remembrance.

Or maybe just Fred. (Glen?)

(Someone suggested a slide. It would certainly be easier on the knees.)

Flower grow from the cracks.

When I come back up the hill I am careful to have some sort of chocolate in my backpack. Heaven knows there could be an emergency.

Eggs, buffalo milk, bread. Peas that the kids will shell, kneeling and giggling together. Unzipping the pods.

Sometimes I want the whole earth to be small enough that I

could care for it, like an egg. It is too beautiful for me, and there are the bells on the donkeys, ringing again. Every piece of clover hurts, every patch of moss, small flowers. I don't know their names. Oh the distance, the peaks should soften, and I would lay my head down.

May 16, 2009

Lately it seems like I am thwarted at every turn. But not thwarted in love, in company, in fresh air, in greenery, in good food, or in baby kisses. So *every* turn is an exaggeration. What I am thwarted in is concentration and reliable Internet access.

Wow, this is a really similar story to so many other that I've shared. *Really, Rae?* you're thinking. *Seriously? You're having problems with Internet access and a clear space to concentrate on writing? We're shocked. No really, we'd never have guessed.*

You guys are so sarcastic. But really, I have so many emails to respond to. (I got your email by the way! I'm so sorry that I'm late in getting back to you!) And then I sit down to do it and one of the kids starts trying to pull off the head of another of the kids, so I decide to wait until the little lambs are sleeping, and when I finally sigh and settle down to do it, WHAM! a lightning bolt sizzles my computer. No it doesn't, but inexplicably the Internet connection is down.

So I of course switch gears and sit and show Renee and Cat and Becca home videos of the children that they already see every single day. *Here's Leafy singing. Here's Leafy dancing. Here's Chinua singing and dancing while driving. Look how cute everyone is! Look how little they are!* And you get the point.

I do have some real ideas stuck in my brain—things I want to tell you and show you. Thoughts on waste and what we do with our trash. (I have lots of thoughts on this—the last year of my life has been spent wrestling with trash and trying to cut down on waste. If there was a theme song to the year it would be... uh.... some kind of garbage related song. I can't think of one right now.) Thoughts on community, on meditation, on life.

*

Today we woke up and Chinua asked me if I wanted to go for a walk. I said yes, and that is what we did. We walked to the waterfall in Bhagsu—down the hill, another kilometer to the waterfall, and one back, and back up the hill. I have superhero kids. And a Superstar Husband who made the last trek up the hill with a baby in the carrier, a Leafy boy on his shoulders, and a backpack on.

It was one of those memorable days when you are so, so tired, but so happy, and you know that you will be talking about the waterfall for a long time, and you are glad that you do things like this, even when they make you tired. Kind of like life.

By the way, did you know that I turned 29 almost a week ago? On my birthday I managed to play pin-the-tail-on-the-donkey, ride on a seesaw, and ride on a thing that I can't remember the word for... spinning thing, really dangerous, launches children into the air like sacks of potatoes, like a carousel but not... is there even a name for it? Anyway, I felt like I turned 9, rather than 29.

And about the seesaw, Kai says that it's like a scale for people, and when I was too heavy on my end, he called Kenya over, saying "we need another orange on this side!" He's learned that from living in India. I can't remember if I've ever seen a scale with weights in North America, but it's all they use at the markets here.

May 23, 2009

First of all, I'm all right. I'm telling you now because this story is about going to the hospital.

Second of all, this may be a rampant galloping case of over-

200

sharing. Consider yourself warned.

Yesterday I went to the hospital in a storm. It was a wonderful storm, truly deserving of the title of storm. There were great gusting winds, hail, sheets of horizontal rain, stunning lightning forks, booms of thunder that made us all shake a little in our socks. Not surprisingly, the power went out.

While this was going on, I was feeling some strong pain in the lower left part of my abdomen, where I had an ectopic pregnancy two years ago. This pain could be anything from ovulation to pre-menstrual cramps, to whatever whatever, but I couldn't be sure. I haven't had a period since Solo was born. I'm at risk for another ectopic pregnancy because of scar tissue. After reading on the Internet about symptoms, I decided to be safe and go to the Tibetan hospital to get an ultrasound. Becca and Catherine came up to watch the kids, since Chinua was out, and off I went, umbrella in hand.

I walked along the upper road to a spot where I met a taxi, just past a mudslide which I scooted over by climbing up the hillside a little. There are two notable things about the upper road during this end of the storm:

1. The smell of the forest and hillside after the rain was absolutely, incredibly glorious. Wet leaves, wet dirt, wet warm pine needles. The sun was starting to shine even though it was still pouring rain. I looked all around me for the rainbow. Then we started to drive a little and:

2. There was the rainbow, and not just one but two. The lower one was the clearest that I've seen in years. I could see every color. I could see across our valley and the rainbow was touching our house. The upper rainbow was lighter and I pointed both of them out to the taxi driver. He chuckled.

Not too much is remarkable about the drive except for the

201

insane traffic jam that occurred. It was a typical case of large trucks on a small road. With much yelling and gesturing, about thirty men had it cleared up... in a while.

When I reached the hospital, I talked with some Tibetan doctors for a while. The main one, a young, tall doctor who had apparently (from his accent) spent some time in Britain, decided to take me down to the lab to see if they would give me a pregnancy test, even though the lab was closed for the day. The lab technician kindly agreed to put some of my pee on a stick.

"I'll just get you a small bottle," said the doctor, pointing out the bathroom to me. I assumed that it was a language issue, this mention of small bottle. Of course we don't pee in bottles!

When he returned, however, he held in his hand a Small Bottle. It was actually the prototype for the Small Bottle. All Small Bottles have forever been fashioned in the shape of this Small Bottle.

Do you know how, when you get liquid medicine in a shot, there is that bottle with the rubber stopper that holds the medicine? And then they poke the needle in and it goes up into the syringe? That bottle is what he brought me. It was TINY. And the size of the opening was the diameter of a pencil.

I was slightly taken aback, but after years of pregnancy and childbirth I have faith in my skillz. So I took the bottle from him with barely a twitch, and had a look at the bathroom. It was a typical Indian bathroom, a small closet-sized room with a squatty potty and a tap in the wall for water. Alright.

But then the light wouldn't turn on. I tried a few times, and then closed the door to experiment with how much light would come in. None. Not a crack of light. Okay, maybe a crack, I won't exaggerate, but the point is that I couldn't see my hand in front of my face.

I called down to the radiologist, "The light won't turn on!" He

answered, "Of course. There is no electricity in the whole building."
Oh yes, the storm.

So it was down to this. I needed to pee in a bottle on the floor in a pitch-black closet. And I was totally prepared to do it. This may be the pinnacle of cultural adjustment for me. I dove into the bathroom, after trying to memorize the position of the squatty potty. (I didn't want to step *into* it.) Somehow, I positioned myself, and then I was busy with the task of trying to aim my pee into a tiny hole with no vision. It was sort of like a blind video game, except with pee all over my hand.

I couldn't even see to check if I had been successful at all, but I went on faith that *something* had to have made it. After standing, feeling around in the dark for the door handle, and opening the door a crack, I could see that I was victorious! I stumbled out of the dark bathroom triumphantly, holding my Small Bottle high! Two Tibetan nurses turned to look at me with concern, then went back to what they were doing. It is hard to ruffle Tibetan people.

I washed my hands. I washed them well.

The test was negative. I'm probably having some cramps, or maybe it was nothing. At any rate, the pain is mostly gone and I feel a little silly and a little glad that I made it successfully over one more Indian hurdle.

(Although this post is very silly, it was an emotional day. It was sad to relive those days around the loss of our fourth baby, and I came home cloudy and sad. Then my family cheered me up and I was just thankful not to go through it again.)

May 26, 2009

Dear Solo,

And just like that, you are nine months old.

203

You scoot, you have one tooth (and are cutting at least three more oh help us Sweet Mercy please cut those teeth already Solo before I run off into the hills) and you like to put anything you find into your mouth. 90% of my current waking time is now devoted to scanning the floors around you in search of debris. There must be no debris within pinching sight of you at any time. Sigh.

It is a joyful thing, for a family to have a baby to dote on. Kenya bosses you around, Kai tickles you until I tell him, Stop Already, and Leafy hugs you and loves you. When Kenya is sad, she usually hunts for any warm body to cuddle with, and often these days, it's you. Perhaps because you don't turn to her and ask her to please stop crying so loudly in your ear, rather, you turn your head and look at her quizzically, as if to say, "What new game is this?"

We love you! What more can I say? At any moment, someone is playing with you... maybe your Aunty Becca, or Tripta, our neighbor, or Cat, or you are kicking and screaming with glee because you caught sight of Kai, your oldest brother whom you look at with what can only be called hero worship. I have never seen anyone as delighted with another person's mere presence as you are with Kai. Is it his large deer eyes? Or maybe it is his six-year-old self, hyper and leaping out of his skin, which matches your nine-month-old super-charged leaping out of your skin exactly? At any rate, he has only to appear in your peripheral vision and you are over the moon.

You've mastered "food" and "more" with baby sign. Good job, laddie. Although we really really need to get you some sort of high chair, because now that you can scoot, feeding you has become a rodeo event. We used to just sit you on the floor, but there are so many interesting things in the room! How can you sit still and allow yourself to be fed? Straps, my son, the answer is straps.

Who do you look like? It's kind of funny, because you look like Leafy (almost exactly, except he was about seven shades darker, even at your age) and you look like me. Simultaneously, which is weird, because I've always thought that Leafy and I look the least alike in the whole family. Genes. What can you say about them? I suppose that most of all, you look like you.

And oh, no letter to you would be complete without the mention of you and your numnums (Mama's milk). You *love* *numnums*. If there was one thing that you could share with the world, it would be that you. Love. Your. Numnums. I peeked at your brother's nine-month letter and it mentioned his love of numnums too, and the fact that sometimes the strength of his desire for numnums made holding him feel like wrestling a beaver, as he tried to get into the right place. What a perfect metaphor! Wrestling a beaver. Only with you, (you are a giant baby) the metaphor would be more accurate if we said wrestling a baby polar bear.

Sometimes when we lie in bed and nurse, I curl around you a bit, and our tummies are touching, and I stroke your hair. You hold my hand and I think that I have never in my life had so much love in me.

It's probably true. You and your brothers and sister have swelled my heart to ridiculous proportions.

Love,

Your Mama

june

June 4, 2009

Enough is enough. It's getting ridiculous. The book must be written before it dies a sad death. I must invest in this. I *will* invest in this.

There has been an unexpected and welcome turn of events here in our house. We have a babysitter! I'm actually looking for someone more long term who can travel with us and hang out with the kids. Just enough so that I can write, and sometimes go out with Chinua while he plays concerts in the evenings, or go to a meditation in the *middle of the day*. It's a bit of a pipe dream, but we'll see. For the time being, I've been asking around here. "Do you know of anyone who can watch kids? They have to speak good English."

Since we moved out of the house that Jaya lived in, I've always had a neighbor helping me for a couple of hours in the mornings. For me, the things that are oh-so-necessary, but really bust my butt when I'm homeschooling with a baby and daily meditations happening on my rooftop and communal lunches (in Goa) are the floor cleaning and the dinner dishes.

In Goa, my next-door neighbor, Maria, helps me. I love Maria, oh how I love her. She is like a brilliant shining star in my day, always laughing and joking. When we first got here, to the mountains, we met a woman named Tripta who lost her husband to cancer two months before we arrived. She is responsible for her elderly in-laws and her three teenaged kids, and now her husband is gone. He used to run a shop, but she is dependent on their guest house for income now, a house that is heavily mortgaged. We have been looking into other ways that we can help her, but when I asked her if there is anyone she knew who might want a cleaning job, she almost started jumping up and down with her hand in the air. She needed the job.

Tripta calls Solo "Giptu." I truly think that "Giptu" has become such a healing part of Tripta's life. In the end, playing with him for a few minutes every day doesn't really make her life better, but it's one time that she is really, really smiling. She's always suggesting that when I go back to "Israel" (I keep telling her that I'm not from Israel, but she either forgets or doesn't believe me) that I leave Solo with her. And then she tells him that I'm not his mama, she is. He is such a perfect little baby for India, too, where everyone pinches cheeks and talks to him. When Tripta talks to him he smiles back and touches her face and gabbles away and gives her round-mouthed baby kisses on her cheeks.

One day a girl came over who was interested in watching the kids. She was with another neighbor of ours. She was very shy and wouldn't really talk to Chinua or I. I mentioned that we could give it a try, having her watch the kids. But all she would say to the neighbor was, "What time do I come? And how much will you pay me?" Chinua was pretty sure that it wouldn't work. The kids are pretty rambunctious. I mean, they are kids.

Tripta was at the house at the time and the next day she brought her thirteen-year-old son over. *Ankit can watch your kids,* was the gist of what she said. At first I was skeptical, because he's only thirteen, but then we came up with a plan.

So now Ankit comes over every morning with Tripta, and plays with the kids outside for a couple of hours while she works. I sit in my back bedroom with my manuscript strewn all over my bed, writing, and the kids run and scream and play. Sometimes they play soccer, sometimes they climb trees, and sometimes they hide behind boulders. It's pretty much perfect in many ways. Tripta is here for back up, I am here for back up, and the kids have someone a little more mature than them to play with, someone who is also almost a kid himself. It's pretty fun.

The only thing is that I don't trust him with Solo yet. So if Solo is sleeping, woo hoo! If not, I type with one eye on Solo while he does the inch worm around the room and chews on my books. *It's still better than nothing.* In this way I've been writing 1000 words a day. Not the greatest, but not bad for a homeschooling/cooking/community-minded/mother of four.

I made another practical change to my life the day before yesterday. Chinua is away for a couple weeks. So grocery shopping has been an issue. Grocery shopping means walking down the mountainside with a backpack, usually in the morning when the vegetable sellers still have vegetables. The other day I was completely stressed out, and I had to sit back on my heels and investigate why.

I was trying to get the kids working on personal schoolwork while I got ready to get the groceries, so my sister could supervise them working, and I was keeping one eye on the clock so that I could be back in time to write. It was not all that sustainable. So I gave the owner of one of the shops down the hill a call. And forty minutes later, my groceries were delivered. *It was like magic.*

I'm known for doing things the hard way. So this easy thing of asking someone to bring me my groceries was an amazing discovery for me. And just like that, school time got much easier. Things are often time-constrained here. I can't go in the afternoons because the veggie stalls are too often all out of spinach, or peas, or carrots. And I can't go in the mornings because of school, and all that it takes for me to get my family ready in the morning. So it was amazing to find a solution.

Now all I have to do is find the right tailor. Starts and stops and starts and stops. Life.

June 8, 2009

You may be wondering how my new set up with groceries and babysitting is working.

Groceries: Awesome. Awesome, awesome, awesome. This morning I called down, and forty-five minutes later the groceries were delivered to my door. I'm paying the porter personally, and a little more than is normal, so the whole employment bit feels good too.

The only thing: today I asked for two bhaingan (eggplant), and they heard two *kilos.* Eggplant is not particularly heavy, so now I have a fridge FULL of eggplant. I batter fried slices of two of them tonight, and said to my sister... two down, only thirty-two to go. I exaggerate. But Kai couldn't get enough of the batter-fried bhaingan, so that's a silver lining. You've gotta love a kid who loves eggplant. (I was not one of them.)

(Of course, as I said to my husband on that fateful day nine years ago when we ate the cockroach in Bangkok, *anything* tastes good when it's fried with garlic and salt.)

Babysitting: Sometimes I want to pull my hair out. My writing times tend to be full of so many interruptions that I am tempted to crawl under my bed and never come out at all. There are water problems, a puppy runs into the house, Solo wakes up. Somebody needs me at the door and it turns out to be some weird masseuse guy with dirty bottles of oil. "Why did you interrupt me for that?" I ask Ankit. "He said you called him here," he replied. Which is a strange business strategy for a masseuse: the outright lie. Like I'd say, "Oh? I called you here? I guess I just forgot! Okay! Massage away with your dusty oils and strange tools!"

But there is something about employing someone so that I can write. I've turned into a machine. I will get my 1000 words out or die trying. No matter how many interruptions, I've been managing. It's been good. Tonight was another story, though. I asked Ankit to come over at 8:00 so that I could go out with my sister for a little while. He came, and sat patiently while I tried for what seemed like forever to put Solo to bed. This is how the evening went.

8:30- Finally Solo gets off to sleep. My back is breaking. (Have I mentioned that this is a very heavy child?)

8:34- I am trying to play a movie on my computer for Ankit. I have the wrong hard drive. Arggh.

8:36- Kenya is "itchy." She heard a bug. Something was on her forehead and that makes her want to cry and cry and cry, because something was on her forehead. She's scared of her bed now. She can't sleep.

8:46- I'm lying in bed beside Kenya, stroking her face. She's still crying, clutching me every few minutes, saying, "I'm sooorrrry," and "I can't sleep." Finally I ask her if she wants to sleep in my bed. I move her and it's like magic; all her itches go away, and sleep comes quickly.

8:56- Success with the DVD for Ankit!

9:00- Finally out the door with Becca, I heave a huge frustrated sigh and refrain from throwing rocks. Where should we go? I'm so tired, Solo is teething and I haven't been getting much sleep. It seems too hard to walk down the mountain, so we decide to walk over to the closer village. Maybe we can have a lassi or something.

9:20- "Becca," I say, "this restaurant seems depressing to me." We hand the menus back and decide to walk back over to the restaurant near our house. It's familiar.

9:35- When we get to the restaurant near our house, I have to go to the bathroom. When I get out I see Tripta (the restaurant is on her rooftop) and she laughs at me because my hair is up in a wrap. She thinks it looks silly.

9:40- The phone rings. I can hear Solo crying. "I'll be right there," I say.

*

Well, we had a nice hike through the moonlight. So, that's how that's going. But I'm sure it's the same for any parents of young children anywhere. It's funny, isn't it? I feel as though I can stretch so far, with my kids, but when they are up past their bedtimes, I'm like, wait, what? I was with you all day! I fed you and watered you and we read together and played! Now that part's done! What's going ON?

Stttreeeeetttch. I will one day be the most flexible person ever to roam this earth. Metaphorically speaking. (Rubs aching back.) Maybe I should get that masseuse back here.

June 10, 2009

I've been having some trouble treasuring my life. (And some trouble feeling treasured.)

The days stretch and there are teeth forcing their way slowly through my youngest son's gums. He is not sleeping, and neither am I. (Are you sure that I am loved?)

I hold him a lot. And then I snap at people. And then I cringe. (*I don't feel lovable.*)

But there are glimmers. (*Do you love me, Maker?*)

Love glimmers, like tonight when my back was aching and I lay on the cool concrete floor and all three of the older kids lined up and lay with their heads on my belly, like a group of kittens. Kenya stroked my face and told me, "I haven't seen you cry in a long time." (*The answer comes: A very loud YES!*)

"When was the last time you saw me cry?" I ask. No one can remember. "I think sometime in America when you and Daddy were talking and you were sad," someone says. They are wrong. They saw me cry in Goa, when we arrived. When we were there, this place that I am in now, comfortable and in a house and out in the sun, in the breeze, on a rooftop, this place would have seemed like paradise. Why am I so dry and stubborn, adjusting to good things and finding something new to complain about? (*Life King, are you sure that you love me? Because I know that I love you, that I would curl myself up next to your breastbone if only I could, that I love the things you make and I would run off of a hillside with lemmings, I would breathe under water, I would stampede, I would fly, I would become the peak of a mountain, just for the joy of it.*)

There are other glimmers. Tonight we ate fiddlehead ferns that our neighbor brought us from the shady glades of the forests near the waterfall. Becca watched everyone this morning so that I could sleep. Math is going well, we are all healthy, and I gave Tripta some of the eggplants. In turn, she gave me some potatoes from her garden. (*Yes, again, an 'I love you' but not a shrill yes.*)

It's better if I sit down and paint. It's better if I am singing my way through the day. It's better if I am getting some sleep. It's better if I am not thinking too hard about all that I should be. (*Not an exasperated yes, either, like 'Yes, already. Jeez.'*)

Here's a comedic glimmer. More than a glimmer, a flash of light like someone on the opposite hilltop has lifted their glass of water in the sunlight, to take a sip.

Yesterday we were walking home, and Leafy was running on ahead. Lately he's been doing what Becca calls the Forrest Gump version of running: we set out, and he starts running and just keeps on RUN-NING. He's almost always within sight, and we are usually on a straight path around the hillside when he's doing this. But yesterday we had to take a left, to go up the hill, and he kept on to the right and down. Kai and Kenya got a whiff of this, and they took off after him, while Becca and I calmly plodded along, blissfully unaware of the drama about to take place. I saw them disappear around a curve and said, "Hey kids! You're going the wrong way!"

They yelled back that they were bringing Leafy home. Becca went to go see what was up, and I loitered on the path with Solo, giving lame little waves to people who climbed past me. When we were finally all together, I heard the story. Leafy had just kept on running down the stone path, with Kenya and Kai in frantic pursuit, Kenya calling out to hikers who were headed in the opposite direction: "*Please* help us catch him!" By the time they all caught up, he was resting on a rock, and they were practically all the way down the hill.

It was pretty funny. He then turned around and ran up the hill, to our house. I don't know what's up with this running thing, but it is a glimmer.

There are many glimmers, and I am trying to treasure these days, minutes, hours. I am tired, but with my pencil held weakly in one hand I am sketching something for us all to remember when we are older. Making chapati in the kitchen, playing cards, sitting on a blanket with knitting and pencils and a rubber dinosaur. Lots of baby kisses.

(Not shrill, not exasperated, but more like a humming, a thrumming, a whirring, like the wing beats of a thousand birds. They all shout yes yes! You are loved you are loved! The earth beneath your feet is humming with it, whispering: Beloved. Lay your head down. Let it swell up and over you. Be loved. This is the biggest truth, the greatest truth: The Maker, The Life King, He loves you. Climb into it. Don't hide cringing in the corner, walk out and let it find you. The days are like a long line ahead of you and in them is the capacity for a great stomping, chummy, heart-easing, devastating love that you must open yourself up to.

It is your life work.)

June 16, 2009

We are as sick as dogs. My darling Becca left and the next day we could barely crawl out of bed. Or, I could barely crawl out of bed. Trouble is, all these kids! And my Superstar Husband returns tomorrow.

I didn't want to call anyone, for fear of contaminating them. I prayed, instead. When my friend Ute showed up in my hallway, (just to check on us) I burst into tears. "What can I do?" she asked. And she proceeded to wash dishes and prepare dinner, read to cranky sick kids and sweep.

Today I am feeling... well, like a dishrag if a dishrag had sensitive skin, a bad cough, and a sore throat. But Ute came over again, and did more reading, more washing dishes, and she chopped vegetables, although I was able to pull myself together enough to make soup.

I am a very proud person, the bad kind of proud. I like to have everything together. I don't like to have people come over and find everything a mess and me out of it and everyone whiny and cranky. Which is why I think I find myself in situations all the time where I have to ask for help. It's more of God whittling away at my character. What will I be when he is done?

June 18, 2009

Stories

Once upon a time Rae's husband came home from Turkey. He had been away for almost three weeks. She was so so happy, and showed him so by hunkering down with a high fever for the whole day, telling her husband from her fever dreams that black people weren't allowed to enlist in the U.S. military during World War I. It was very upsetting to her. She may even have cried a little.

   *

  Once upon a time there was a boy named Kai who was obsessed with the word *Mister*. Also, *Missus* or *Miss*. Almost every noun was supposed to start with one of these words, according to this boy. So the family read "Green Eggs and Mr. Ham" with Mr. Sam I Am as the star. They ate Mr. Porridge for breakfast, went to Mr. Bed at night, and sang Mrs. Songs. They loved to eat Mr. Mangos, and Mrs. Bananas. And their favorite time of day was when they got to play in Mr. Outside.

   *

Once upon a time there was a dog who thought she lived at Rae's house. Rae saw her milling around for a couple of days, and then took a closer look, finally seeing a tag with a phone number on it. She called the number on the tag, and made a new friend. But why didn't Rae look sooner? That's the mystery of the story. Maybe it was because of the fever. Maybe it was because she couldn't be bothered, or because there is always some dog on her porch. When she was asked by the dog's owner whether she had fed the dog, she said no, and the owner was glad, because if she was hungry she'd be less likely to run away again. But then Rae's daughter said, "I fed her my biscuits!"

*

Once upon a time Rae's baby was pushing out his fourth tooth in about a week. But that's okay, because Rae thought secretly that sleeping was overrated anyway.

*

Once upon a time Rae was walking along a path towards her home when she saw a Himalayan woman, wearing her shawl on her head, standing beside a pile of iron window grates. Rae made some sort of interested exclamation about how interesting it was! Window grates! A pile of them! Next to the woman! and the woman took this as encouragement to impress on Rae the need for Rae to carry one of them down the hill. Rae made a faint protest about the fact that she was already carrying things, including a new broom, and the woman chose a slightly smaller iron window grate for her. She was left with no choice, carrying the window grate in a trembling arm, as other women exclaimed and laughed at her on their way back up the path to carry more window grates.

*

Once upon a time, Rae was so, so tired. And so happy that Chinua was back. And it all mingled together in a great wash of giddiness, like a wave.

June 22, 2009

If you've ever sat on your unmade bed slumped into a shape like a letter 'C', if you've ever hit your foot on the bottom of a chair and messed up your toenail polish, if you've ever spoken sharply to your kids and then found out that they were innocent, if you've ever run out of money, run out of time, run out of patience...

If you've ever been too hot, forgotten to drink enough water, stopped exercising for a year... If you've ever put your head down on

216

a concrete floor and given up, only to peel yourself up and continue washing dishes a few minutes later, if you've ever been late for dinner or paying a bill, if you've ever sighed overly loudly and then been caught peeking to see if anyone noticed...

If you've ever been so bored your teeth hurt, if you've ever looked at the days before you with dismay, if you've ever looked at your face in the mirror with dismay, if you've ever made a bad hair decision, if you've ever bumped your head really hard and then cussed and then felt bad because you just happened to be on camera, if you've ever blamed people just to make yourself feel better, if you've ever been a blamosaurus rex...

If you've ever had a cough for days and days and days, if you've ever broken a tooth on popcorn, if anyone has ever found glass in your food, if you've ever looked at crafting blogs and despaired, if you've ever woken up and realized that you are pretty sure that you are totally mediocre...

Well, the following story is for you.

Once upon a time there was a girl who lived in India, and she was a girl, but she was also a mother, which means that if she was having a bad day she wasn't allowed to lock her bedroom door and refuse to come out. (It's just kind of one of the rules, if you're a girl and a mom. Also if you're just a mom.)

So this girl who was a mom was having water problems at her house again, and she had a couple of wise friends who had spent a lot of time in the mysterious land of India. These friends told her, "If you want to get anything done, you have to get mad!" The girl wasn't at all sure that she could act angry to someone, but she thought she'd give it a shot. So she called her landlord, (again) and she said, "Listen, I just can't live this way anymore. I'm spending all my money to send my laundry out, I can't cook, we can't bathe. This is ridiculous!"

She didn't sound angry, but she did succeed in appearing rather pathetic. And she learned from the landlord that all had been done that could be done, and nothing more could be solved with the water crisis until the monsoon. They would just have a little bit of water, each and every day.

And this is what happened to the girl: she pulled one sleeve until it turned inside out, and the other sleeve until it just tore right off her shirt, and then she hopped on one foot in a circle, and she turned red and then she began to weep. The water thing was taking too many thoughts, and the thoughts became bumpy, and the thoughts were not smooth, the way she liked her thoughts to be. And the children had grown fangs.

So she cried. She sat down on the floor and cried and cried, and soon all the things that were sad but that she hadn't cried about (because she was a girl AND a mom) were filling up her head and demanding that tears be dedicated to them too. And then the neighbors began to line up and write small things on pieces of paper, things that needed to be cried about, and then the Internets joined in, and the girl who was a mom wept until her tears formed their own clouds and a great storm came. The great storm turned into a great monsoon and after a few days, the water came rushing into all the tanks in the village.

All the villagers were very happy, plus they'd had their sad things cried over, and so they bought the girl who was a mom a bathtub of her very own, so she could soak her old feet in it and then rub some nice smelling lotion into them.

And it was all because the girl who was a mom had let herself cry. (There's no rule against it!)

The End

June 23, 2009

Another Glimpse into the mind of my youngest son:

Now that I am able to pull myself to a standing position, I will do so at any and every opportunity! No one will be able to stop me! I will be a STANDING BABY!

Mama would like me to go to sleep, I can tell, and though I am tired, there is simply nothing better than standing. I will pull myself to standing!

She has just come in for a little bout of singing, I see. Little does she know that singing is no use against the mighty stand. It doesn't matter what you sing, Mama: Twinkle twinkle, You are my Solo (to the tune of You are my Sunshine- Mama is witty), Jesus Loves Me... Nothing will work. For no matter how tired I am, I will continue to pull myself to my feet, and then cry because I can't get back down. This is my superpower.

She is sighing and complaining about her back for some reason, but I am still standing with my little red mouth open, I can sense a victory! I will stand, I will stand, I will stand. I wonder... if I butt my head against her shirt with my mouth open will I get numnums? Yes, yes I will!

She has laid me back down again, and I will not put up with this. In another minute I'll stand again, and that'll show her! In just another minute. Perhaps if I just put my thumb in my mouth... perhaps... Zzzzzzzz.

June 27, 2009

We are going on a little adventure tomorrow. I'm ready to get out of here for a few days. It's true that we live in India, (which is adventurous) but it's also true that we rarely venture beyond walking distance, and if that, only to buy paper, go to the tailor, or get some cough drops. (Though sometimes we drop in at the local Korean restaurant.)

Tomorrow our hired jeep will pick us up at the nearby road. We will walk along the stony path, down the stairs, along the creek bed, and up the hill, and then off we go in the jeep to Manali. I think the journey takes 7 hours, but I don't think that's calculated for children.

*

It was quiet, today, in the Stage Carriage, until Cate asked if I had heard that Michael Jackson died. She was sitting in front of me, beside a Tibetan woman wearing the *chupa*–the traditional Tibetan dress. The Stage Carriage is a jeep for public transportation. It has three bench seats, and doesn't drive for anything less than four people per row. It's a cozy ride. (And it's really called a stage carriage.) For 10 rupees, you can hop in the Stage Carriage in McLeod Ganj and ride to lower Dharamsala, where you can find a tailor to make you yet more children's clothes which your children will grow out of in six months.

Anyway. Suddenly the jeep was alive with discussion. The Tibetan woman beside Cate shook her head.

"It's because he was trying to make himself whiter," she said.

A Polish Buddhist nun in maroon robes was sitting next to me.

"His music was so so beautiful. Did you like him?" she asked

"I like his music very much," I said. "But I think his story is very sad. He got too famous, too young."

"Yes," the Polish Buddhist nun continued, "he gave all of himself away, and had nothing left for him."

Cate was still talking with the Tibetan lady up front. "Yes, he was very young, it's very sad," she said.

"Everyone, everywhere, is sad about him dying," said the Tibetan lady.

"And did you ever see his DVDs? He was such a great dancer," added the Buddhist nun.

And I shook my head. Reminiscing about Michael Jackson in India in the Stage Carriage with these two ladies was almost too much for my grip on reality.

*

Sometimes when your husband is away and you are tired and not getting a lot of sleep and you live somewhere far from where you have lived before, you might have a small crisis and cut your hair, which is what I did, back when Chinua was in Turkey.

But the good news is, I only cut off the bottom half. I emerged from the bathroom with a handful of dreadlocks that had been with me for almost seven years. My neck is much cooler, but I needed it cleaned up and made the same length, so I headed to the barber.

I should have known better, because what part of "I just want it tidied up," sounds like "Go ahead and shave it?" The lower part of my head is very bare now. At least I can say that I've been to an Indian barber. And it really is *so* much cooler.

july

July 2, 2009

Amazing things in Manali:

* Animals! Angora goats, sheep, yaks, snakes, and one beloved bear. (Kenya, our resident adorer of animals, is of course right smack in the center of everything.)

* An old Himalayan village with carefully crafted wooden buildings, stables on the first floor of the homes for the sake of the heat. Women walking up the hillsides, carrying basket after basket of greens on their backs for their cows. My favorite is when the purple clover is perched on the very top.

* The traditional village women here wear handwoven wool wraps. One day I saw a woman weaving one. She let me watch her for a while, but declined a photo.

* Orchards everywhere with teenager apples in the middle of growing up to be adult apples.

* The monsoon has come. I still get nervous with the really

heavy rains, not yet used to the fact that it's completely normal. Everyone has been waiting for the rains. We are so glad for them.

* Good conversations and good coffee.

* A long walk through a forest.

* Solo is no longer a baby who is content to sit quietly with us while we wait for our food in a restaurant. Chinua and I pass him back and forth like a football, each of us holding him until we can't amuse him any longer. Kai, on the other hand, simply looks for a chess set. Things get complicated, though, when he is playing with Kenya and she becomes frustrated and starts knocking over the pieces.

* A beautiful music jam with a Swiss accordion player, Israeli guitarist, and Chinua on the mandolin. The Swiss couple happened to have a tin whistle and I played along, although it has been a couple of years since I have practiced. The muscle memory was somewhere back there, waiting. As we played, pieces came back to me bits at a time, like a small child waking up from a nap.

* Tomorrow we leave, piling into the jeep, singing, playing 20 questions, excited to get home to our house and kitchen. (Mama is excited to make herself numerous cups of tea in the morning.)

July 6, 2009

Today the kids cornered me.

"We need to get a yak," Kai said, truly serious.

"A yak?" I repeated, a little dumbfounded. "What would we do with one?"

"We don't have *any* animals," Kenya added, doing her wide eye thing and waving her face in front of mine, in case I wasn't paying attention.

"We don't have anything, not even a cow, or a buffalo," said Kai.

"We don't have a GOAT, or a chicken, or a SNAKE. Or a

rabbit, or a cat, or a dog..."

"Or a sheep!"

We do have Solo, but I suppose that's not enough.

*

My husband is a juggler. He's tried to teach me, but I just can't keep everything in the air.

And that makes me wonder about my life, how I keep trying and trying to keep it all suspended, hitting each of my palms at precisely the right moment.

1000 words... beans on to soak... time for math... Solo and the potty... burn the trash... painting... someone coming over for dinner... prayer in the morning... pick up dominoes... listen to the kids reading aloud... emails... phone calls... time to deworm...

A breeze comes. It has been sunny for two days, and today I'm hoping for a great big storm, a rouser and a crasher, something that will sweep through and happily scare us. Just a little thunder and lightning and a real downpour.

God knows we need it.

July 9, 2009

My dad would like to know the symptoms telling me it is time to deworm... does he really want to know?

Actually, we don't really have a lot of symptoms, other than slightly run down immune systems, which could be anything, really, but they say in India to deworm every six months. We missed the first six months, so here we go a year! Or thirteen months, really. *Reary*, as one of my British friends would say, with a *Briyant!* and an *Innit?* on the side.

Other British friends would say *Brilliant*, very carefully, and *Is That So?* and *As it Were*, and *Isn't It?*

I love British accents, how they are all over the map (quite!) and

224

full of mild surprise (lovely!) and inexplicable turns of phrase (innit?).

Other things I love:

*How it rained yesterday and the air that came to me through the window was so sweet and fern-like that my knees wobbled a bit.

*That many travelers have given us their umbrellas as they've left, so now we have forty-two umbrellas.

*Brown rice.

*Kai: "If you ever need to find a mouse, just come find me, because I'm *really good* at knowing where things are *just just by hearing them.*"

*My new plot graph for my book, which makes me feel as though it's possible to finish it even though I never *write* it, like it's a *magic* plot graph or something. (The babysitting thing with Ankit didn't work out, in the end. It was an interesting month. Half of the time I wrote, and half of the time I was sure I had adopted a fifth kid.)

*Chinua when he's in that one silly mood where he can't stop laughing and he reminds me of the nine-year-old he must have been.

*Possibility. I line up every morning with my hands out, no matter how tired I was the night before. I'm in the queue! I believe!

*Forcing myself to do things I don't necessarily want to do and then rewarding myself with small squares of chocolate gently placed between biscuits afterwards.

*Spinach.

*The thighs that belong to Solo.

*Indian steel shops where they sell all the plates, cups, bowls, pots and pans, and tiffins that you could ever desire. Cate's been known to love a good steel shop, too. And who wouldn't? Once you get into stainless steel, there's no going back.

*Waiting for a package in the mail.

*Leafy, who, incidentally, clogged an outside drain so badly (by putting things into the fascinating open hole at the top of it) that four people who work for my landlady spent half a day unclogging it. A part of a one of the broken umbrellas was in it. The most ambitious thing he put into the drain? A whole toilet brush. We've had a talk, since then, and I've threatened him a few times, so hopefully he'll refrain from his wild drain-clogging ways.

*How the kids sometimes collapse in laughter.

*Hope that does not disappoint.

*Bhagsu cake: a delicious concoction of a shortbread crust, caramel middle, and hard chocolate top. So good.

*A good Skype call, like the one I had with my parents the other day, or the one Becca and I had with Matty when she was still here.

*And Kenya, daughter of mine, with her fearlessness and inquisitiveness.

July 14, 2009

On Getting Well

I almost never get sick, which is why it's frustrating that for days lately I've felt knocked down by different viruses. My digestive system is perfect. Lovely. Plenty of fiber, no yuckiness. I won't get any more detailed than that, but let's just say that I take pride in my digestive accomplishments. But these weird viruses—terrible.

Like this last one, which threw me for a loop. It started with a headache so strong that I couldn't get out of bed. I was only in a large amount of pain (as opposed to a monstrous amount of pain) if I lay very still. When Chinua passed me Solo so that I could nurse him, he of course was his usual exuberant self and ended up knocking his head against mine a few times. It felt like he had brought an ice pick into the bed with him. Good gracious, he's a violent baby.

Anyway, the next day it had moved into my upper spine, and as we walked down into town to celebrate a friend's birthday, every step vibrated in different pain decibels all around my vertebrae. The next day? Lower back and kidneys. Very strange. Very mysterious. No fever.

Today I'm feeling better but still not myself. I'm going to get well, take supplements, eat sprouts, get my immune system back in order. And that concludes my long illness memo. Thank you for attending.

On Putting the Right Pants on

This morning Solo woke up and popped his face next to mine, making that wrinkly-nosed-bared-teeth grin that he's been making lately. (He starts in his bed and ends up in mine. Sometimes I wake up next to him with virtually no memory of collecting him from his bed in the middle of the night.)

As I was rubbing at my eyes, trying to wake up, I noticed Leafy lurking around the doorway (as he does if he wakes up before Kai or Kenya) wearing the pants that Kenya had been wearing when she went to sleep the night before. It was strange. I rubbed away and tried to figure it out, then gave up when I felt the headache coming back from the strain.

The kids of course busted their guts laughing when they saw Leafy wearing Kenya's pants. And then she said, "But I peed in those pants!!" Ha ha ha. Turns out she peed in the middle of the night, got up, took her pants off and put new pants on, and then when Leafy woke up and his pants were peed on, he took them off and put on a random pair of pants that he found on the floor—Kenya's pee pants. (Are you still following me?)

It's a regular pee party around here! Come on over, we can all pee in our pants and then switch! Like musical chairs! Only smellier. (Sigh.)

On Marathons

Today, when we were sitting around the table doing schoolwork, Leafy set up a little computer and speaker set for himself. The computer was a small yellow wooden box that we use for toys. The speakers were some math manipulatives. He set them up on the floor, and proceeded to beat box and dance for about half an hour. It was very cool and very distracting.

Then he pressed an invisible button on the computer and speakers, and said, "Whoa, I was just dancing for four days."

On Bathing

I've finally figured out how to get my older kids really bathing themselves. In water shortages, it doesn't work to let them hop into a shower themselves, because the *whole world* is at stake if they let that water run too long and I can't flush a toilet later. And then sometimes the showers don't work, the hot water in the bathrooms doesn't work, everything is spotty.

But a good old bucket bath is perfect. I give them a bucket of really warm water, tell them to get wet and soapy and rinse off, and Voila! Two kids down, two to go.

On Chai

At the heart of every Indian woman is the desire to make good chai. So when I go to Tripta's house and she makes chai, she looks at me inquiringly afterwards. "Ohhhhh. Good chai," I say. "Thank you Didi," (sister) she replies, with a modestly gratified look.

I know exactly how she feels. The other day some guys were over, practicing music for a concert that they are putting on with Chinua. They play such great music: Darius, a British-Iranian guy who's been playing violin since he was four, Itai, an Israeli drummer, and my husband on mandolin and Turkish saz, playing Celtic songs, gypsy songs, and an Egyptian folk song: Beautiful.

I made chai, and then while in the kitchen I heard Darius raving about it. "This is proper chai: perfect ginger, perfect sugar, not too strong... Perfect."

I felt rather smug.

On Aging

Isn't it funny how having kids makes you feel young and old at the same time? So often I find myself turning into a crone, standing hunched over my cutting board in the kitchen, slicing onions with tears in my eyes, barking "Calm DOWN!" to the kids who are jubilantly racing through the house, destroying everything in their path. They fall down in fits of giggles, and I'm dismally muttering in the corner, "You better pick that up when you're done with it," and "I said *calm down!*" And I realize that at that moment, everyone else in the house is *so much more fun* than me. I'm raining on the parade.

And simultaneously, I feel very young, because of the sheer ratio of hours of Lego play to hours of non-Lego play in my life.

On What it Feels Like to Really Swing on Vines through the Jungle

You would get your face scratched by other trees, I would think. And you would get bugs in your mouth. And then there would be all those jolts and swoops and thunks.

But then there would be moments of truly flying, when the whole jungle flows past you and you can see it so clearly and smell the flowered breeze, and that's how I felt today. It was just a normal day, but I was feeling better and I could see, again, as if for the first time, the true value of what I've been given. Bantering with Kai, receiving baby kisses from Solo, I laughed so many times today, and I felt so glad.

July 20, 2009

The monsoon here has been lovely so far. We have great, cracking storms in the afternoons and night times, and often when we wake the world is sparkling and the sun is rising to shine for a few hours before the rain comes again. It is humid, but not moldy. It is cool, but not cold. Sometimes the lightning at night is nearly constant, and I wake up to watch it flicker in the distance with a rhythmic pulsing, almost the regularity of a heartbeat.

Our house has been full. We have new neighbors, an Israeli family and an Australian family, and there are four new children in our apartment building. Yesterday everyone was tumbling in and out of the house, playing tag (or "chasies" as the Australian neighbors call it) or hide and seek, washing the mud pies out of their clothing, drinking water or showing me the stubbed toe they'd gotten from one of the rocks.

In the evening some friends from up the mountain came down for dinner. I over-salted the food and everyone pushed it around on their plates politely and took great big gulps of water. We washed up and drank tulsi tea and talked until it was time for them to take their long trek back up the mountain to bed.

The concert the boys were practicing for took place on Saturday night. No one was sure what to expect, but in the end, the room was packed, even vibrating slightly from the dancing in the back. The fiddler/violinist had never played a concert like it before. Used to an opera house, he was full of the thrill of playing for an audience that he could interact with.

So. I've been cooking and cleaning and teaching and shooing kids in and out of the house. (Depending on whether it's raining or not.) I've been reading the book of John in the Bible (and being blown away) and knitting a washcloth and drinking tea rather than coffee these days. I've been making plans and avoiding writing. I've been dreaming of Goa. I've been walking up and down hills and glancing furtively at scarves, thinking that one of these days I really should buy one. (Did you know that I've never bought myself a scarf? They've all been gifts. I'm afraid of buying a scarf, just like I'm afraid of buying most clothes. There's too much choice. It's paralyzing.)

The house is always in a state of being picked up and put away— as soon as we finish, we need to start again. Same thing with the kitchen. It is always time to feed everyone. These rhythms become part of us, and I'm thinking that if I can just be living in a rhythmic way, all the little bumps will be more like dancing.

July 22, 2009

If you heard the explosions in my house earlier, don't worry. Nothing was being detonated, that's just the sound of eggplants when they're roasting on the gas stove and they pop. I know! I was a little scared, too, before I realized what it was.

I made a little song in my head today. It went like this: "Don't put too much salt in the food, don't put too much salt in the food..... don't put too much salt in the food..." and you get the picture.

It worked, and a little Leafy Boy followed me into the kitchen after he'd cleaned his plate of food to tell me, "You're such a good cooker, Mama."

"Awww," I said. "Did you like it?"

"It was delicious."

Gosh, charmer, get to a woman's heart, why don't you?

July 24, 2009

Ugh.

It happens, I knew it did. In fact, I expected that it would happen more than it has. We haven't really been sick—like Indian gut sick. Everyone's been growing and twitching and leaping from high objects to demonstrate their caped superhero abilities. Everyone eats mangos and papayas with gusto, waits for the apples to be ripe patiently, starts fiddling with tape and paper and crayons practically before the day begins.

And then my littlest guy started having yucky poos, but more than yucky. Yucky with mucus and blood.

Scary!

I took him to the doctor a few days ago, and it was one of those experiences where the doctor barely listens to you, and you want to shake him and say, I could diagnose better than this! But you don't, because you didn't go to medical school and he has the medicines. He told me that the yucky poos were caused by his cough, a slight bronchial infection which wasn't concerning me. *It was not the reason I went to the doctor.* He prescribed antibiotics for the cough. (Again, not the reason I brought Solo to the doctor.)

So, today, when the poos were still yucky and scary, I took him to the Tibetan hospital (remember the place with the pee sample fiasco?) with a poo sample with me, and they:

1. listened

2. did lab work

3. diagnosed

Turns out my baby has amoebic dysentery. Amoebic dysentery!!!
My BABY. (Wrings hands.) (Shakes head.) (Runs over to sleeping
Solo's bed to kiss him again.)

The only way I can even imagine that he got amoebas is from the
bath water, which he's been splashing rather enthusiastically lately.
They gave us the stuff to take care of it, and we left with Solo singing
in my ear and flirting with the doctors over my shoulder. He has
been so active, so happy, so easy-going. It's crazy that he's been sick
with amoebas. Most adults would have been stuck in bed, sure that
they were dying.

Now I'm wondering about everyone else. I think that in the
next few days, I'm going to go down to the hospital with a whole lot
of poo, from all the different members of my family. Labeled, of
course. Amoebas can be asymptomatic, so it would be good to get
us all checked out.

Stool samples for everyone! Just me and my bags of poo and the
rickshaw driver, vs. dirty rotten amoebas up in my family's business.

July 26, 2009

Solo is all right. Better than all right, even. Thriving, crawling,
wrestling alligators, trying to steal bread from my plate, learning how
to use his teeth and not to use his teeth, smashing me in the face
with his mouth when I ask for a kiss, drooling on all of us, making
friends everywhere he goes.

Yelling "No!" Attempting escapes out the front door. Wriggling
and shrieking if he catches sight of one of his siblings. Cuddling up
in bed. Dancing.

And laughing.

July 27, 2009

To be honest, my brain is barely functioning right now. And still I am sitting down at the page (screen), because it is often in times like this that I find myself writing a post that is something I'll be glad I wrote later.

It was a full day. A good day. Chinua was out doing some photography, so I made dinner and put the kids to bed, which is no easy feat, mostly because I started making dinner at 4:00 and finished at 7:30. (Why? Solo, of course, is the answer.)

Dinner was a hit. I've been thankful lately for little snippets of healthy choices from my kids, like when Leafy says that his favorite food is rice and vegetables, or when Kai enthuses about how he loves cauliflower more than any other food in the world. It's taken a while, but they love our way of eating here. And they can handle spicy foods now. All it took was time.

On Friday we are taking a train to Delhi, to register Solo's birth and get him a passport. The boy will finally have a nationality, and it will be American, given that his brothers and sisters all have U.S. passports. I'm really excited for a little trip to Delhi (trying not to think too much about what the weather will be like there—hot!) because I want to check out some book printers and fabric shops and tailors. Oh, I have my ideas. I'm always full of ideas.

Our living situation here has become so sweet, since now we have these great downstairs neighbors at the height of the monsoon. I went down to bring one neighbor half of the fresh milk that we're sharing, and borrowed some sugar to bring back up for my coffee. We're neighbors like *that*. Later, when the neighbor was looking for his daughters, he knocked on my door and asked "Permission to come aboard?"

It wasn't just talk. They really are sailors. They sailed from Australia to South India, then ran out of wind early in the season, and decided to stop in India until the winds change. (Like Mary Poppins.) They then drove all the way up here in an old Ambassador car. This is kind of a big deal—it's not at all easy to drive a car across India. They are wonderful, adventurous neighbors, and the kids play together really well, although familiarity is starting to kick in. ("You *always*... you *never*." I could tell them from experience that these words are not helpful.)

Some other friends from up the hill called this afternoon and asked if they could come over to watch *The Office* for a while. I said of course, and down they came to lounge on our bed and laugh over the complete awkwardness of the best show on TV.

I'm very thankful for the ways we can open our home. I'm thankful that people are comfortable coming over, that we eat together and share, that we drink pots of chai, that even at the very end of the day, when I'm beside myself with trying to get Solo to sleep, at those moments when I'm muttering away in my brain (I'm too tired for this, I hate days like today, I hate my life, this is too much for me) I can still hear some muffled giggling in my home from friends watching a funny show, and sigh, and know that it's going to be alright.

This is what I have learned about hospitality:

1. No one cares if your house is perfectly clean. What everyone craves is to be *welcome*.

2. The smallest things are gestures of inclusion. A cup of tea, the offer of your kitchen if they'd like to make themselves a sandwich.

3. Children are very hospitable, if you allow them to be.

4. You can fall apart, even with people over. You can say, "What a day, I'm so tired." People want to help.

5. The world is full of lonely people. Invite someone in.

august

August 3, 2009

In Delhi the first thing we noticed was the heat, which wrapped around us lovingly in a thick wet hug. Without much rain, this monsoon season has been almost unbearable, with everyone watching the skies for some cooling precipitation. The next thing I noticed was the stuff everywhere! Living on the mountainside, like we have been, makes a visit to the capital a jaw-dropping experience. And then I noticed that our snot was already turning black.

The pollution has improved here, though, in the years since they instituted green fuel technology in the auto rickshaws and buses. The auto rickshaws themselves are like small yellow and green beetles, swarming by the hundreds, overtaking and passing the larger, more sluggish automobiles on the road. Some of the vehicles are ridiculous—in already tight spaces, giant SUV's make driving almost impossible.

Then there are the people, the millions of them. The row of men napping on their bicycle rickshaws on the side of the road, cracked heels dangling off the vinyled edges of the seats. The acrobat beggar children who flip on the sides of the roads to get us to look at them, wanting money for their child labor efforts. The colorful saris, the dupattas and scarves everywhere.

Sometimes in culture-colliding moments, I feel the world tilt like I have a severe case of vertigo. Such was the case today at the U.S. Embassy, when I sat in the waiting room and watched the woman with the freckles dispense advice and forms with a Mid-Western accent, her comfortably padded figure an ideal of smiles and friendliness. The room slid dangerously from left to right, the chairs all stacking up on one another with my strong sense of dislocation. Where were we? Technically America, but in the center of our India.

Now I have broken away for a moment, jubilant with the success of our passport mission, knowing that Solo's passport will be in our hands in two weeks, with a train ticket for tomorrow night in hand, hard-won by Chinua. I'm running around to do some shopping, looking around in Khan market, which is another culture collision. I'm here because there are stores here that I can't find elsewhere. It's a strange place, guarded by security companies to keep touts and beggars out, which makes it a simple shopping experience, but a little uncomfortable, since everyone seems to be so much cleaner and wealthier than I am. Should I be here? Or should the security guard stop me at the entrance?

It is much like the embassy today, where I wiped my baby's head, damp with sweat, and considered our flowy and sun-faded clothing, comparing our dirty, cheerful selves with the pressed clothing of the other inhabitants of the waiting room. The damp curls on the sides of Kenya's face trickled sweat down her cheeks and I wondered how the others had managed to arrive at the embassy perspiration-free. Possibly they jumped from air-conditioned car to air-conditioned

237

waiting room, rather than piling into an auto rickshaw like the six of us.

I can't imagine a mall in the West where some people are kept out and others are let in. On the other hand, at malls in the West there are often strict No Soliciting signs on the doors, which would definitely prevent the men who trail me for blocks, demanding that I pay attention to their handkerchiefs or towels or chess sets. (I particularly love the way the chess wallahs react to my "no," offering hopefully, "backgammon?" as though I possibly detest chess but am an avid backgammon player.)

Have I idealized the West? Or is it true that a working child would not be allowed to turn flips on her face on the dirt on the side of the road? It's hard not to blame the government here. And then there is the woman we met so many years ago, a beggar with a baby who called out "Chinua!" as we walked down the street. She marveled at our four children, none of whom we had ten years ago when we saw her last, when we spent each day sharing a meal with her.

It's a homecoming in a way, this Main Bazaar in Paharganj, the backpacker's ghetto. I spot the guest houses where I hid away, my teenaged self in utter shock at the way the world had been ticking away in the dirt so far from me in my clean Canadian cul-de-sac. The beggar woman looks amazing, clean and healthy, barely any older, walking home with us to make sure that Chinua will take her out for a meal. I consider this woman, young, with a home, with English skills better than most people I meet in India. She is so friendly and lovely that she must have a different opportunity somewhere else. But maybe the begging life is addictive. I mean, she's famous around the world, in a way, she has friends from every country. It's a lot more exciting than working in a factory somewhere.

Everything here has something that contradicts it. With a mind like mine, always in overdrive, it is difficult to be at rest. No matter where I go, there are questions and answers, and there are contradicting answers. Now I will go and find Kai a birthday present (ahead of time) in a mall where I am an outsider, just a hippie in a well-dressed throng, trying to find something that will not break in a day. I am both wealthy and not, and very aware of both.

August 7, 2009

It looks like we are in for a wet month. (When I wrote of the monsoon not coming I was referring to Delhi and the surrounding areas, not here in the mountains where it is alive and well.) The monsoon has taken its real grip now, with tight fists and claws clambering up the mossy stones on our hill. Everything is green! Bright, shameless green. There are ferns throwing themselves up under the trees in the forest, climbing right up onto the trees themselves and swarming over the trunks. There is moss growing between the stones and on the stones, which makes for careful climbing down the hills. The corn on the terraces is taller than us now, and we walk in a narrow hallway, gently sprayed by the water that has collected on the tassels.

It would be a very green view, if we could see it. Instead we are wrapped in a dense fog almost all the time. It clears up and then reasserts itself very quickly, and we are busy running in and out putting the clothes out to dry, then bringing them in when it starts raining again. I have been washing the mold off different parts of the kitchen every day.

We compensate by turning the lights on even in the day, playing loud music and card games, reading in a pile. We can still snuggle, because though it is wet, it is not hot.

When I think of how afraid I was, just a year ago, how displaced and terrified I felt, it is like a page turning. I look at myself now, weaving between cornstalks and sitting in auto rickshaws, and a whole different kind of light floods the inside of me. I am so thankful. I have come through fear into rest, and trusting God has been the only way through. It's another story to add to my stones of remembrance.

August 8, 2009

This evening, after a day of hard rain and fog, there was so much sky that it seemed impossible. Kai and I glimpsed pink clouds over the hilltop through the tiny kitchen window, and we ran outside to see the rest. I had Solo in my arms. Chinua was away, and the kids and I had just finished dinner. Aloo Gobhi; potatoes and cauliflower~ their favorite. I'd thrown in carrots for the orange color.

We didn't look down into the valley, because all the radiance was up and over the mountains. Great swathes of pink cloud contrasted with sky of a blue that was the first blue ever seen; a newborn blue. Kenya danced on tiptoe in leftover puddles and said, "This is soooo beautiful! Even as beautiful as a *rainbow*!"

To the left was an intense monochrome, layers of clouds tipped silver and grey and feather white. Steel clouds and platinum. I looked for a minute, but, my heart full of my love for color, turned my face back up to watch the pinks and blues shift and change for as long as they were there.

After a while, I looked around me, and there, down on the path, was my husband, holding a closed umbrella that was almost the same blue as that sky. He was smiling, watching me watch the clouds and their journey. I had no idea how long he'd been there.

He smiled into my eyes from that far away and at that moment a whole flock of birds broke into flight inside me. They almost carried me off into the sunset I'd been watching, but... ah well. Everything was shifting to dark blues and greys, and so we carried the color along inside with us. It was time for pajamas and goodnight stories and the well lit circle of home.

August 11, 2009

I've written about the extreme anxiety I used to experience, years ago. I don't know how to describe to you how crippling it was. It caused rage, panic, and overreaction to very small things. I couldn't see my way around it. It was completely irrational—in the midst of it everyone around me looked like an enemy. I was wild-eyed and irrational. I hurt myself. I struck out at my husband. I struggled with this for years. And I prayed, I went to counseling, I read fifty books, I tried everything. Nothing would dislodge the knot of fear that went with me everywhere I went. I completely lost the ability to enjoy myself, to have fun, to relax. Writing here helped a lot. But it didn't help everything.

There was the night that I constructed an elaborate art installation on my floor with melted wax and burnt paper and rose petals, thinking, "maybe someone will notice." I remember the time I reached out to a woman I trusted, telling her how bad things were inside my head. Her response was, "You're okay, Rae. Really, of all people, *you* have to be okay." She was referring to the fact that we worked with street kids at the time, and quite frequently people were falling to pieces all around us. *Someone* needed to be strong, to be stable for everyone else.

But what if it wasn't me?

In the end, it was my relationship with my kids that was the last straw. I found myself shaking with anger and anxiety, barely containing myself, staring at three tiny children who stared back at me with huge eyes. And then I read a book. Not any type of self-help book, just a novel with a character who condemned her mother, who was an alcoholic, for not taking the steps she needed to keep her children safe from herself. And I shook myself, because it occurred to me for the first time that it was *my responsibility.*

There wasn't going to be any knight in shining armor. I wanted someone to rescue me, to notice my struggles and pull me out, but actually, I needed to be the one to ask for help. I was so close to asking already, and then two more things happened. 1) I had a panic attack so severe that I had to pull the car I was driving over because I couldn't breathe. And 2) I lost a baby due to an ectopic pregnancy. Because I was already back and forth, seeing the doctor, we talked about my mental health. I told her everything. She prescribed medication that deals with social anxiety disorder. It was April of 2007, a time when everything changed for me.

I remember the first day I went for a drive and found that I was happy. It felt like the first time in years that I wasn't afraid. And so. It's funny, before I admitted how sick I was and gave in, I was so afraid of the way taking medication would affect my relationship with God. But without the barrier of my imbalance, I find myself walking through each day with the ability to trust, rather than the sickening feeling that I can't get out, I can't get out.

I was too concerned for my family to take serious steps towards suicide, but a day didn't go by when I didn't feel that the only way out of my own mind (which was poisoning me with a crippling fear) was through death.

I'm so glad that I found out it wasn't true.

When I look back on all the poems I wrote then, they all have images of hurting, clenched stomachs, of not being able to let go, of shoulders rigid and tight, of the need for escape. Images of people as wolves, of panic in the grocery store, of sabotage. I am so thankful, now, for the ability to relax in my own skin. I still have stress, I still have to remember to give my worries over to my Father. The difference is that it is possible for me, now.

This is the way He is; Broken things are made new.

Oh friends, I am so broken. But being renewed every day.

August 22, 2009

Today I woke up and tidied the house. I threw away broken toys and burned the paper trash. I put the books back on the shelf in that nice neat way that I love and I put all the crayons back in the crayon bowl and the pencil crayons back in the pencil crayon cup. I washed my trash can. And I wrote, because I can't spend any time away from my characters or they hate me.

Then it was time to meet Chinua at the Israeli restaurant for jachnun, the delicious bready deliciousness served on Shabbat. We love its Yemeni goodness.

After that we came home, and a couple that I've been inviting over finally decided to come. We sat and talked in my living room until more neighbors stopped by. Then we all chatted, and we drank some chai that I made, except the first couple, who declined because it was Shabbat and they didn't drink things that were prepared on Shabbat. (But I am a goy, I thought to myself, surely I could prepare it. I guess it doesn't work that way.)

And then it was time for dinner, and later, time to observe the stars, and breathe in the cool night air, and fulfill the many requests for water and blankets and this stuffed animal or that one, tucking small people in to sleep until the next morning comes, hopefully sunny and light.

August 24, 2009

Chinua took the kids out this afternoon for a rousing game of

243

backgammon, so that I could write. Of course, he can keep the kids here while I write, but he probably had a bit of cabin fever. You have to have cabin fever, to want to take Solo to a nearby café while you attempt to play backgammon. Solo's presence is not *conducive* to the playing of backgammon. Or any other board game or card game for that matter. Which is why the kids are always asking me to do something about his habit of crawling over the chess board or eating the jack of hearts.

"What do you want me to do?" I ask them. I'm helpless. "Play your games on the table," I say. I mean, I *tell* him not to eat the cards, but he turns a deaf ear.

August 30, 2009

Oh dear me, am I ever in a funkedy funk funk.

An I-fed-my-baby-kidney-beans-and-he-didn't-fall-asleep-until-4:30-in-the-morning funk.

An I'm-worried-about-money funk.

A look-at-the-big-stack-of-work-in-front-of-me-and-no-brains-left-to-do-it funk.

An I-miss-my-family-and-friends funk.

A non-stop-rain-and-fog funk. The monsoon is romantic, is necessary, is green, but gets old with cabin-fevered kids and very little space. Thank God for water colors.

Other things I'm thankful for include:
* food on our table
* the lush beauty all around me
* the many impromptu hugs Kai has been giving me
* Chinua playing the mandolin in my living room right now
* the prospect of sleep (maybe) tonight
* coffee and chocolate
* Tripta

* train rides, long walks, learning about space, movies, cuddles, a cat appearing in my house, drop-ins from friends, the cheesecake Cate recently discovered that actually tastes like cheesecake, muesli, chilies, and Jane Austen.

(Deep breath, dive into the day, don't sulk in the corner, give more because there is always a spring welling up for you and you will not be empty.)

september

September 1, 2009

Today Kai turned seven. I made pancakes with Nutella and fried eggs (the fried eggs were by special request) and we sang. He was up long before I was, but still wanted to eat breakfast in bed.

We had an early birthday party last week because some friends were leaving and we really wanted to include them, so today was just about pancakes and badminton and video game time and a special dinner out with Daddy.

I absolutely love Kai. He's just the coolest kid.

September 3, 2009

Yesterday I went to a cooking class with my neighbor. She was meeting me there, so I walked down the hill alone. We live on the side of a wide ravine. On our side is one village, and on the other side is another. The light as I was coming down the hill made the houses on the other side of the ravine glow so that I had to stop and catch my breath from the loveliness. The sun was out for the first time in days and there was that beautiful late afternoon light. My feet were almost too buoyant to hold me down.

The cooking class was excellent. Of all the food I've ever had in India, nothing has compared to the food that comes out of an Indian woman's kitchen. We sat on the floor and chopped vegetables together. I learned to cook a new dish (Malai Kofta) and to use a new spice (kasoori methi. I cook with fresh methi in Goa, but never knew before now that it was available dried). The teacher's outdoor kitchen was in a small earthen house with cow dung plastered walls.

She told us many things. "In India, the man is king. His wife must do whatever he says." "School is very expensive now, which is why I only have one child." and "My husband used to be a mountaineering guide. Seven years ago he fell, and now he is paralyzed from the neck down. Now I work very hard."

We all ate together. I told them about going to Burkina Faso and hearing that the way I ate with my hands (the Indian way) was wrong. Instead of pushing the food in with my thumb, I needed to do more of a scoop and turn with the fingers. I never did get it right, the West African way. I'm pretty good with the Indian way.

*

Tripta keeps joking about how I should leave Solo with her when we go, so that he can learn Hindi, and I can collect him next April. As she continues in her jokes, I wonder if she's actually serious. Whether or not she's joking, the answer is a resounding NO.

Seven is already a very affectionate age for Kai. I believe I've had more hugs in the last three days than I had the entire year that he was six. I love seven.

All of our train tickets are booked. We leave on the 19th, and

247

will be in Goa (with stops on the way) by the 5th of October. I can barely wait.

September 10, 2009

"Mama," Kenya calls from the next room where she is busily combing her My Little Pony's hair. "What does a comb *do*, anyway?"

I laugh to myself as I pour my coffee. "It takes the knots out," I say.

"Oh," she says, and her voice sounds disappointed. "I thought it made your hair *longer*."

*

She is five years old and doesn't know what a comb is for. It's all you can expect, really, from a little girl who has had dreadlocks since she was two. I combed and braided her hair until I had an operation to remove a tumor in my neck. Coming home from the hospital I couldn't face the snarl that her hair had become during my recovery, and thus began the beautiful dreadlocks of the Kenya sister.

I didn't teach her about the use of a comb because I figured it was obvious. It wasn't obvious, as it turns out.

We don't make a big deal about dreadlocks, in our house. Most of our family has them. But we don't have to make a big deal about Kenya's dreadlocks, because practically everyone else does.

*

We are walking down the hill into Bhagsu, and Kenya suddenly says, "I want you to be the beautiful one, the most beautiful one in the world! I don't want to be beautiful."

I attempt to digest this. "Why?" I ask.

"Because then no one would talk to me and tell me I'm beautiful. Even when they don't say anything, I can tell that they are talking to each other about me."

The extraordinary thing about this conversation is that Kenya is so completely outside of herself most of the time that I had no idea she even noticed the people pointing at her, talking about her. I knew she dodged many of the reaching fingers aimed at her hair, and declined an answer when people oohed and aahed over her. But she spends most of her time drawing, or running, or climbing, or falling down, or coaxing snails along to places that are safe from our snail-smashing neighbor, or making snakes out of modeling clay and curling them up in their nice soft beds. ("Look, Mama!" she said, the other day. "This one is a *teenager* snake and it's bigger than its *Mama!*") She also loves to crack eggs, peel garlic, and make her bed. She is the originator of most of the pretend games that are played around here, and if she uses the word *beautiful*, it's usually to describe a dress or a butterfly.

"Oh, Kenya," I said. "You shouldn't wish to be different than you are. The most important things are being kind and polite, anyway." I thought was being sage. And I know there are many other important things, but I was mainly talking about when she's out in the world, where people point and stare.

"I know, Mama," she said. Not really exasperated, but ten steps ahead of me. "But I can be *those* things and not be beautiful. I just wish you were the one."

Thinking about it, as we walked along, hand in hand, I realized that she wasn't really talking about beauty. Those are just the words people have used when they've pointed her out. And believe me, there are many, many beautiful little girls in the villages of India. As much as I think Kenya's a stunner, I know that she's a rose in a rose garden.

She was talking about attention, about being different. She would like to shift it to me, someone bigger and stronger in her life.

This is one thing I can't do for her, though. I can't shift attention from her to me. She will always be mixed-race, she will always be different, no matter where we live. And it's good for her to be among the people of India, who are so kind to children. She is not teased for being different. But she will have to learn how to bear attention, to take on its weight and then smile and shrug it off.

It was a small moment, this little conversation of ours, and the monkeys on the road soon drove it out of our heads, but it showed me that she is paying attention, and that she notices. I can't take the strain away from my daughter, the strain of being noticed, but she is always welcome to turn and meet my eyes when it is becoming a bit much. We can make a quick exit, the two of us, and go and rescue some snails. Or slugs, she rescues them too.

September 12, 2009

The other day was a writing day for me. Chinua has been giving me all of Friday to write and get some work done on the book and another project I've been working on, and I LOVE it. I feel like for the first time in seven years I can really focus. Or, focus as well as one can when one's children keep opening the door and asking if you are done with the computer yet because they'd like to watch a movie, or as focused as one can be when one's baby crawls to the door of the room that he KNOWS one is in, and when it doesn't open, bangs on it, yelling, with two open palms.

I take what I can get.

This Friday, however, I needed to try to get a truck up to our house to pick up the boxes that we are sending to Goa by mail. (Since we travel by train, the post is the easiest way to get things like our books, toys, and anything else we don't want to carry on our backs to our house down south.) I really didn't want to do it on a Friday. It's my special day, see? But I also saw the wisdom in not putting it off.

Chinua said, "I don't want you to do anything that's going to make you angry later, because I don't want you to be angry." Fair enough. I needed to do what was necessary and deal with it in my own cantankerous soul, rather than letting everyone know how put out I was by doing this work for them, and they'd better appreciate it, because my whole *day* was ruined, practically my whole *life*. Also, it was raining.

I made myself a list:

Tips for Making a Lame Day Better
(by me)
1. Draw stuff
2. Take photos
3. Talk to people
4. Notice things
*

Well, I couldn't take the camera because it was raining and I was walking, and my little camera is broken, so we only have the big one. And I didn't draw anything. But I did talk to people. And I did notice stuff.

I noticed a cow walking down a steep flight of stairs, onto the street below. I've never seen anything like it before! I peered up the stairs, to see what the attraction was. Nothing up there. When I asked her what she was doing, she totally ignored me.

I also noticed, when I took my mobile phone to the shop to have it looked at (it's not working), that the man checked to see if my battery was full by ducking his head down and putting it in his mouth. The battery, not the phone. I thought this was odd.

I bought scarves. And I talked to the man in the shop where I bought scarves. (Me buying scarves is a big deal!) He showed me some nice wall hangings, but I didn't buy any.

I talked to my pregnant friend when I bumped into her on the street. I noticed that her eyes are a very brilliant blue.

I talked to the jeep men about bringing the jeep to my house. I asked them how far they could bring it, and they said, only to the *upper road*. I asked them to bring it down the steep *sort of road* and along the *non road* and up the stairs and over the *definitely not a road*, but they stared at the ground and muttered. So I asked if they could just bring it down the steep *sort of road*, and they stared off into the air and muttered. My problem in India, you see, is that I am far too polite.

I loitered all day, waiting for the rain to stop because we can't move our stuff in the rain. The rain never did stop, but I talked to a few more people, including a couple of begging kids, a Tibetan tailor, and a man from Mumbai whose wife teaches a cooking class.

Finally (when the rain let me know it was not a day for me to move boxes) I went home and found my family.

So I didn't get anything done, but I noticed some things and I talked to some people. All in all, not a bad day. And at the end of it, I wasn't angry.

Epilogue

This morning the sky was a big bowl of glazed blue pottery, and our neighbor, who is moving his stuff as well, persuaded a taxi driver to come all the way to the *definitely not a road*. Chinua and Cate loaded the boxes up, had them stitched in white cotton in the Indian way, and had them sent off at the post office by noon. I spent the morning drinking two tiny cups of coffee and cleaning, and that was that.

September 14, 2009

The other day Kai was asking me if there was a way to avoid paying money for electricity."Ye-es," I said. "If you have solar power or wind power or hydro power from your own equipment, you won't have to pay money."

Leafy looked up from turning somersaults on my bed. "Solar power," he said, "is an orange ball of power that you hold in your hands and it makes you strong."

We all just looked at him.

This is my Leafy Boy. Spending his days in the wilderness of his imagination, surfacing only for cuddles and food and sometimes even not for those, since he can remain in his world of pretend: food can fuel any amount of pretending and cuddles can be between a mama dog and her puppy.

When he's naughty I have to come very close to him. "Leafy, look at me." He usually avoids it, looking wildly around or covering his face with his hands. "Leafy, look at my eyes." When I can get him to really tune into me, then we can talk. He's brilliant, telling stories and dancing almost from waking to sleeping. He's a flash of light, a comic imp, and he's still sorting out what the difference is between truth and what he's convinced himself is true.

He's amazing. I'm rather privileged to be around this little mind in the growing stages. If nothing else, it's just a lot of fun.

(But I think there will be big somethings in this kid's life.)

September 15, 2009

I had just finished cooking when the boys showed up. The rajma was bubbling away, and all the other food was ready. The boys brought a drum, a violin, a guitar, and our friend Oshan, who had a fistful of flyers. "All right, kids!" he shouted when he had some breath back in him after the kids tackled him. "Time to color flyers!" We sat down around the table with cups of colored pencils and crayons and started in on the concert flyers.

"You color very neatly, Oshan," I said.

"Yes," he said. "I'm the best colorer in the whole world, pretty much." I love British hippies, because they may look wild, but their accents give them away. When I was having juice with Oshan and Darius last week, they used the words "mollycoddle" and "persnickety" in a ten minute span of time. Not to mention that when I walked up, Darius was eating baked beans on toast; a food that is utterly mysterious to me.

"Well," I said, feeling that he'd better be brought down a peg or two, "you're not very *creative* at coloring, are you?" He held out his work and looked at it. "No, no I'm not, am I? I'm more simple, really."

The boys and Chinua discussed where they would practice for the upcoming concert, and the rest of us sat at the table with our crayons. When they decided to go to the nearby restaurant where the Nepali cooks work, Darius asked if the art entourage could please accompany them. I hemmed and hawed, since I had just finished making dinner, but in the end, decided that time spent with these friends was time well spent, and we could eat the food I'd made tomorrow. So we all rounded up jackets and left.

And we colored more flyers, and we ate. And there was a hailstorm, and it grew increasingly cold, and you can sense the impending doom, can't you?

On the way back, Chinua lovingly hiked back up the hill with me, so I wouldn't have to do it alone in the dark, and we all shivered (when we leave in three days we won't shiver again until perhaps next April) and I thought thankfully about the fact that our house had been warming up all day in the sun, and would be pretty warm, compared with how frigid it was outside.

And then we reached our door, and we smelled the smoke. Chinua and I looked at each other, wide-eyed. "I didn't... I'm not... I thought," I said, cleverly, and dashed into a huge cloud of smoke which escaped when I opened the door. The smoke pursued the children around the veranda. First, I turned off the stove. Then we began to open every window, every door, to let the horrific smell out. Not only the smell of burnt beans, but the smell of burnt pan. We gathered around outside, glumly, looking into the pot which Chinua illuminated with his flashlight. Nasty black bubbly beans, all charred and stuck to the bottom of the once-pan.

Bummer.

Now our house is refreshingly chilly, and still smells of something you'd rather not be close to. Kenya said, very distraught, "We should check all of those *things*, before we leave, shouldn't we?"

"I did check, I looked a few times. I didn't realize it was still on."

"What about looking under the pot, to see if the fire is going?"

"Yes, that would be the best thing, wouldn't it." Yes, yes it would.

September 20, 2009

I will miss:

The shape of the range of hills behind my house; the way it curved itself like a bowl, and on clear nights all the stars fell into that bowl.

This everyday lesson: the only way to tackle a steep pathway up a long hill is head in, ready, one step at a time, with willingness to breathe hard.

Rain.

Tripta, who hugged me and cried.

The freshness of the air. It's a different kind of air up there, and the sky robed itself in glory on many, many evenings.

*

Now we are nowhere and everywhere, in between places, in between trains in Delhi, one of the most populous cities on earth.

We are the tiniest people in a great heaving, working mass, waiting for our train to take us away from here.

September 24, 2009

I bought a sari today.

We arrived in Varanasi a couple of days ago, but I haven't found time to get out and use the Internet until this very moment.

This is deep India. Crowded, lovely, the India of merchants who fling saris and sheets while you sit and drink tea on their cushioned floor, trying to make your decisions about which color, which fabric, which print.

Imagine the house that we are staying in with our dear friends, in a rare peaceful spot beside the Ganga. A maharaja house from a long ago era, with crumbling curved white archways surrounding a courtyard that has a mango tree presiding over it. Power only sometimes, tea several times a day, hibiscus flowers and bougainvillea climbing the walls. Yesterday there was a monsoon rain and running across the quickly flooded courtyard, instantly sodden, I felt that I was at home.

September 28, 2009

In India there is a river called the Ganga.

On one part of this river, there is a city which is said to be the longest standing living city in the world. Many people come to this city to burn their dead and spread the ashes, to study music, and to find India at its most potent.

Along the Ganga, there are rows of steps, called ghats. The other day, just before sunset, we went out for a little walk along the ghats. I've done this many times, back when I was nineteen and twenty years old.

Let me tell you, the ghats are a different place when you have children. They become wild terrain, a place for climbing and sliding, and mothers shudder because they know these ghats have the filth of a thousand years etched into their stone surfaces. And still the children climb.

The ghats are covered with mud and silt from the river at certain times of year, because the river rises in the swell of the water from the Himalayas, and then settles itself back down again. Sometimes children step onto the mud, believing it will be solid beneath them, and instead their feet are sucked in and covered. They have to be pulled out with a loud SCHWELP!

And the children's mothers shudder and cover their heads with their hands, because they have seen the dead water buffalos and goats thrown in the river. And they have stepped over the piles after the men have their morning poos, right there on the ghats. They sigh and pull out the wipes and the hand sanitizer. And they sit and have a chai together, just like old times, but with more rescuing of chai cups going on.

I wish I could show you the look of longing that comes over my daughter's face if she ever spots a snake. She is a snake charmer's dream customer. What will she become, this girl who so willingly twines snakes around her and then reaches out for them and whispers to them?

It has been hard to find time to blog here because we don't have the Internet at the house we are staying at, and the power is off from 9:00 in the morning until 12:00 and again from 3:00 until 6:00 in the evening. It is hot in that way that slumps you a little and makes you shrink from the normal bustle of folding laundry and picking up. But we have been having a wonderful time. Our friends here are

257

october

October 3, 2009

Yesterday I stumbled over a dead cat, and then saw a dog with a large piece missing out of the back of his neck. I sat and had tea at the tailors, then returned to the home of my friends and had coffee under the mango tree. Once I chose a cycle rickshaw wallah who looked old and desperate, and it took me three times as long to get where I was going, because his rickshaw was broken. And another time I chose the first cycle rickshaw wallah who yelled at me, and we zipped home at breakneck speed, smashing into the wheel of an oncoming cycle rickshaw when we spent too long in the oncoming lane while passing a fruit cart.

This city and the country it embodies are like this. The best and worst, all in one parcel. A beggar with missing limbs lolling on the ground like a piece of trash. That's a person down there, but everyone is walking on by. A circle of women laughing and pinching your baby's cheeks. Flowers garlanding the necks of loved ones, lights on the river. God is here, like he is everywhere else. He sits in the dust with the beggar, watches the light change in the daily flow of his creation, and he never doesn't see. His heart hurts for it all, even when I am too far away to know about the boy in the tailor's shop who just got cuffed over the head.

We're getting on the train tonight after an incredibly rich time with our friends. We love our Aussie friends and their ridiculously wonderful hospitality. We will miss them.

GOA AGAIN

Coming back to Arambol, our beach in Goa, was the first homecoming we experienced in India. We moved back into our house and found that familiar things were suddenly there to welcome us, and all that hard work of making a little home had paid off. Things got better and better as time went on, the more memories we made and the more we invested our hearts and time into our meditation center and our life in Goa.

october

October 7, 2009

We are back in Goa. Leafy is overwhelmed with delight. He won't stop hugging me. All of his favorite coconut trees came and gathered around in our yard, to greet him.

There is a new gate and driveway and a concrete courtyard at our house. It is a vast improvement. There is also a lot of fungus and mold to deal with, which is not a vast improvement. I'm a little overwhelmed by all that I need to get done. But one step at a time is a good pace.

Cultural transition feels a bit like playing Memory. You turn a card over, hoping it will match the card you already have, the one with your homeland stamped on it. It never matches. Maybe you squint for a moment, through the light in a certain forest, or at a particular stone formation, but then, no, it's not the same card. The trees are shaped differently, and the light hits them in a funny way. It is not your forest, after all.

It is beautiful to see new things, again and again, but it can be a

263

little disconcerting. It is a very long game of Memory, and you are never winning.

More than the beauty or the sense of welcome from the people here, the thing that strikes me about returning to Goa is that I am finally finding matching cards. The first card is not the homeland card— instead, it is last year, when we had Solo, or when we researched dolphins, or when we bought the bread from the bread man with the squeaky horn.

I turn them over and they match and it is bliss. I'm almost as delighted as Leafy.

October 10, 2009

When Goa became our home, all Kenya's drawings of houses became multi-colored, and always featured a few birds, some caterpillars, some worms, and at least one butterfly. When we moved to the mountains, her drawings changed. The houses weren't as colorful. Suddenly, there were large mountains. Sometimes the houses were tiny in comparison, and the sun was just peeking over the hills.

Now we have come back and we have a new landscape of color around us. Everyone is repainting after the heavy rains, the village is busy with cleaning and painting and the houses are the same, but wear new faces. Next door the house is lime green with cantaloupe highlights! And out the back, what color was that house before? I can't remember, but now it is a brilliant blue. An eye-straining blue that keeps coming even when you are no longer looking. It is lovely. Three things that Goan people love are fireworks, color, and fish. As one man told me, chicken is for special, but fish is good every day.

There have been late rains this year. They've caused flooding and problems, but also weather which is cool for the time of year.

264

And the rain soaks my laundry on the line when I forget to take it in at night. I go out in the morning and it is sodden and embarrassed.

Did I ever not like palm trees? Did I ever compare them to sticks with hair, back when I was eighteen and I had moved to San Diego from my deep cool forests of Canada? That must not have been me. The palm tree is not only about coconuts or dates or the symbol of relaxation. It is about a wild symmetry of lines and fronds and straight trunks with an explosion right where the tree touches the sky.

And then there is the sorrow of the broken times we live in. Trash in the streams, plastic on the beach, trash washing up on the river beds. The creation is tired—it is not being treated well. I hurt with it. Beauty and pain always seem to come together. Fear creeps in as well. Is it okay to love anything so much? I remember I felt this way when I first had the babies—as if they would be taken away. But what does this say about how we perceive God to be? As if, after giving a child a birthday present, we would hover over them, waiting to see if they liked it too much and then snatching it out of their hands.

He gives us good gifts. The appropriate response would be thank you, I guess.

So, *Thank You.*

October 15, 2009

There is so much work to be done, especially in a family of six. It almost never stops. When one load of laundry is taken off the line, another is ready to go on. When one meal is cleaned up, it's almost time to begin the next. Sometimes we even work very hard for leisure (as any mama who has gone camping knows).

A woman can work very hard. She can organize and make lists, and she can tidy and straighten and wash and reorganize and dunk

265

her baby in a bath and dress him and put him to bed. But not all of a woman is made to work. The soul of a woman contains so much more—there is a girl-child inside, ready to play! Sometimes the girl-child is upset, because there has been no time to play, no time to laze around and read on a window seat on a rainy day.

But there is work to do. There must be a way to bring the two together! Surely God did not make us to forget how to be children (Jesus suggested the very opposite when he said, "Unless you become like children, you will not see the Kingdom of God") and surely he is not a great taskmaster, always hovering and waiting for us to account for ourselves.

My dear friend in Varanasi said to me, when were were talking about making pots and pots of chai and running around and serving and hosting, "But what about the Girl inside?!" Other people may forget the girl-child, but I don't think we should forget her. And if you are a man, you should not forget your boy-child. Actually, this is one of my favorite things about my husband. The small boy is always lingering just below the surface, so close that sometimes they are one and the same. Sometimes that boy bursts through (often!) and rolls on the floor laughing or picks up a sword to play with the kids. I want to be like this.

And yet, the children who are children both on the inside and the outside, they need to eat!

So. I am making a list of ways to play while I work. Tomorrow I will show you my list. I think I will illustrate it and put it somewhere in my house, somewhere I will not forget it. It is necessary, for my survival, as a woman, a girl-child, and a seeker of the Kingdom of God.

October 16, 2009

Well, not to be a tease or anything, but I didn't get my list done.

It's taking more time than I thought it would, because I really want it to be a good list, a fun list, a thought-provoking list that I can consult on a day that is dragging its heels through the cow pies. And I went to the market today and it is the day before Diwali, one of India's biggest festivals, and it was CRAZY.

(Just before we left the Himalayas, when we were all skipping down to Chinua's concert with the Turbans, Leafy came running back up the trail crying, with a face that was black with something gooey. "Did you fall in mud?" I asked, as he was approaching. "No, it wasn't muuudddd!" he wailed. And then he was surprisingly calm and cheery, while I was very grossed out (as well as impressed by his skillz), because he had tripped and and fallen in perfect alignment with a Leafy-face-sized fresh cow pie. It was a soft landing, you could say that for it.)

There are things that will hold us back from being playful.

*Worry.

*The idea that we aren't allowed to enjoy what we do.

*Lack of imagination.

*Lack of wonder.

*Self-consciousness. There is something very beautiful about sitting and watching the play of young children, who pay no attention to anything but the thing they are focused on. And *right now*, there is a man just outside my house, taking a bucket bath at the well, STARKERS. He is not self conscious. Let us all take him as our example.

One way I've learned to deal with self-consciousness is to pay more attention to what I am seeing than what people are thinking of me. It helps, especially being a foreigner in a staring country. I don't care what people are thinking of me, because *look at the pretty colors!* And *are those lemon cucumbers?*

And again, it all comes back to being like little children. My children don't lack imagination or wonder, are only a little self-conscious, and don't worry all that much. They definitely have no problem with enjoying themselves. Thoroughly.

I think I have come to a place where I am very capable at rolling up my sleeves and getting down to business. I no longer cringe at my time being thrown around like whitewash, and I do love the creative work of raising a family. But I get the Super Mom label all too often, the "You're a Hero" words more than I like, because the Super Mom image creates distance and throws up an instant fence.

And I do reach for my work hard defenses ("I work so hard!) all too often, but I want to be the child that is loved and whole and not perfect. Loved. Whole. (Though broken, what a paradox.) Not perfect.

Full of wonder. Not wondering if anyone is noticing how hard I am working.

October 21, 2009

*

HOW TO
PLAY
and
STILL DO
your
WORK
(some ideas)

*

1. Write To Do lists that are fun to look at
(doodles and colors)
AND include fun things on them.
for example:
*buy milk

268

*fold laundry
*GO jump in a puddle
*wash more laundry
(including your puddle-jumping clothes)

2. Please remember to turn on some music
because it changes the electro-magnetic currents in your
twiddly thorax swamp-buster,
making you more apt to have a good time.

3. Switch on your senses.
Play with the bubbles that the dish soap makes and notice
how the water feels, splashing over your wrists.
smell everything.
(at least, smell the *clean* things)
When you fold clothes, group them by color,
or test yourself to see how neatly you can put the edges together.
then sit back and admire your work

4. Invite the Little Helpers along.
sometimes they slow things down, but they make
everything more fun.
(and you are teaching them, and one day you will
blink and they will *actually be helping*.)
show them how to make dirty things shiny.
get them to use the rolling pin, the broom, the
vacuum cleaner,
the vegetable peeler,
even the KNIVES
(with supervision)

5. Name your appliances. Name your pots and pans.
Use their names when you're talking about them.

6. Put signs everywhere that say important things like:
open me for birdsong
on the window.

7. Fresh flowers whenever possible.
Origami ones when not.
(origami is a very orderly way of having fun, good for the
anxious times, like knitting. maybe you can knit yourself
some flowers.)

8. imagine that you are the Only Living Daughter of the
last king of the tribe of Vindakoo and that your survival depends on
your task.
only if you finish washing the dishes in the Gigantic Sink
can the key to the labyrinth drop into your hands. once you
mop the floors, you will be able to come through the labyrinth
and get to your tribe.
(and save them!)
(hey, I *said* play. I'm not ashamed!)

9. be a World Famous Documentarian.
(documenting yourself)
you can do it *crocodile hunter style,*
narrating your way through the wild things all around you
(this especially works if you are wrestling
young boys)
or *rivers and tides style*,
where everything you do is a temporary work of art and

there is a hushed silence as you
Chop Tomatoes.

10. On that note, make sculptures!
Use the Lego, the couch cushions, cucumber slices,
potato peelings.
They will be temporary, but they will probably entertain your family.

11. Play with food because kitchen time can be too serious.
Make faces from vegetables, make cities, draw your children's names
and create animals.
then eat them.

Have fun!
Give thanks.
*

the end
*

October 24, 2009

Robbery is not as fun as making believe that you are a warrior princess. Obviously. Even if you lie awake thinking about how you could catch the robber if you only had the chance, (maybe you could bash him around the shins a little with a plastic cricket bat, just a little, just so he wouldn't get away before the villagers came out and grabbed him) it's still not the fun kind of lying awake, more the speedy mind kind of lying awake.

Is there a fun kind of lying awake?

Is there a way of posting any lucid thoughts when you are seriously sleep-deprived and you are weaning your baby, which has you lopsided physically and emotionally?

A thief broke into my neighbor's house a week ago, while she was away. He took a bunch of stuff and then moved on to Cate's house, behind my house. There, he was surprised and chased off by a guest who was sleeping in the living room. The guest was too disoriented for pursuit, but he probably saved Cate's house from being ransacked, since she was also out of town.

It did not escape our notice that both of the people who were robbed or had a robbery attempt made on them were away. Someone knew this.

I went through the twelve stages of post-robbery trauma, admittedly in proxy, since I wasn't actually robbed: curdling stomach juices, adrenaline, fear, apathy, anger, betrayal, ice-cream cravings, acceptance, squinty-eyed looks at all the men of a certain age who might have run off with a pocketful of money, the cessation of the squinty-eyed looks, returning to saying hi cheerily to everyone, and gossip. Well, it's not really gossip, but I spoke a lot with my Goan neighbor, Maria, about it. Since she knows almost no English and I know only a few words (and counting!) of Konkani, our discussions are very limited. We click our tongues a lot, and shake our heads. "This man is very bad," I say, and she shakes her head. "This no good," she says. "This first time. This seven years foreigners coming, no thief." And we click our tongues and shake our heads.

Then, last night when I was up with the boy in my house who has never slept through the night and hopefully will before he ages even one more month, there was another robbery.

I heard shouting, and then I saw running, and there were flashlights, and more shouting, and more running, and pretty soon all the neighbors were gathering on the road and in front of my house. There was a lot of yelling, and a description from the old man who had seen the thieves and shouted first, and then a repeat description, and then lots of questions about which way they ran, and then their route was described a few hundred times. Then real progress! In their flight they had dropped the laptop that they stole! And also, they had left their shoes behind.

Lots more shouting. Finally, I toddled back to bed. It was about 3:00 in the morning. Did I mention that I am on single-parent duty for the next couple of weeks?

We have changed the locks on our doors.

I was so shocked after the first theft. And then I wondered why I was so shocked. As though I don't know that the world is full of grasping, full of people with less, people with a broken conscience, people who need drugs, people who will steal tools from a non-profit organization, people who will walk away with the guitar of someone who tried to help them. Last night I was shocked at the thief's boldness in coming back to the same place, and walking into a house with people in it, but more, I noticed how the darkness of the whole thing was making the light even brighter.

There is a great decency in this village. Everyone expresses concern—people have been in tears because this has happened here. And then, in the middle of the night, the people in the area banded together to try and figure out what to do, to shout and race uselessly into the jungle, searching, to commiserate, to shake their heads and cluck, and to simply be together. It's the kind of thing they totally take for granted, but I don't, because it's not every place that has everyone from the elderly to the very young rushing towards the scene of the crime to do whatever they can to help. You more often find people retreating behind locked doors and watching behind their blinds as the police arrive.

October 27, 2009

I'm so exhausted. There doesn't seem to be anything left of me. I search in my sleeves, after the kids have fallen asleep, and my arms have fallen away. I can't carry a single thing, and I slip through cracks in doorways, even when I not planning to enter. I wonder if there is anything remaining, anything that has not been taken by cooking and talking and staining furniture and teaching.

The phone rings. I cringe. When it is like this, I know I am in a bad way.

And yet, things are not bad. There is always another stone to leap on, just in front of me, whether or not I am in spectral form, whether or not there is any solidity to me. I jump from stone to stone. I take my time.

Small fish make their way through the river below. The sun is blinding me as it flashes off their scales.

Solo really started walking today. Flash!

Kenya drew a beautiful picture of Jason and the Golden Fleece. Flash!

Leafy said, "What if I took my head off, and it grew small little bones that became feet, and small little bones that became arms, and it walked around all by itself and drank water?" Flash!

These things reminds me to watch for fish. Flash! Don't stop seeing their beautiful, rainbowy scales, even if you are just barely able to stumble from stone to stone.

October 29, 2009

I am plummeting, for some reason. These days my heart is constantly sad. But even so, I can look all around me and see a blessing there, and there, and there. Right over there! Maybe the counting of these blessings, like beads on a rosary or tiny pebbles that I rub in my hands, is the most important kind of noticing. I feel like I am sinking, and so now I need to say thank you over and over again, because there is no sinking harder to come back from than self pity. I know myself enough to know that at some point I will come floating back to the surface. For now, I need to become even more still, to notice the simple, beautiful things that are following me and to say yes to each one, to welcome them in, because they are the hands of my Master, bringing me along.

Here are some beautiful things from this day:

1. There is a small toad who sits on my back stoop every evening, just outside the door. He blinks at me when I go outside. I make a sweeping gesture to let him know he can come in, but he never takes me up on my offer. He just sits there. I'm not sure why. Maybe he is bashful. He is a bashful toad, but he wants to sit just outside and be quiet, and maybe listen to my music, when it is playing in the evenings and the children are sleeping and the air has begun to cool down.

2. My little hibiscus bush has three buds that will most likely flower tomorrow. I pruned it and now it seems to be putting buds out everywhere. There are buds for tomorrow and some for the next day. The flowers are bright yellow with a red heart. I want more flowers in my life. I will head to the nursery sometime in the next week, I think.

3. I have a papaya which will be perfect for breakfast, along with the yogurt I am making.

4. This evening the kids and I went to the birthday party of a little boy that we met in the mountains, whose family is now here. We sat and talked and went for a walk and the kids were wild and the parents sought peace, and it was good and companionable.

5. Solo is possibly the cutest thing I have ever seen, these days. Talking earnestly to me. Standing up, taking steps, falling. Standing up, taking steps, falling. Shrieking with delight. This one's a good one. I think we'll keep him.

november

November 2, 2009

This is what I did today. I got up and had a coffee while putting muesli and yogurt in bowls. I noticed again just how lovely the sunrise over the coconut trees is. Then I noticed that there is still furniture waiting to be stained in the courtyard. And then I put that thought right out of my head.

I watered the garden and cleaned up the little things, put away laundry and supervised Kai and Kenya washing the breakfast dishes. They like to pretend they are running a restaurant while they do the dishes, so today I told them they were worthless donkeys and they were both going to lose their jobs if they didn't stop rubbing suds up around their elbows. Actually, Diary, I didn't really say the worthless donkeys part, but I could have.

Then we sat at the table and wrote down what the kids need to get finished this week in their school work. How many exercises in math, what they need to write, and how many times I would like them to break off their pencil leads while juggling their pencils, whine "I didn't mean to! I don't know how it happened!" and then dump all of the pencils on the ground in a mad search for the pencil sharpener. Many, many times, is what I wrote down. We may as well expect it.

I would have to say that not a ton of work got done today, because there were many interruptions. But we did all of our reading, and tomorrow is a new day. I need to work on the interruptions, because my neighbors don't always understand about homeschooling. I need to draw good *boundaries*, Diary dear, and you know I'm terrible at it.

I started cooking around noon, and I made dahl and rice and subzhi, with some more interruptions thrown in. I also did the second kimchi step, so the kimchi should be ready in a day or two. I love cooking, but I love making things that are a little strange even more. Like kimchi and yogurt and peanut butter and muesli. Not that they're strange in and of themselves, but they aren't just a meal, they are something more.

Then we ate, and Solo was kind enough to make us a rice carpet. He also stood up in his seat and waved his bum around to the music, which caused everyone at the table to nearly die of laughter. Sometimes I wonder why I bother feeding anyone. They could live on cracking themselves up.

Later the kids watched Tom and Jerry, which is their primary source of historical information about things prior to the 21st Century. I consider it very educational. We have many, many episodes, and some date back pretty far, so that if I say, while we are reading, "blah blah blah phonograph... hey, do you guys even know what a phonograph is?" they will say, "Yeah, we saw one on Tom and Jerry!" This also goes for a phone that plugs into the wall, and a hobo with a kerchief on a stick, something Kai is always pretending to be.

After Tom and Jerry, it was time for the sea. I rushed around flutteringly, getting nothing done, before finally getting out the door and then coming back in several more times because I had forgotten things. We met friends at the sea and I sat in the shallow water and tried to prevent Solo from diving in, since he feels that he is invincible. The boys all used the bodyboards and Leafy got a little more bold about going out further. I saw a friend from Dharamkot, and we talked about our summers. The moon rose, looking like a gigantic golden coin, and the tide came in swiftly, soaking our towels. Then we walked home and Kai and Leafy cried all the way, while Kenya and Solo were troupers. They like to take turns like that. Everyone misses Daddy. I hosed them off outside before we all took a shower and I noted again that I really need to tell my landlord that the hot water on my shower is not working.

We had scrambled eggs and bread for dinner, and I didn't forget to cut up the fruit. It was a beautiful, simple day, Diary dearest. There was such a sense of camaraderie between us today, and when it is here, it is almost physical, something that reaches out and embraces us all. We touch each other impulsively. We say we love each other too many times. I listen more, and the kids try a little harder to get along. It is this kind of companionship that makes me really love being a family.

November 3, 2009

I talked with the painter (about the meditation space floor) the plumber, and the builder today. I don't want my landlord to build a gigantic wall around our house, but he wants to. We'll see what happens. I put finish on a set of shelves, and stirred the kimchi. I listened to Kai read, trying to figure out whether I should continue having him read at the level he's at, since he's obviously a little bored by it. But he still guesses at words, mostly at names.

278

I held some beautiful words from Chinua like a jewel all day long. I'm completely over the being apart thing, just *over* it. But it's not for much longer.

And do you know what happens tomorrow? Do you know? Renee flies in!

I am going to bed a happy woman, with a messy house because I can't do one more thing. I'll pay for it in the morning. I'm just counting the cost over here.

November 5, 2009

I fell into bed exhausted, after going to the goodbye dinner for some friends that I have known for six months now. There were too many kids in one restaurant, let me say.

What else? Solo has taken to walking around the house pulling his wooden pull-toy behind him. It's so cute that it's ridiculous, especially the serious, responsible way in which he does it.

I need to rearrange my furniture.

Chinua is coming home today!

Renee is here and jet-lagged. She slept on my couch for six hours in the middle of the day yesterday. She brought gifts from home and I barely could contain myself.

November 6, 2009

Last night I fell asleep when the kids did, which was very romantic on my husband's first evening home. I think I felt safe and my body just collapsed. I'm fighting some sickness.

Renee was an angel and watched the kids while I went to the airport with Cypriano, my house owner and taxi driver. I grow exhausted driving so far here, so I took the easy way out, and spent an hour catching up on reading. I was reading a novel about the

U.S., and blinked whenever I happened to look up, very surprised to find myself in India.

I find the local airport a very interesting place to hang out. I've spent some time there over the last year and a half, waiting to greet beloved people, noting all the strange shapes of people whom I haven't seen before. Today I stood outside, trying to get a piece of shade, hot in the sudden humidity that has returned. People spilled out the doors, everyone grumpy in the inconvenience of flight, noses wrinkled as they withstood the calls of taxi drivers and hotel touts. This is a slow airport, nothing like Delhi, or Mumbai. Even the taxi drivers are fairly lackadaisical, falling back when you tell them you're not interested, rather than pursuing with increasing volume.

I've been living in one village or another for the last year and a half, used to people who mostly dress alike. In Goa it is Indian house-dresses or the Catholic A-line dresses that fall just below the knees. In the Himalayas, it was salwar kameez with a dupatta tied around the head. The men in my village here wear shorts and no shirts most of the time, with a towel draped over one shoulder for modesty. The men in the Himalayas wore Gaddi hats with vests over white shirts, herding their goats and cows. So it was strange to see all these modern Indian people at the airport. They seemed very pale, and they were wearing many different things, not just one traditional costume. Many women wore glittering saris and had perfect pedicures, while some had cropped hair and were wearing jeans and t-shirts. One woman was wearing a toque (a beanie) with a button-up shirt and a swishy skirt. She seemed odd there. Just as I must have seemed to the people around me. She and her husband, who was wearing many gold chains around his neck with a pink shirt that was slightly open at the collar, welcomed two irritated-looking men who seemed to be hardly able to walk. The woman and her husband walked quickly, after taking the suitcases, leaving the two other men toddling in their wake.

I watched, and watched, and waited.

And then there he was, and he was beaming. "I hardly wanted to expect that you would be here," he said, "just in case you weren't." On the way home we ate baklava that he brought from Israel, and we looked at each other. I told him my experience of reading the book in the car and feeling like I left the country, and he nodded and exclaims, "I know! Isn't that strange?" It's so good to have him back. He is my perfect grown-up.

November 7, 2009

The other day I was riding through the jungle on the scooter and I smelled the most blissful smell. As it turns out, it was not burning trash, it was a climbing rose that a village woman had woven onto a trellis. I knew immediately that it was time to get some roses.

So, today Renee and Kenya and I drove to the next sort-of-big town to purchase ourselves some roses for the garden. Wonderfully, they were only 20 rupees for each plant. (About 45 cents.) The plants are pretty small, but they'll grow. We also bought some more hibiscus and a night blooming flower and some little green fluffy froo-froo things, to make things look more lush and less like a construction site.

Soon daily meditation will start up, and then maybe some concerts, and I hope that during meditation, the scent of roses will come floating up to us, and that during a concert, we will breathe in the fragrance of the blooms of a cousin of jasmine.

November 8, 2009

I planted four of the rose bushes today. They are blooming, to answer my mom's question. They smell lovely, but I still have to get right up to them and stick my nose inside the flower to smell them. Not that I'm complaining.

So here's something strange. I bought ratkirani, which I told you about—the queen of the night flowering tree. My house owner and next door neighbor were happy to see this lovely flower, but a little agitated, because they say it brings snakes. So I googled it. On one site I saw mention of it bringing snakes (in India) but they said that the cure is to plant a C Diurnium plant beside it. When I looked into it a little, I found that it is called dinkiraja in Hindi, meaning king of the day. Apparently the king and queen will keep one another in line. I'll be looking into it.

I'm learning to ask for help. The kids and Renee and I parked down by the cliffs tonight, and then walked along them to the fresh lake. We swam for a while, and Solo learned to blow bubbles in the water. (I swear the kid is turning into a fish.) Then we headed back for a bite to eat, and I called my husband.

I called him to come and help me reverse the car from the precarious parking space I had found for it. Imagine a very old tiny van, parked facing downhill on a narrow Indian street, just after a T intersection. To get out I needed to put it into reverse with the stick shift (and the clutch is always funny in reverse) while turning into a busy intersection, (ha ha, I can't believe I just called it a busy intersection. Not a busy intersection, but one with many people standing around it) while not hitting anyone.

I was dreading it while we were swimming, dreading it while we were walking, dreading it while we were eating. And then the realization came to me: I don't need to spend my life in dread! I can phone a friend! A friend who loves to help a wife in trouble. And he rode the scooter down, in the rain, just to back the van up (it wasn't easy, even for him) and then I hopped in the driver's seat and we headed away. I could have done it, I know I could have. But I'm learning that even if I have the capability to do something, I can still ask for help. And then at the end of the day there isn't even anybody keeping score, no one ready to say, "You used up your coupons on that one. You should have saved them for when you really needed help, because now you have a flat tire and no spare."

I'm thankful that the lessons I'm learning are good ones, about love and trust and admitting when you are weak and you need someone to floor the gas and let off the clutch and speed backwards without running anyone over, because for whatever reason, you just can't do it yourself.

November 9, 2009

I think I'll call it: Rae's Red Floor. Because what happens when you paint a floor red and then regret it? You cannot unpaint it, that's what happens. So everyone agrees to live with it.

The floor in the meditation center on my rooftop was a mixture of paint powder and cement, and it was lovely, but almost impossible to clean. Cleaning it was like trying to clean a piece of sandpaper, so we ran around holding our hands under people's plates as a preventative measure to anyone dropping anything on it. And then the painter was telling me that it was impossible to seal, which now I'm thinking - hmm? Because isn't concrete lacquer a thing? We had a concrete floor in the North, and it was sealed with something sealish. Or something lacquerish. I don't really know my terminology. It might be some whatsit compound.

(I don't have concrete floors in my house downstairs. I have fancy marble floors, with the emphasis on the fancy—they have large orange stripes and veins running through them on the diagonal. It was too late, when we realized that we could have had more input on the floors in the house. We could have said, "something grey and plain!" but instead we showed up with open mouths, turning our slack-jawed selves into smiling, nodding, slightly stunned foreigners when our landlords proudly wanted to know if we loved our floors. Marble floors are quite the thing, here. And marble is cheaper than wood.)

Anyway, so I wanted to do something nice while Cate and Chinua were gone, and the floors needed to be dealt with. Somehow the paint happened. *I don't know. It wasn't me.*

No, no. That's not true. It was me, there's no use trying to fool anyone. It's nice. Just a little... shiny. And red. We like it. Really. Cate has been very gracious, considering the fact that I tattooed her baby— the meditation space that she oversaw being built from the very first step last year. Rae's Red Floors. I'm a little down about it.

In other news, there was a pig slaughtering party in our front yard this morning! Which means that a Goan Catholic feast is going on, and I believe this one is the feast of the Holy Cross. I asked my neighbor what the feast was, and she looked blank for a minute, and then said, "Jesus." I don't know how I feel about the pig butchering. On one hand, I have no problem with people raising and harvesting their meat. No problem at all. These spoiled pigs have the run of the village and the surrounding jungle, they lead happy lives, and then someone eats them. As far as meat goes—though I find pork disgusting—it's great, this free range animal that helps to keep snakes away. And then there's the community of all the guys in the neighborhood getting together and hacking away with choppers. It's camaraderie!

And it's disgusting. And very close to my house. And my kids love to watch. I draw a line at watching the actual slaughtering. It will go on, with or without my approval. As it should.

Here's another tangent. Yesterday, just before I called Chinua for my sanity, we were eating at a restaurant here, and one of the dishes came with (surprise!) black mushrooms in it. There is nothing more disgusting than black mushrooms to me, and I couldn't eat it. Kenya tried it, and her input was that it tasted like millipede, at which point I nearly sprayed the table with my food, I found that so funny. Millipedes are filled with juices that come out if your baby pulls one apart or someone accidentally runs over one with a scooter (we don't do these things on purpose, we are insect lovers around here) and Kenya has never eaten one, but they smell terrible. She was astutely inferring that the black mushrooms taste as bad as millipedes smell. That's my girl.

Just as an aside: I stopped having Kai read aloud to me, feeling better about his little reading bumps becoming smooth over time. Now he is speeding merrily along. I hand him a book which is supposed to be the week's worth of reading, and an hour later he says he's finished. It was just the tediousness of reading aloud that was making him sigh and pretend to fall asleep, even when I told him that it wasn't funny, repeatedly, ending with an elbow in the ribs. I've been concerned about his reading and writing abilities being so far apart, but I guess I'll just let him run off with the reading, and treat them as totally separate things.

The end. One new member of our little community just arrived, so I'll go to say hello now.

November 12, 2009

Last night I slept through the night for the first time in almost two years. I feel amazing. I feel surges of patience and fuzzy goodwill and cheer that weren't there before. Solo slept through the night also, and he also claims to feel amazing. More kissing power.

When I say his full name, Solomon, he imitates me by saying, "Nomen nomen nomen." And then my heart stops because he's adorable.

Tomorrow I will take a writing day. And all I can say is that it's *about time*. The people in my novel are laying on their backs, holding their hands out to me limply, calling in their frail voices, "We'll dieeee if you don't bring us to liiiifffe."

The rain stopped today and I got the rest of the plants in the ground. I bashed my shin on a stool when the power went out and I was trying to get a candle, and then I yelled at the kids for leaving the stool there, which is really not fair, since I wouldn't have said anything about it if I hadn't bashed my leg so hard that there was an instant lump. Then I hugged them and kissed them. And held my leg and moaned a bit.

November 13, 2009

"... and in His temple all cry, 'Glory!'"
on the scooter, I see rice hay heaped golden in fields...
glory!
I move into the shade of the jungle, and the sweet cool air sweeps me clean...
glory!
back into the sun, there are hills covered in cashew trees...
glory!
the wind catches me as I cross the river, blasts me from the side and I take big gulps...
glory!
some flower somewhere has a heady scent...
glory!
Langur monkeys play on the road, staring at me with their old black faces as I pass...
glory!
the clouds pile up on one another, and as one covers the sun I am

286

reminded of something, but can't think of what, I only know that such a yearning has overtaken me, it pulls me forward and I just keep going.

November 15, 2009

There were cyclone-like winds last night. Again. The power was out all evening. We filled our house with candles and I sleepily lounged around because candles make me sluggish and content. Then, just as I was drifting off to sleep, the power came back and so did all the lights! Then the clicking from light switch to light switch, tired feet on an unforgiving floor.

Cyclone Phyan swept through this week. One story that has come out of it is of three men who survived in the sea by clinging to plastic bottles and then were shouted at and turned away at the Government Hospital near the capital, here in Goa. I'd like to point out that my son and I were treated very badly at this same hospital, that I suspect they are trained to be heartless, and that in fact I suspect them to be part of the axis of evil.

There are good hospitals here. Decent hospitals. That one? I'm not sure what they're playing at, but it's tough to imagine shouting at three men who have just been shipwrecked and stayed afloat for 24 hours, who have broken arms and concussions. It's impossible to imagine tossing them out on their ears! They did end up getting treatment in one of the good hospitals.

The cyclone was pretty rough. It came out of the blue and a lot of fishermen were killed. No one from our village, because it just happened to be a Catholic feast day, and the fishermen weren't out in their boats. I'm thankful that no one nearby was hurt or killed, but I'm feeling sad for the other families.

November 16, 2009

Here's a conversation that I eavesdropped on:
Leafy: "What if I cut a bear in half?"
Kai and Kenya in unison: "That would be really terrible, Leafy!"
Leafy: "But I would clean the knife!"
Kai: "No, not terrible for the knife. (Laughter.) Terrible for the bear!"
Kenya: "A bear is an animal, Leafy."
Kai: "Yeah, how would you feel if someone killed you!"
Kenya: "It would hurt the bear."
Leafy: "It's a bad bear. If it tried to kill me I would cut it in half!"
Kenya: "A bear is a wild animal! We can't kill wild animals!"
Kai: "If you kill a bear, then you should be killed."
Leafy: "MAMA! Kai SAID..." and then I stepped in.
*

A conversation I was a part of:
Leafy: "What's for breakfast, oatmeal or mu-sell-li?"
Me: "I just woke up, I don't know wait-and-see."
Leafy: "What? (Laughs.) "Who's Andsee?"
Me: "Nooooo. Wait. And. See."
Kenya: "Yeah. And Antsy is the lady who's visiting Cate."
Me: "No, Kenya, that's Nancy."

November 21, 2009

Last night we had a talking circle to come to consensus about a decision that needed to be made in the community. There weren't too many of us, just Cate, Chinua, Johanna, Renee, and me. Everyone who is here so far.

For those who aren't familiar with rainbow gatherings and rainbow culture, in a talking circle you pass a talking stick around and the only person speaking is the person with the stick. If you have nothing to say, you can pass the stick to the next person. When

288

you are trying to come to consensus, you pass the stick until there is silence and then you make your decisions, taking as much time as possible for everyone to come to the same conclusion, hence; consensus. It is very different from voting. We have been working more with consensus for the last year and a half; previously our community had very different ways of making decisions.

I love the talking circle and the talking stick.

For a big time interrupter like me, the kind of girl who gets all upset and impassioned by my opinions, who gets threatened by other people's opinions, the talking stick is a barrier of love.

In love, I will listen and not interrupt. I will love my neighbor by hearing her, and as I am forced to listen until she gives up the stick, I love her and love her and eventually I come past hearing my own responses in my head and into hearing the very real words that are coming out of her mouth.

I hear my neighbor.

Last night we passed the stick around the circle three times and then we had consensus. It was lovely. It helps to pray first, I think, to ask the Spirit of God to help bring agreement, although we forgot last night and prayed afterward instead. The prayer still stuck.

I love the circle. Everyone can say something, no matter how old or young they are, no matter how new or seasoned they are.

Our stick is from the Sinai and has a wreath of blue leaves painted on it by our lovely friend Cat from Canada.

I've been tripping through my days talking to carpenters and plumbers, painters and landlords, and one Russian lady who I can't seem to convince that I don't have a babysitting service. Yesterday I really thought we were clear on it, because I had someone translate for me, but then today she dropped her son off while I was away and Chinua was home. It is baffling. Chinua talked to her again when

289

she came back (when she arrived he didn't realize she was going to leave) and told her that she cannot drop him off, and that she needs to call before coming. We often have people drop in, but there seem to be boundary issues in this case.

November 23, 2009

The other day Leafy drew a beautiful picture of me in the sand, with his finger. You know how there are the natural swings of motherhood; the days of clumsiness and grief, and the days of moment after perfect moment? Or, in actuality, they are much more connected than that... Leafy draws a portrait of me that stuns me with its grace, and then he cries all the way home because there is sand on his belly. Kenya is so much a little girl that I catch myself staring at her, open-mouthed, because the very fact of her being a little girl makes me feel more free, but then she cries all the way home because I let Kai take a turn pushing the stroller.

Sigh.

And then I see them bend together to lift the stroller over the loose sand, puzzling out a problem for themselves and finding a way, and I believe again that the shining moments are much more weighty than the others.

Update on the confusing am I or am I not a preschool issue: I think we have it cleared up now. Chinua was pretty clear (stronger than me? less apologetic?) when the lady got back on the day she dropped her son off, that a) we are not babysitters, and b) she should call before she brings her son over, but they are welcome to come and play. Together.

I think it was a combination of a) a language barrier, b) the fact that many foreigners here *do* open up kindergartens for other international kids, c) the fact that I homeschool my kids, something that is not done in many countries and is very strange to some

290

people, d) the fact that someone TOLD her that I had a school, and e) her own boundary issues. But she is very sweet, and I'm glad we have it straight now. It was just funny there for a minute, because on the phone, I'd be saying "I am not a babysitter. I do not have a preschool. I do not babysit other people's kids." and she'd say, "Maybe we can talk about it when I come to your school." Oh dear. Oh dear oh dear oh dear. At one point, I said to Chinua, "Maybe I should just open a preschool."

This is the way my brain works, which is why it's good for me to have people around who say, "Rae, you really don't want to do that." And then I say, "Oh, you're right. I don't."

November 29, 2009

It is my writing day today and I am at the studio that a few of us are sharing this year. It's a tiny house with two rooms, owned by a local fisherman's family. The fishermen are the brothers of my neighbor, Maria.

I am in a small room with a peaked roof. The walls are all white, and the roof is covered with the red clay tiles that they use here in South India. Right now the family is cooking over a wood fire outside, and it's smoking really badly and it has crept up under the roof until the house is full of smoke. My eyes are burning.

I am sitting at a simple wooden table with my computer, drinking a cup of coffee. I have my small electric burner over here, so I can keep making cups of coffee whenever I feel like I am going to fall asleep, which seems to be my body's response to the great strain of so much creative output. I am trying to write a whole lot today, since I spent yesterday on the scooter, trying to get all the rent money for my landlord. It's never easy to get a lot of money here, and he wanted it for the remaining months that we will be in Goa. Something about a loan that he needs to pay off so he won't have to

291

december

December 4, 2009

Is it an ocean of grace? Or an ocean of regrets? Are we what we do? Or how we feel? Or something different, something in between, something the size and shape of the perfect smooth rock that you close your hand around, just to feel its weight.

I have been struggling with anxiety again lately. It's okay, I'm okay. It is not fear, I have nothing to fear. It is a sort of discomfort in my own skin. I can't relax, can't enjoy. But I'm learning to observe it from the outside. The best way is to be the author, the painter, showing what I see, not bringing things into the tangle. I am learning to be silent, to silence the seething within with patience and gentleness.

Those are not true feelings, Ducky, just fold that laundry and make it really smooth.

It's okay to sit and read for a minute, don't jump up just yet, Love.

Did you see that glimpse of river through the jungle?

Did you see those short cows in the road, confused and clustered around each other? I laughed, you can laugh, too.

You haven't done anything wrong.

*

I've been picking up hitchhikers lately, on my scooter. Not who you might think of, when you think of a hitchhiker. These are old ladies, looking for a ride to the village center. I almost wrote elderly, and then I deleted it, because the term doesn't seem to apply here. They are old, but not elderly. They wear saris, but sometimes tucked up between their legs, like a dhoti. They are carrying their bags for the market.

They are surprised when I stop. And they hop on the back, sitting side saddle, the way traditional women do, and some are so light that I can barely tell they are there, while some rock the scooter a bit and I have to re-evaluate the way we take the turns. I drive slowly.

And then I have made a friend for life.

*

I haven't been the best friend to myself. Today we meditated on the wisdom that comes from above, that is first pure, then peaceable, then gentle, then open to reason, then sincere... There were others, I don't have a Bible on hand right now. (You can read it in James 3:13-18) Gentleness is a great gift. I will ask for it and wield it in my house, with my family, spread it on my table like a cloth, throw it on the walls like a bucket of water, so it runs down and covers all of our mistakes (and hopefully washes some of the crayon off the walls.) And then I will wrap it around the small stone that I have in my hand, like a blanket.

December 9, 2009

Haiku for my children:

Kai
water on the floor
experiment gone awry
clean it up yourself
*

Kenya
forceful affection
your love is exuberant.
don't jump on our heads
*

Solo
you talk all day long
conversing with no real words.
you don't seem to mind
*

Leafy
imagination
boy with a cape and a sword
come back to earth soon

December 12, 2009

I have some exciting news and a rumor. The exciting news is
that I ordered my oven today; a little metal box that I can set over
my gas burner and make heavenly concoctions in, if everyone is
lucky. Or maybe just meatloaf. Beanloaf. Lentil-loaf. Charred
sneakers. I'm very excited.

The rumor that's going around is that I officially finished the
first draft of my novel last weekend and am now working on
revisions. A novel that I started in the Redwoods, continued in
Sacramento, continued even more in Goa, worked on in the
Himalayas, and finished in this studio.

That's the juicy gossip around here, anyway. I can neither confirm nor deny it.

December 18, 2009

This story starts with a carpenter.

No, not that carpenter.

Although, while I've had this carpenter working around my house I've been imagining Jesus working in his father's workshop with all the shavings, teaming up to hold a beam in place, giving someone an estimate. "No, that's for the materials only. *These* are the labor charges." I wonder what kind of wood he used. Cedars of Lebanon?

I think he was probably taller than my carpenter, who is about five foot two. But probably he wasn't taller than me. I am five foot eleven. It's not likely, anyway.

I hired my carpenter to build a few pieces of furniture that have been missing from our lives. I designed and drew out the furniture, and then explained each piece, taking about fifteen minutes, with the help of an interpreter,. When the furniture came, every piece of it was off in some way, by a foot or six inches. There was a bookcase that was two feet wide rather than a foot wide. It happens. The bunk-beds that I ordered looked great, but the guard rail was completely missing. The head and foot were missing from the top as well; it was just flat across the top of the upper bed. Not so safe. So my carpenter came back and installed a belated guard rail, and then painted it.

This is where my story really starts. (That was the preamble.)

The day after the carpenter painted, I was having a difficult morning because too many things were going on and I couldn't focus on school. I was rushing around, cleaning up, moving the laundry along, trying to get the dishes washed, retelling the kids to get dressed and ready to sit down and read together. Solo had something in his hand; a small packet wrapped in newspaper and I hurriedly took it from him.

Poof! He and the floor around us were instantly covered in a fine red powder. Powdered pigment, the dye that the carpenter had been mixing his paint with. It was a mess, a really big mess.

I did what I normally do in such circumstances. I tried to slow way, way down and appreciate the situation. It was too good of a mess not to share, so I took Solo outside and held him out at arm's length to show him to Miriam and Johanna, across the way in the little house that they share.

"Johanna!" I called.

She came out and promptly fell over from fright.

Yeah, I hadn't really considered the fact that the pigment looked a lot like blood. Oh, okay, exactly like blood. Whoops. When all the fright was sorted out we admired the mess, and then I went and hosed him down.

That was the introduction to the day.

Later, Leafy, Kai, Kenya, and I were headed to the doctor to get treatment for a skin infection that the boys have. The great health that my children usually enjoy prevents me from uttering all the complaining that I could possibly spew forth on the subject of minor maladies like skin infections, which are annoyances to two active boys and a busy mama. But anyway, we were on our way and I had elected to take a taxi because I didn't feel up to the drive that day. It was a long drive—we were headed to the capital, and it was midday. The sun was high in the sky and all of the ground was baking in it. And then we got caught in the traffic jam of the decade. We couldn't go forward, couldn't go back, and soon we found that people were on strike, that they had shut down the bridge into the capital.

No one knew when the road would be open again. Meanwhile, we were stuck there like cockroaches, and the car couldn't turn around because the two way highway was separated by a large hill. The kids and I got out and they scrambled up the scrubby hillside to play in the dirt for a minute. We took shelter in the shade of a truck, whose driver stared. All of the people on their way to the airport tried to figure out whether they could reschedule their flights. The pregnant girl from Bombay in the big car in front of us dashed out to throw up in the bushes. The men from the pregnant girl's car had a discussion with me about Kenya's hair. After about an hour, all of the people on the buses started to evacuate and walk.

"How far is it?" I asked Alex, our taxi driver.

"About six kilometres," he said. I made a quick decision.

"Meet me at the hospital when you get through," I said.

And we walked off. I carried Leafy, and Kenya and Kai walked very nicely. It was either walk or bake a while longer, and at least this way we got closer to some of the river breezes. People walked all around us, and when we reached the strike scene I was relieved to see that it was very peaceful. Men were lying in front of traffic with newspapers on their faces. The police weren't beating anyone.

"Oh!" said Kai. "So that's what caused the traffic jam." Like it's totally normal for people to lie on the road in front of traffic. I'm amazed, sometimes, at what my kids take in stride.

Walking over the bridge was hard because there was no shade and it is a very long bridge. We were hot and thirsty. We felt like pilgrims on our way somewhere, heading through the desert, gypsies moving through a dusty plain. And then there was the river and a barge moved downstream, with three great pyramids of dirt. We ran to get to the place where it would intersect the bridge, so we could stand exactly over it as it passed underneath. After the bridge we put our hands out and stopped traffic to cross the streets. It still wasn't moving very quickly, even on this side of the bridge, so it wasn't hard.

We stopped in a shady little restaurant and had water. We washed our hands and faces. We found a rickshaw and wearily arrived at the hospital, a little flushed.

I guess it makes me think about parenting and what it all means. At my house I can't always get things to run as smoothly as I want them to. I keep up with the laundry and then suddenly lapse and no one has any clothes. I wake up to dishes in the sink after collapsing in bed at night. There are often cut up pieces of paper all over the floor. Sometimes I pick things up myself that the kids should be putting away, because I just can't bring myself to try to get them to do it. I have this ideal where everything flows along and we are all clean and no one has skin infections or is taking medications and we sit down gently to read together without red dye on our clothes.

But a lesson for now is that sometimes parenting is walking along a hot road with my children, and how they see me react. Can we be curious still? Will we run to see the barge float right under us, watching the barge man watch us on his pyramids of dirt? We will, and we did, and so we move along in wonder and love, not clean all the time, and in stops and starts. But I think we are learning the right lessons, all of us, still.

And Solo is alright—just the slightest bit pink.

December 26, 2009

So what is it that we have been doing, that has kept me away from this computer for so long?

We have been coughing and blowing our noses, but that is not it. That is not all.

First, there were our gift projects. I found some lovely cotton canvas-y type fabric in the Mapusa market and had cloth grocery bags made by my new fabulous tailors.

    * A note on the tailors. I've had so much trouble with tailors over the last year that I've seriously considered just buying a sewing machine and making all the kids' clothes myself, something I would *love* to do if I had a clone who could finish my book and host all the people who come over every day. If there were two of me maybe we could get it all done. What I did instead was took a deep breath and walked into every Nepali shop that I've been avoiding here in my tourist town since I arrived. I hate shopping. Remember? Loathe it. And there is nothing that will frighten an anti-shopper like myself more than an overabundance of choice. So I took an afternoon and forced myself to go and talk to all the tailors. I found some with a wide open space in the back of their shop, so they were practically outside, but with a shade cover. Good working conditions. Check. Polite, not smarmy. Check. Understood what I meant. Check. Good stitching on the samples. Check. I found my dream tailors and I have loved everything they've made. Wonderful, because the kids always need clothes and there are no thrift stores here and don't even get me started on the horridness of things that are sold in the shops. *

    So anyway, I had the bags made, and then the kids drew simple designs and embroidered them. The gifts were a hit. We gave them to our neighbors and close friends. We decorated our Christmas tree; this year a tiny spruce. We got the rooftop ready for a Christmas party that we had on Christmas Eve.

    And then we had the party. It was so sweet. There was plenty of food, and the decorations were so peaceful and nice (Miriam and Johanna made stars out of paper and palm fronds) and I read the Christmas story while the kids acted it out. The child who played Mary had a bit of a nervous problem of picking her nose, so the video may prove to be an embarrassment one day. We sang carols in parts, and Chinua performed his arrangement of the Little Drummer Boy, which never fails to bring me to tears. The guests went away happy and blessed.

Christmas day was beautiful and sweet, except for my sleep deprivation from being up at midnight Mass. Oh, the kids were so excited and Chinua and I made crepes together and then friends came over with hula hoops they had made for the kids, and the other members of the Turbans (the band Chinua played with in the Himalayas) showed up (we haven't seen them since we left the mountains) and then we went for a family swim. I've been worn out, lately, and missing my family back in Canada, so this soft, sandy Christmas was just what I needed. God always knows, doesn't he? He always, always knows.

january

January 14, 2010

I had some big plans fall apart recently. I was planning a trip to Ethiopia to visit my friends who live there and work in a children's home. Everything was ready. I've been needing to take some time away, I wanted to visit good friends who I haven't seen in a long time, and I wanted to find out about ways that we can help them.

I had my tickets. I was set to leave on the 19th.

And then I found out that India has changed its visa regulations completely. If I leave now, I won't be allowed back into the country for two months, even though I am here on a five year visa. It has never been this way before, and Chinua has been in and out to Amsterdam, Turkey, and Israel since we moved here. But, everything has changed, and the timing wasn't the greatest.

It goes without saying that I can't take a two month vacation from my family. So I won't leave until we are ready to be gone from here for two months or more; probably not until this summer.

I'm adjusting and getting over it. I only cried a little. I will still be going away for a little rest, probably somewhere close by, but not getting a whiff of another place, which is what I felt I needed. I'm sad that I'm not going to see my friends. I really, really was looking forward to it.

Anyway.

I just watched a video about the earthquake in Haiti and my heart broke. It is an important part of being human to be able to put yourself in the place of someone else and imagine what it must be like to be them. In a time of loss my troubles begin to reveal themselves as very small, very normal troubles.

January 21, 2010

Silence. Hmmmm. I'm entering a new stage of culture shock that I like to refer to as "I have no connection with the rest of the world" stage. Is there a rest of the world? Or is there only my veggie stall and coconut grove and small dirty market in the middle of nowhere? I'm inclined to think the second in my heart. But I know there is a rest of the world in my mind. So I'll go with *mind* rather than *emotion*. The world is round, it's been shown.

Sometimes when I think of writing I wonder if I am standing on the edge of a floating carpet on the sea, throwing words into the wind. They blow back at me and stick to my face like cobwebs. I know it's not true, but I feel separated from everything outside of this little square I'm standing on. I want to endeavor to keep throwing words out there.

So here is a question for you. Do you ever belatedly add something to your "to do" list, just so you can cross it off, after you've already done it? I do. I just did. There are all sorts of ways to pull yourself out of being overwhelmed.

I'm sorry that I write so much about being overwhelmed. I think it is my normal state of being.

It may be the seventeen-month-old climber/run-away/dog-lover (this one is really challenging in a country with a lot of street dogs)/rock-eater. He is so beautiful and so exhausting.

January 23, 2010

Today we threw a birthday party for Leafy. He turned four with a flourish and a crown and a birthday hat combined. We played games. I baked a cake in my stovetop oven. Someone referred to my oven today as the space missile, because it is so unwieldy and made of tin. The cake turned out perfectly, which totally surprised me.

The day after tomorrow I leave for a week to a) finish my book and b) rest. I don't know if I'll make it through a week. I'm already doubting myself, going, but I know I really need it.

I'm ignoring the rest of the housework tonight after a day of baking and games and snacks and a wee bit of babysitting. Ignoring ignoring, tra la la...

going to

bed!

January 27, 2010

I am in the backpacker's India of my late teens and early twenties, staying in a little guest house with plywood walls that are cracked and sagging. I am showering in cold water, standing over the squat toilet, toweling off carefully.

When I got up this morning I hurried to the shower, hoping to be the first there. I didn't need to worry. Apparently my fellow backpackers aren't up at 7:00 for the shower, not having jumped out of bed as soon as they opened their eyes and it was light. I can't help it! I need to see the world, the sun is up and I am exploring.

I love this. I paid 50 rupees extra to have two windows in my room. One is a little one about a foot and a half by two feet, with a view of the roof of the building next door. I'm glad I paid the extra. The air was unbelievably fresh this morning. It is January, and the coolness off the river is delightful.

I had Indian breakfast at a little restaurant around the corner. It was bhaji paratha: fried flat bread and a potato curry. Mosquitoes were biting my ankles, so I brought my legs up and crossed them on the seat (this is, after all, India) but later the owner of the establishment came by and rebuked me.

"Put your legs down," he said. "Sit properly."

I was instantly aware that I am no longer the venerated mother of four, queen of my chaotic household, drinking my espresso and cream amid fluttering limbs of people under eight. I am just your ordinary backpacker, a budget traveler, with unkempt hair (dreadlocks) and Nescafé in my cup. I have traded respect for a bit of peace and quiet for a few days. I notice how differently I am treated when I am alone. I don't have the weight of my family in a country where family is everything.

January 28, 2010

I drove away from Panjim, the capital of Goa, this morning on my scooter. In Panjim I walked around and took photos of buildings and a few people, I saw a movie in a theater (the last time I saw a movie in a theater was in April of 2008) and I had a massage. It was beautiful. But I was ready to leave.

I drove south for two and a half hours, and my bottom was numb when I got here. I drove through cashew forests which smelled heavenly because the cashew flowers are in bloom. And I drove through forests of eucalyptus which were stunning and alien. I haven't seen anything like them in North Goa. I felt like I was back in California, except that I was on the left side of the road. I stopped completely at one point because a man was trying to tease me on the scooter, riding up beside me and staying there, trying to get me to look at him, speeding up when I sped up, slowing down when I slowed down. I've had one man do that before, and it's so dangerous. The only thing to do is either smash into him on my scooter (not a good idea) or stop at a market and wait for him to be really far away. I did the second.

Now I am at a small beach in the south, staying in a beach hut. A beach hut! I can't believe the luxury. It is behind one of the beach shack restaurants, made of coconut fronds with a cow dung floor. I swam today, and read some, and edited three chapters. I walked up and down the beach a few times, climbing over the wonderful boulders at one end of the beach. I'm flinching a little at the prices of the food.

It's a part of Goa that the vacationers experience, a part that I haven't, really, with my house and my homeschooling and my children. I need the municipal market, I need things, I have appointments, I have a pretty firm schedule. But today I have only a backpack and a computer in a hut on the beach, and the comfortable knowledge that I will be with my family soon again. What a vacation. I'm a blessed girl.

Thank heaven it's a working vacation. I'd be so, so bored if I wasn't working on the book. It's a writer's dream, really, write for a couple of hours, then take a walk. Read for a while, then write again. Walk again. Go for a scooter ride. Do research on agents and what a book synopsis is.

The characters in my next book are banging around in my head. I have to finish this one, quick! Although I'll miss these folks, I really will.

PS: Reality check on the whole paradise thing: Last night after I wrote this there was a big fight in front of my hut. A very angry

British woman punched a very drunk British man and then screamed at him for a while, telling him he was an alcoholic and he'd better stay the eff away from her friend. STAY THE EFF AWAY! And on and on. A while went by and then they were dragging the very drunk man away to put him to bed somewhere. Then I heard a woman say, outside my hut, "But there's shoes out here!" just before they went to open my door to put the man in my hut! I leapt out of bed and opened the door before they could.

"Oh! Sorry," one of the women said. I should say! Can't a girl get a little peace and quiet?

January 29, 2010

I've been up to my elbows in my book all day. I'll tell you two secrets:

1. I love the smell of burning cow dung. I really, really do. Every time I drive by and smell it, I sigh a long sigh and then I think, *that's* India.

2. If one more person that I've only known for two minutes castigates me for homeschooling my children and harangues me about their socialization (and I mean harangue, not express interest, or gently debate) I'm going to jab them in the chin with a fork and say "How's that for socialization?"

There are limits.

January 31, 2010

I don't actually make a habit of jabbing people with forks.

Indian people here are unused to the idea of homeschooling, but open to it. I am almost never challenged on it by the locals. In many countries in Europe, it is illegal, so unheard of! Their school system tends to be more thorough, and they don't have the pioneer background of North Americans, which many people in a way feel that they can return to. Teaching our own kids, back to the multi grade school system, stuff like that.

The woman I met the other day had no desire to listen. She would ask me something and then interrupt when I tried to answer. I think she felt that she was being honest, but for a first meeting, it felt incredibly judgmental to me, especially from someone who didn't have kids. She seemed to believe that I haven't thought about my decisions and the pros and cons of them at all.

I don't have a very strong stance on homeschooling. I have a strong stance on creative and interesting education for kids. I like literature-based curriculum. I like a lot of imagination. I like Singapore Math. Weighing all the options (and boy do I weigh them. I weigh them and weigh them and weigh them again. And then I measure them with a teeny tiny measuring stick that I carry in my wallet) I believe (and Chinua believes with me) that homeschooling is best for us right now. For our particular mix, at this particular time, in this particular village.

So there you are. And yes, socialization. Ahhhh, socialization. Well, I can say, that the only way I learned to socialize in school was to stay away from the mean kids and anyone who looked cool and hide in the art room. It's a form of socialization, I guess.

My kids have friends from Italy and Germany and England and India. They have adult friends and kid friends. And they have each other. They may complain to us about their upbringing, when they get older, but I think they will enter the adult world with grace and confidence and the ability to be flexible. I know that they have a voracious curiosity about the world around them, and that they can find Turkey and Israel and India and Germany and Russia and Canada and the U.S. and ... well, you get the point... on an unmarked map, because they've learned that the shapes on maps are

308

real places, and it might be possible for them to see them someday. Kai would like to be an explorer when he grows up. I'm not sure what he will explore, but... he has time to figure it out.

So there you go, my views on homeschooling. Maybe one day we will live in a place that has the school of our dreams, and I will say, "Off you go! Off you GO! Get out of my hair and get someone else to teach you stuff!" Or maybe I will teach them until college. Who knows? We take it from year to year. And I think for mothers that the feisty guilt demon is always gnawing away at your shoes, and you just need to put your fork in your pocket and kick that guilt thing in the head, like it deserves.

february

February 13, 2010

It is 5:00 in the evening here. The light is getting softer and the wind is picking up, like it does in the evenings at this time of year. I am on our rooftop, looking at red stones and multicolored glass panes, watching the wind move the coconut fronds. A man in the village is getting married tomorrow, and the tape of wedding music has begun its long loop.

I've been on the rooftop since early morning. Sending out query letters, my self-confidence dying a little more with each click of the "send" button. Did I mention that I finished the book on my writing vacation? And did I mention that I've been home for two weeks? Just in case you're thinking that I'm on a really, really long vacation. But today is my writing day and instead of writing, I'm, well, beginning my journey to publication. I want you to read the book.

I'm writing this now, and it's feeding me. The wind in the leaves feeds me, the breath of God feeds me, hanging laundry on the line feeds me, and writing feeds me. Also, finding treasures on the shore, a scooter ride through the jungle, and cooking good food.

I'm nobody important, that's what I feel when I look through all the agency websites. But that's what I find to be beautiful about life, that we're nobody important, just small, lovely people who extend a hand of welcome to one another. My book is about small, lovely people, my life is full of small, lovely people, and every day I meet another person who is fascinating and insightful and nobody important at all.

Kai, who barely acknowledges that he missed me when I went away, had his own way of letting me know he was glad I was back. Almost as soon as he saw me, he asked if I would like to help him and Kenya build their new invention: a bacteria smasher. Inviting me to help him build it was his way of welcoming me home. Of telling me that I was important. Every little frond, every little brick, every pane of glass. Every small trouble, every word, every little blogger, every one of our long, tiring, beauty-filled days.

February 15, 2010

The Query Letter I *didn't* write—a spoof:

Dear Agent,

I have a super fantastic book that I wrote, and I think it will make us both rich and famous! LOL! There are a few reasons that I think this.

1. Because you are totally awesome, obviously, I read your website and it sounds like you are the most awesome person on the planet! LOL!

2. Because my husband really likes the book. He told me he couldn't put it down. And you should know that my husband isn't the type of husband that would say that it was good just because I

311

wrote it. He's actually a really picky person. Really picky, and he's totally honest, too. So if he says he likes something, HE REALLY LIKES IT! LOL! For example, when we were trying to pick a title, he told me that if I said the word "landscape" one more time, he was going to throw me out the door. Landscape. Landscaaaaape. Sounds good to me, but I trust my husband! Did I mention that he's in this really cool band?

Anyway,

3. Because my friend Renee likes it and sometimes she calls me to read a line she really likes to me, and then I'm all, "Why did you like it?" because I really like to talk about it. I'm like that with writing, but not with cooking, because when I cook and people like it, I'm all embarrassed and stuff. And I made a cake the other day and people liked it and one person said I should totally start a cake business, and it was SO EMBARRASSING. But I like it when Renee reads paragraphs that she likes to me.

What have I been doing for the last few years? Well.... I've been doing lots of stuff, like cooking (I already said that) and sometimes I go for a scooter ride in the jungle, and I have this blog that's just amazing, you should totally read it, and I take care of my kids and then sometimes I write down funny things they say! I read all the time! And I do a lot of laundry. I also homeschool my kids. And I know a lot of people from all around the world.

Is that a good biography?

Okay, so... think about it. Let me know in the next day or so, because this offer's hot and you'd better jump on it! LOL!

All my love,

Rachel xoxoxoxo

February 26, 2010

I was sick, but I'm feeling much, much better. I had some kind of brief, violent flu. I've been taking it easy. Sort of. I'm not very good at taking it easy. Today I'm going to Mapusa, so I can run errands in the hot sun! I will buy some plants and some fabric, drop off my trash, and peer at the steel shops. I don't really need any steel right now, but I wish I did.

The air here has been unbelievable lately. So clean, and the sky is so blue, and it hurts, it's so beautiful.

march

March 6, 2010

Today was an up/down/up/down kind of day. I believe that this what they call a *roller coaster*.

First I had some highly skilled parenting moments in which I had the following conversation:

Me: "Kai, will you please water the garden for me? We need to go and meet Claudia at the beach and I'm running late."

Kai: "I can't. I'm too tired, and I don't want to."

Me: "Fine then! Just wait until the next time you want help! I'm not going to help you!"

Kai: "What?" (Genuinely baffled.)

You're welcome for the stellar example of boundary setting, including a nice wallop of impossible consequences. No help for you, kiddo! That's what you get for being so unhelpful! Of course, I blame my lapse on the fact that I sometimes turn into a nine-year-old, without warning. It's not my fault!

But then the kids and I made it out and met my friend for

breakfast on the beach. She was leaving today to go traveling to other places in India (with Renee! Ack, Renee-less and Claudia-less! Double blow!) and we had coffee and gazed at the ocean in the distance and tried to tell each other how much we mean to one another.

The kids played, and Solo tackled the other babies, just like I've trained him to. I've tried to warn him, though. Go for the toddlers that have older brothers and sisters! Because those first-time parents can be lethally protective. To his credit, he doesn't mean to attack the toddlers. He just gives really big hugs and then if you start pulling him away because the other kid is shrieking, he kicks at them, for good measure. Sigh.

A man yelled at me for getting in his way in traffic. I cried.

Then we ate grapes and cheese and bread and I had a blissful hour of doing embroidery work on a skirt I was making for Claudia while listening to This American Life. I think it may be my favorite way to spend an afternoon.

Then Solo pulled a mayonnaise jar off of the counter and it shattered on the floor. Let me tell you, my friends, that you haven't experienced the true bliss of life until you've combed your fingers through gelatin-like mayonnaise on a marble floor, pulling pieces of glass out. There is nothing to equal the greasiness, the potential danger, the pure fatty sharpness of it.

And it was time to say goodbye at the taxi. Big hugs and kisses and Claudia and Renee spun off, a little late, to catch their train. I love my friends. I will miss them.

Back to the house and while I was making dinner, Solo broke my favorite coffee cup, which was nice because I loved it and I didn't want it anyway! Stupid coffee cup! So smooth in the hand, so brown, so perfectly sized and shaped. I'm glad I'm rid of it!

But around the dinner table I was filled with this warm rush of love for all their crazy selves. I love this family. I love these kids. I even love these kinds of days, when Solo makes me crazy, and then runs into the room, teeth first in that way he has, just to throw his arms around my legs and try to kiss my knee cap. I love that he lets me pinch his cheeks (gently and ceaselessly) and I love the conversation that never stops swelling and ebbing all around me. I love goodbyes sometimes, because we try to say what we feel shy to say at other times.

Also, I love Ira Glass and my blooming bougainvillea and going to the vegetable stand to find the perfect purple cabbage. Life, in other words. God and his eternal goodness.

March 11, 2010

Yesterday I went to the market on my scooter, in the town about forty-five minutes from where I live. I bought some fabric from a man who refused to let me pay my bill before he could give me tea. He told me that next time I come, I must have a samosa, too. While I was driving, many thoughts went through my head, as thoughts always do when I am traveling in the luxury of my own company.

Isn't it amazing that a landscape can wind itself into you? How you may not have noticed every lovely detail when you were new and raw in your transition, but now, two years later, that lone magnolia tree in a field can bring you to tears? Or the egrets, the great white birds, friends of cows and water buffalos, winging over the emerald rice paddies, the egrets that have you waving after them foolishly, able to do nothing more than put your hand up toward the sky as if you thought you could touch them.

How you love even the dustiness, the color of it, all the lonely dusty roads and fields, crisscrossing like veins over a vast country.

India is certainly majestic. But it is not mine, not really, because I am from somewhere else.

316

We are preparing to go back for a visit, soon, to Canada and the U.S. I am thoughtful and sorrowful and excited and over the moon. And scared. And happy. And thoughtful.

But what I wanted to talk about, on this rambling evening, is the shape our community takes. Chinua and I have lived in community for all of our married lives, and for many years before. In fact, in the whole time we've been married, we've only spend five months out of intentional community. We've lived in many different situations. There was the big house in San Francisco, with people everywhere—in all the kitchens, falling down the stairs, spilling out of the windows. That was fun. There was the house in Arcata, always changing. For a while it was all boys and me, and then it was a few couples with newborns, and then we moved back to San Francisco to a largish flat with all our babies and had lots of crazy fun interspersed with whispered fights in the hallways. That was crazy. And then we lived at the Land. A couple of times. There's lots to say about all of it, but what I will say is that I really love all those people I lived with, and I really believe in community.

This is the shape our community in Goa takes now: There aren't so many of us, really. There have been six of us (adults) committed to being here for six months of the year. We have three small houses close together and one a little farther away. Our courtyards touch. We eat lunch together every day. We take turns cooking, and we have a circle once a week to decide who will cook on what day.

We are a meditation community, and we are followers of Jesus. We do daily meditation in the Christian and Judaic traditions, and we focus especially on the Divine Presence of God among us. In our weekly circle we also decide who will guide each meditation.

The committed people in our community keep the structure running, but it is an open community, which means that we have a lot of visitors. The meditations are open to whoever would like to experience this kind of meditation, and lunch is always an open invitation. It's great, really, because we get the best of whoever is cooking; everyone can put their all into one or two meals a week. Lunch in my family is the biggest meal, and dinner is usually pretty snacky. Sandwiches, or omelettes, or leftovers.

We live close together (the meditation space is on my rooftop) but Chinua and I and our family are the only ones living in our house. (Thank goodness, because we only have two bedrooms.) I love this. We run in and out of each other's kitchens, but we can find our own space, too.

Sometimes the rhythm of it all (the lunches every day, the other meetings we have) gets repetitive to me, since every other waking hour is filled with the restraints of family life, but I remind myself that if I can sigh into the structure of it, into the restraint (as a friend of mine once said) I will gain the freedom to learn to truly love.

Our vision is for a Jesus focused, creative community exploring art and music as well as the disciplines of meditation and prayer and worship, in an international hub. Goa is the place for us, right now. We will be back here in October, for our third season.

March 16, 2010

The book was *nearly* finished, it turns out. I'm currently diving into a second revision, (sort of, that doesn't count all the times I rewrote it while I was writing my "first" draft) while attempting to finish the homeschool year and pack up the house. We are leaving in two weeks. We're going to Thailand! I'm so excited!

I keep trying to get Leafy excited about it, but he insists that he wants to go to Leafy-land. He gets the word Thailand confused with the word Kai-land. Kai-land was invented by Kai when we first started traveling, as a sort of ideal country. All the kids have one. In

Kenya's, everything is made of chocolate. Also in Kai's, but his has the added twist of a convenient way to dispose of dead bodies.

"In my country, you just eat someone after they die!" he told me.

"Yuck!" I said.

"What?" he said. "All of you is chocolate, there, even your insides!"

"Still," I said. "Yuck."

*

I'm very seriously considering the self-publishing route. We'll see.

It is dark everywhere and the crickets are singing and there are strains of music coming from every direction. Solo has a new way of smiling which makes him even cuter. I waded through three chapters today, and now I think I can go to bed.

March 19, 2010

Today I pulled out the warm clothes that I'll pack just in case it's still on the chilly side in Canada. Right now it is very hot here, hot and humid, so I don't even like to touch warm things. Don't even like to look at them. You want to show me your sweater? NO THANKS. Unless you can take a picture of yourself wearing it in the snow, because that balances things. I can handle that.

March 23, 2010

I made a video recently and noticed something. It's funny, isn't it? How you put it all into the camera and put a soundtrack to it, and suddenly you appreciate how much it's all worth? You see them anew, see their smiles and hear their chirpy fast-forward mouse voices. You see the baby, smiling sweetly, fresh from his nap. You think, wow, the houses are really cute.

You stop thinking, why does concrete have to hold so much

heat? You don't see the kidney-stone/colitis combo your husband has been suffering from for three weeks, or the massive skin infection you're recovering from. You don't see the ant bites, smell the trash burning. You don't see the struggles you have with feeling like you are never quite good enough. As a mom, as a friend, as a wife. Nobody is complaining about being bored, no one is fighting. No one is falling off the three short steps and bashing their head on the bottom one and being rushed to the hospital to get sixteen stitches.

Leafy fell, yesterday, when I wasn't here. He was just hanging out on the front steps, but he slipped or tripped, or something. There was blood everywhere. You could see his precious Leafy skull. And then later, all stitched up and much better, all he could talk about was that now he looks like a Transformer. He's amazing, that kid.

I guess I am writing this because I don't want to be a fraud. It is not all pretty. But it is very blessed, very good, and we are very thankful. We trade some things for others. Clean spaces for wide spaces, well-built houses for houses close together.

I am a typical neurotic basket case. I question myself every day. I mostly keep it inside, keep it simple, and just continue.

I'm starting to think that the ability to accept the love of God is more than just a bonus, it is an essential part of my faith. If I, as a Christian, can't receive love from God, then what can I do? If I am low, dragging my belly on the ground, constantly prostrating myself rather than holding my head in the sun? I only have words, then. But my loud message, the one that I carry, is like a wave beating on the wall of the lie that is constantly vibrating under our ground, under the whole earth, poisoning the air. It causes all the brokenness and pain; the lie: "The Creator does not love you. He does not want you, he doesn't like you."

So my life work is first to practice being loved. He is loving, so I am lovely. I practice this, I bring it into me, I walk farther and farther through the dust of the constant lying, the constant travail and evil of the opposite. Of the names unloved, irredeemable, screw up, simply worthless. It's a good life work, being loved.

Second, to practice love. To see the loved ones all around me and to extend an open hand. To be gracious, to be clear, to sing with ringing tones the very truth that keeps our bones together. We are loved!

I often have a picture or a story that I return to, in meditation. Lately I think about an ashram. I've read many things about ashrams, but one thing is that in an ashram with a human guru, there is so much hope deferred, so much competition for the slightest bit of attention, the slightest glance from the guru. Oh, if he would notice me, oh, maybe if I get close enough, maybe if I prove myself... he passed and again he didn't see me. Maybe if I give more money?

In my picture of the ashram where Jesus lives, the guru (Jesus), has enough attention for every person there. He envelops and fills at once. He gives a gentle reassuring touch on the arm, his eyes are understanding, he sits among a busy crowd and there is always enough.

My heart is filled with thankfulness. I will practice this. Next time I feel like I'm not enough, I will remind myself that I am loved. That there is enough room for all of us.

March 28, 2010

Today I've been ignored, sneered at, ogled, patronized, put in my place, and confounded. I've also been smiled at, spoken nicely to, helped, and complimented. I may have thrown a small fit at the foreign registration office when I was *finally* driven over my limit at one too many obstacles in my path. This was after I returned to the xerox shop three times, drove back and forth between different departments in different cities seven times, and filled out two forms in triplicate. At one point, I may have had tears in my eyes, muttering under my breath, "This is it, they've beat me."

There are certain rules you have to relearn, in India. I know this, and I'm skilled at it. It won't do to get angry at people crowding a counter in an office, for instance, because the concept of a queue (or a line) is not prevalent. So don't yell and get angry! You're wasting your breath! Or take staring, for example. Staring is a perfectly acceptable social recreation. There's no point beseeching the heavens over it (although you can ask a group of rowdy men to leave you alone, or threaten them with your shoe, like my friend does to particularly naughty ones) because people watch each other here. They will stare at you, a car accident, a cat in a tree, children on the playground, or a foreigner tying his shoe. (There is a whole other meaning to rubbernecking here, as I saw the other day again when I witnessed dozens of men parking their scooters to peer at a car that had driven off the road.)

One rule that I find hard to unlearn, in the area of bureaucracy, is my assumption that a well-ordered list of requirements, including future needs, will be given to me when I apply for something. For instance, in my world I am told that to get the exit permit I need for my son, I will have to visit the Secretariat with copies of my passport and visa, a copy of his birth certificate, and a printout of my plane ticket. Then I will need to wait four days and return to start the application at the Foreign Registration Office, after paying the visa fees at the Secretariat. I will need to bring three passport photos with me.

Sounds reasonable, right?

This is the way it really goes:

I show up at the Foreign Registration Office.

"I need an exit permit for my son," I say. "He was born in India."

The man at the FRO tells me, "Go to the Home Office, in the town directly north over the bridge."

I try to find the Home Office (the Secretariat) and drive around for a while before locating it. The man there ignores me for a while, then finally demands to know what I want. I tell him. He is a low-talker, hard to understand. He tells me to hand-write a request for an exit permit and give it to him with copies of my passport and visa and Solo's passport.

"Oh good," I say, "I already have those."

I hand-write the request and bring it back to him with the copies. He looks through them.

"Where is the copy of the birth certificate?" he asks. I look blank.

"You didn't ask me for one," I say.

"You need a copy of the birth certificate," he says.

I leave the compound, drive out to the little town, and make a copy. I bring it back. He looks at it. (There is a whole lot of ignoring and feet shifting and sighing going on in these interactions, but I'm not including all of it.)

"Where is your airline ticket?" he asks.

"You've got to be joking," I say. (Okay, I don't say it.)

"You didn't ask me for one."

"You need a copy of your airline ticket." These rules are beginning to feel very arbitrary to me, and they just might be, because I know that this man can make anything happen that he wants to happen. I leave the compound again, drive out to find an Internet café, find my airline tickets, print them out, and bring them back. The man looks through everything again.

"Come on 27th and pick up a disk at the FRO," he says. "Then come and pay your fees here and you can pick the permit up at the FRO." This means driving back and forth between the two towns again.

"All right," I say, doing some mental math while I walk away. I return to the desk. "The 27th is a Saturday," I say. Are you open on Saturday?"

"The 27th is a Saturday?" he asks, surprised. He changes the date on my documents to the 26th. "Come on 26th," he says.

When I arrive at the FRO on the 26th, they don't have my paperwork.

"You will have to go back to that town to the north to ask them about it," they say.

"And then I can take my permit today?" I ask.

"No!" they say. "The Home Department always makes it sound like that, but now you *start* the application process here, once you get the paperwork and pay your fees. You will have to fill out the applications and make copies and give us three passport photos. Then we will submit your application."

"But I don't have any passport photos. And this is for my son, who is an hour and a half away, at my home."

They shrug. This is when I throw the fit. I'm not ashamed of getting angry. It's a normal part of doing work in India. Sometimes you have to get angry. But I do think I sound pathetic.

"You should give people a list of everything they will need, so they can come prepared! I have come back and forth so many times! Now what should I do? Drive all the way home this afternoon to get passport photos?"

"First get the paperwork," they advise.

My fit earns me a compromise. I drive back and forth four more times, fill out the application in triplicate, xerox many documents, and pay my fees. I earn the right to bring the passport photos when I arrive on Monday to pick up the documents. Despite the fact that I hadn't planned to come back into the Capital the day before we leave (!) I almost kiss the man's hand.

*

My daughter turns six today! She is such a delightful person, such a confident and winning and loving girl. I'm thankful that I get to be in her life. She told Kai that he can have the first turn with any toys she gets. That's the kind of girl she is. (And that's how much she loves her big brother.)

Solo has almost never worn shoes, while he's been growing up. If we are out together, it is at the beach, and otherwise I am carrying him. As a result, he is obsessed with shoes. He feels like the coolest thing in the world when he's wearing them. Oh the simple pleasures of life.

I am wading my way through all the packing and bureaucracy (I am simultaneously embroiled in trying to get my van back on the road in America, despite the obstacles. The DMV may also be a run around, but at least they tell me what I need to do, from start to finish.) We leave in two and a half days! Egads! And I have another trip to the Capital and a birthday party as well! Packing right now for me involves putting everything into plastic bags or tubs or metal trunks to keep it from molding during the monsoon. I have my work cut out for me.

april

April 2, 2010

So I did get the permit after all, and I very nearly told the man who had been helping me that he was my new best friend. We flew through immigration as much as any six tired people can fly through an airport with too many musical instruments on their backs in the middle of the night.

Oof. Red-eye flights with four young children. Not for the faint-hearted. But we are sculpted by India. I do have to say that taking the train in India is a cinch with kids, compared to multiple flights and going through security and trying to keep young people off the luggage belts.

In Thailand I feel as though we have been propelled forward twenty years or so. It's not that there are not modern places or things in India, just that we never seem to be where they are. We live in small fishing villages where people use hundred year old mango tree boats. Or in Himalayan villages with goatherds, on vertical hills.

326

So using the people-mover in the Thai airport was like being shot into the future. It was a like an escalator, but flat, and it curved up and down like a roller coaster. We were stunned and slightly frightened.

I love Thailand! I love the food and the smells, the people. I love this part of Asia. I would love to get to know it all better, to speak some Thai, to understand. I am halfway between delighted and terrified right now, not able to make myself understood. I am doing the Indian head wobble to Thai people, who look at me blankly. I am translating all the prices on the menu into rupees, rather than into dollars, since I think in rupees now. I don't know how many dollars we should spend. I do know how many rupees we should spend.

Leafy very carefully takes his shoes off before entering any shop, something that is not required here.

The kids are intrepid travelers, running down the grassy curbsides, leaping over hedges, pretending to fly, pretending to be anything and everything. As long as they can climb or jump over something, they are happy. Kai likes the food, although sometimes he says it is not spicy enough. Kenya loves the Bangkok cats, although she is a little freaked out by all the smells. She was used to the Indian smells. Solo is capturing the hearts of Thai women everywhere.

I had a minor breakdown in a Thai night market.

Crying, I told my Superstar Husband, "Nothing is familiar. I don't understand anything." He wisely suggested that we leave the market and go back to the guest house. There are too many things to buy. I don't know where to look, nowhere seems safe. In the taxi I was disturbed because someone almost cut into our lane and the driver didn't honk at him.

"I don't understand how people can drive without honking!" I said to Chinua, in tears again.

I am deeply affected by cultural changes. And I'm finding that this is a particularly big change, coming from India after twenty-two months, coming away from my home there, while planning to see my family and friends and then return to India, which is not really my home after all. Oh boy. Time to take a deep breath and just enjoy the jasmine on the side of the roads here, drink the iced coffee, in which they don't skimp on the ice at all.

We love taro root, coconut, pineapple. We love basil and kafir lime leaves and we love small southeast Asian alleys with cooking pots and pointy nosed cats and the steamy humid heat of a Bangkok April.

April 3, 2010

It's just going to be the same thing, over and over again, while we are in Thailand. You might want to skip past these parts.

Everything is so clean! I was examining our guest house today, trying to figure it out. Why is the effect so peaceful? Is it the tiles, how they line up with each other?

Pedestrians have the right of way. Being on the road is just an inch away from death for us in India, my friends.

And... I'm still freaking out. But mildly! Inside! And a word to the wise: Just because there are amazing coffee shops and delicious coffee everywhere doesn't mean you have to drink it all the time! (It adds to the freaking out, friends, it really does.)

I saw a Starbucks today. I shut my eyes and turned in the other direction, pretending it wasn't there. It might have taken me over the edge.

We are in Chiang Mai, in the north. We took a night train last night, which is a pleasant way to travel, even if you have too much stuff with you. Bring snacks though. They charge a bundle for the

328

train food, unlike India.

When Kenya told the man at our guest house her name, he pointed to Leafy and asked, "His name Congo?" I laughed. It was really witty, I've never had anyone ask me that before. Then he started talking about the City Lights Bookstore in San Francisco and the Beat Scene, totally randomly. (It had something to do with wanting dreadlocks, but not wanting to deal with the stigma in Thailand.) And then he refused to give Cate a coconut shake because it's too hot out for coconut.

"Not good for the stomach."

A character. He's helping himself to a little too much of this fine coffee.

April 10, 2010

We have been traveling. We arrived, as you know, in Bangkok on the 31st, then took a night train to Chiang Mai on the 2nd and then we took a bus to Pai on the 6th. Now we are back in Chiang Mai, and we're getting back on that night train tonight to go back to Bangkok.

It has been adventurous, delicious, and very, very hot. Weather in the 40's, averaging around 106 degrees Fahrenheit, for the Americans. Fortunately in Pai, where it was hot like that, it cooled down at night and we may have even pulled a sheet over us.

Yesterday on the bus from Pai to Chiang Mai, I sat with a baby sleeping against my side, looking out into bamboo forests. It is the dry season, and there were controlled burns, so sometimes we would whirl around a corner and see flames among the bamboo, smoke hiding the road until we came through it. It has been hazy since we arrived, though, the haze of pollution and no rain or wind, and the sun was a perfect orange disk in the sky as we traveled on the bus. There were a few rain trees, scattered here and there. I think the rain tree is my favorite tree now. Saman tree is another name for it. It looks like a huge umbrella, with small pink fluffy flowers on its leaves. They smell like heaven, but the saman trees here and in India are so huge that you couldn't get your nose anywhere near the flowers if you tried. Still, they arch over the roads protectively, and that is just as good.

Everything was dried out and withered. I wonder if there is whooping, here, when the first rains come. Singing? Dancing? Sometimes the first rains of monsoon are like that, in India, when it is so hot and the rains finally bring their cooling. I listened to Kai talking with Cate. They noticed a water slide at a carnival, and he said, "Oh, I love water slides! My friend Danny made us the best water slide. Do you remember Danny?" he asked her. "He was from Scotland."

The slide he was talking about was a large piece of linoleum that our friend set on the side of a sand bag slope at a beach shack in Goa. He ran buckets of water down it while the kids flew down, shrieking. Eventually somebody found a hose, and a steady trickle of knobby kneed kids waited their turns, when they were being well behaved, and pushed past each other, when they weren't.

It is amazing to me that this is my son's impression of a water slide. Sometimes he surprises me, my oldest child, growing up, suddenly so different. I returned to our guest house room today, when we were checking out, to give it one last search (always a good idea) and found him placing the remote control carefully beside the TV. "I was cleaning up," he explained, and as I looked around, I saw that he had made the bed and straightened the towels. As we left the room he carefully placed a piece of trash in the trash basket. Who is this child?

Or the other night, when we were at the Sunday Walking Market in Chiang Mai, a beautiful market of hand crafts and food, and he wanted to find out how much the little poached quail eggs were, so he could try them. I watched him speak to the woman at the stall so politely, and he looked like a grown up, suddenly, like he wasn't my seven-year-old son. He listened to her seriously, his wide deer-like eyes trained on her face, and then handed her the money. He came back to our table and ate one of the eggs. "Hmmm," he said. "It tastes *slightly* more bitter than a chicken egg. But it's good!" I just stared at him, I couldn't get enough of him.

And Leafy, the other night, when we walked back to our guest house in the evening, when it was cooling down. He was overflowing, for some reason. He couldn't stop giggling, and when there were disco lights in the street and Chinua stopped to dance, Leafy stayed for a long time after, unable to keep himself from dancing his little groove in a circle of colored lights. Sometimes, lately, he runs and every four steps he flings his arms out and jumps, like he's trying to fly.

And Kenya, dreaming of owning her own elephant. Finding more animals to fall in love with. "I just need to say one last goodbye," she said, when we started to walk away from an elephant that we met on the side of the road. She ran back and gave the elephant's leg a little hug.

We are learning about a new place, contemplating what it will be like to return to North America, taking each day as it comes. In our guest house in Pai, I would get up and pray in the morning, sitting by the river which was so low and sluggish. I brought back homemade yogurt and scones from a bakery, and we drank soy milk, the best you've ever tasted. I bought tiffins, little Indian style lunch containers, and brought home street food for lunch. Wide noodles with chicken, spicy rice. The tiffins were good to have—I'm trying to keep from using styrofoam, but the street food is so much cheaper, and then take-away is so much easier, with four young children. We had bubble tea on the side of one dusty road. We ate whole mangoes. Marveled at them.

One day we went to an organic farm outside of Pai. The lady there took us on a tour, and we saw the bungalows they have built, the nurseries, the mango orchards. She showed us where they ride bikes to run the pump from the well, so they can water the garden or fill the washing machine. It was lovely. The kind Thai woman who showed us around stopped in front of a gigantic swing and pushed the kids, one by one. People here are very kind.

It has also been hard. Traveling with children just is, that's all there is to say. Last night we had an encounter with a stressed-out guesthouse manager who wanted us to keep our children from crying. Keeping Solo from crying when he is tired after a long bus ride is something that I don't yet have the magic button for. We've never had this kind of interaction before in Thailand or India. I cried, of course. Chinua was wonderfully diplomatic.

Soon Song Kran will start; the amazing Thai water festival where everyone throws water on each other for three to six days. I say three to six because there were young children on the roads yesterday, unable to keep themselves from starting. I can't wait, since it has just occurred to me that a city-wide, multiple-day water fight may just be the coolest thing my kids will ever encounter.

April 13, 2010

We are flying in a matter of hours and I am a mess. I am not such a calm person, after all. Okay, the mess is mostly inside, mostly centered in my chest cavity, and if you were looking at me you might think, "How calm she is! Sitting there with her iced coffee and her laptop, perched on her hotel bed!" Do not be deceived. Inside, I am all aflutter.

Here's a tip for you and me. You don't need to answer questions

332

about who you are and what your place in the world is, hours before a flight. Just get your bags together and get ready to go.

April 14, 2010

I'm in the Taipei airport, sitting in an ultra modern, chic transfer area, styled in shades of grey and taupe, with white stamping of birch trees on the wall. Everything is rounded and retro-modern.

Today I am thankful. I am thankful that I will see my family in a few hours, that we will jump up and down and hug each other. I'm thankful that we were able to spend time with Cate in Bangkok. I'm thankful that I'm traveling with this big amoeba-like mass of children who are my own, wriggling and crawling over everything. I'm thankful for a small plumeria farm, glimpsed through tall buildings on the way to the airport this morning. For inflight movies and the peace they so technologically enforce. For comfy seating.

For the gift of these two years away, for the simplification, the self denial, the way I've been shaped into a tougher person.

Nori-flavored potato chips are a new favorite thing. The best chips ever, chips from heaven. I'm thankful for them, too. And flip-flops and my two new comfy t-shirts and water when you're really, really thirsty. And anything green. And a few hours in an airport to simmer down and contemplate. (And chase after Solo.)

Psalm 116 talks about a sacrifice of thanksgiving, which is a funny kind of sacrifice, except when you think that perhaps sacrifice is something that doesn't just pour out, but something you have to rustle around in your deep pockets for. In my case, it's not that I'm unthankful, but that I'm preoccupied by so many questions. Nothing stills my heart like sacrifice; the pebbles I take out and smooth in between my fingers.

333

ABOUT THE AUTHOR

Bio

Rachel Devenish Ford is the wife of one Superstar Husband and the mother of five incredible children. Originally from British Columbia, Canada, she spent seven years working with street youth in California before moving to India to help start a meditation center in the Christian tradition. She can be found eating street food or smelling flowers in many cities in Asia. She currently lives in Northern Thailand, inhaling books, morning air, and seasonal fruit.

She is deep in the revisions of her second novel and the compilation of the second Journey Mama book.

Other works by Rachel Devenish Ford:

The Eve Tree
Trees Tall as Mountains- Book One of the Journey Mama Writings

Reviews

Recommendations and reviews are such an important part of the success of a book. If you enjoyed this book, please take the time to leave a review at Amazon.com or your site of choice.

Don't be afraid of leaving a short review! Even a couple lines will help and will overwhelm the author with waves of gratitude.

Contact

You can contact the author in a plethora of ways:

Email: racheldevenishford@gmail.com

Blog: http://journeymama.com

Facebook: http://www.facebook.com/racheldevenishford

Twitter: http://www.twitter.com/journeymama

Instagram: http://instagram.com/journeymama

Thanks so much for reading.

ACKNOWLEDGEMENTS

I want to thank Cate, Renee, Miriam, and Johanna for being such amazing community friends and neighbors. I'm so thankful for many cups of coffee, tea, and friendship on your porches. Thanks to Matty and Becca for being such a wonderful brother and sister and coming all the way to India to spend time with me. I send all my love and thanks to Leaf, Brendan and Taran—the ghat ninja— for being the warmest welcome to India we ever could have imagined. My heart thanks go out to Jaya for being the perfect partner in crime. Thank you Cat and Jocelyn for being rays of light. Thank you Darius and Oshan for being true friends and bringing great music into all of our lives. And all love and thanks to my traveler family in Goa and the outer reaches of India. You make life wonderful.

The Grace in Small Things idea that was scattered throughout this book was the brainchild of Elan Morgan, of www.schmutzie.com Thanks so much, Elan!

Made in the USA
San Bernardino, CA
23 December 2013